Teaching and Learning the Archaeology of the Contemporary Era

Also available from Bloomsbury

Archaeologies of Conflict, John Carman
Heritage, Communities and Archaeology, Laurajane Smith and Emma Waterton
Using Digital Humanities in the Classroom, 2nd edn, Claire Battershill and
Shawna Ross

Teaching and Learning the Archaeology of the Contemporary Era

Edited by Gabriel Moshenska

BLOOMSBURY ACADEMIC
LONDON • NEW YORK • OXFORD • NEW DELHI • SYDNEY

BLOOMSBURY ACADEMIC
Bloomsbury Publishing Plc
50 Bedford Square, London, WC1B 3DP, UK
1385 Broadway, New York, NY 10018, USA
29 Earlsfort Terrace, Dublin 2, Ireland

BLOOMSBURY, BLOOMSBURY ACADEMIC and the Diana logo are trademarks of
Bloomsbury Publishing Plc

First published in Great Britain in 2024

Copyright © Gabriel Moshenska and Contributors, 2024

Gabriel Moshenska has asserted his right under the Copyright, Designs and Patents Act,
1988, to be identified as Editor of this work.

Cover image: Martin Shields/Alamy Stock Photo

All rights reserved. No part of this publication may be reproduced or transmitted
in any form or by any means, electronic or mechanical, including photocopying,
recording, or any information storage or retrieval system, without prior permission
in writing from the publishers.

Bloomsbury Publishing Plc does not have any control over, or responsibility for,
any third-party websites referred to or in this book. All internet addresses given
in this book were correct at the time of going to press. The author and publisher
regret any inconvenience caused if addresses have changed or sites have ceased
to exist, but can accept no responsibility for any such changes.

A catalogue record for this book is available from the British Library.

Library of Congress Cataloging-in-Publication Data
Names: Moshenska, Gabriel, editor.
Title: Teaching and learning the archaeology of the contemporary era /
edited by Gabriel Moshenska.
Description: London ; New York : Bloomsbury Academic, 2024. |
Includes bibliographical references and index.
Identifiers: LCCN 2023029530 (print) | LCCN 2023029531 (ebook) |
ISBN 9781350335639 (hb) | ISBN 9781350335622 (pb) | ISBN 9781350335646 (epdf)
| ISBN 9781350335653 (ebook)
Subjects: LCSH: Archaeology--Study and teaching. | Archaeology--Social aspects.
Classification: LCC CC83 .T43 2024 (print) | LCC CC83 (ebook) |
DDC 930.1071—dc23/eng/20230630
LC record available at https://lccn.loc.gov/2023029530
LC ebook record available at https://lccn.loc.gov/2023029531

ISBN: HB: 978-1-3503-3563-9
        PB: 978-1-3503-3562-2
        ePDF: 978-1-3503-3564-6
        eBook: 978-1-3503-3565-3

Typeset by RefineCatch Limited, Bungay, Suffolk
Printed and bound in Great Britain

To find out more about our authors and books visit www.bloomsbury.com
and sign up for our newsletters.

This book is dedicated to the memory of Don Henson (1956–2021), whose enthusiasm, expertise and advocacy for archaeological learning continue to inspire.

Contents

List of Figures	ix
Notes on Contributors	xii

Introduction: Pedagogy in Contemporary Archaeology
Gabriel Moshenska   1

Part One Course and Curriculum Development

1 Contemporary Art and Archaeology: Interdisciplinary Pedagogy
and Practice in the Digital University *Antonia Thomas*   19

2 Documenting Wesley College: A Mildly Anarchist Teaching
Encounter *William Caraher*   41

3 Teaching Contemporary Archaeology: The Durham Experience
David Petts   61

Part Two Pedagogical Practices

4 The Henge with a Postcode: The Benefits of Contemporary
Archaeology Fieldtrips *Kenneth Brophy*   81

5 Draw Your Phone: The Cellphone as an Intimate, Everyday
Artefact *Colleen Morgan*   101

6 Walking and Talking around the Bombsites of Bloomsbury
Gabriel Moshenska   113

Part Three Working with Communities

7 Over, Under and In Between: Collaborative Learning from
Landscapes using Contemporary Archaeology *April M. Beisaw*   131

8 Teaching and Learning Difficult Pasts of the Twentieth Century
through Community Archaeology *Tiina Äikäs, Oula Seitsonen, Tuuli
Matila and Vesa-Pekka Herva*   149

viii *Contents*

9   Beyond Zinjanthropus: Historical Archaeology Pedagogy in
    Tanzania *Nancy Rushohora*   167

Part Four The Personal and the Political

10 'We Want School!' Teaching and Learning Contemporary
    Archaeology with Displaced People in Anarchist-Adjacent Spaces
    in Athens, Greece *Rachael Kiddey*   185

11 Archaeologies of the Contemporary World – A Chancy
    Business? *Greg Bailey*   205

12 Education Is Life: Collective Experiences of Practising the
    Archaeology of the Contemporary Past in a Conservative
    Atmosphere *Maryam Dezhamkhooy and Leila Papoli-Yazdi*   225

Index   239

Figures

1.1 Collaborative mapping (object-studio-island) with artists Brendan Colvert and Rosey Priestman during Papay Gyro Nights Contemporary Arts Festival in 2014   23

1.2 Aileen Ogilvie performing in the abandoned space of Perth City Hall in 2020, for her project 'An Talla: Giving a Voice to the Voiceless'   26

1.3 Live drawing by Eòghann MacColl: '(Re)mapping the way: psychogeography in a rural place'. Undertaken as part of the MA Contemporary Art and Archaeology and later presented at FestivalCHAT in 2020   28

1.4 Still from Rebecca Lambert's multimedia 'Underpasses are Liminal Spaces' project   31

1.5 Still from the 'Lines of Rupture, Lines of Flight (Pegwell Bay)' film installation by Lara Band, 2022   33

2.1 Wesley College Campus from the east. Corwin/Larimore Hall in the foreground and Robertson/Sayre Hall in the background   42

2.2 Abandoned laboratory space in Corwin/Larimore Hall   46

2.3 Abandoned iMac dating to around the year 2000 still stands on its table nearly twenty years later   47

2.4 Intimate traces of the building's past life lingered on after abandonment   47

2.5 The north wall of the Corwin Hall recital room, preserving the shape of the proscenium arch   49

2.6 Sayre Hall ceiling reveals evidence for the former coffering   49

2.7 A photo from the 1920s of the Sayre Hall sitting room showing the coffered ceilings   50

2.8 Names of former students carved into the window of Sayre Hall   51

3.1 Dunelm House, Durham University, used as the Durham Student Union building and focus for the 'Adventures in Contemporary Archaeology' recording project, 2018   66

3.2 Durham University Observatory, focus for the 'Adventures in Contemporary Archaeology' recording project, 2019   68

4.1	Location map showing Balfarg's position (left) and the Archaeology Trail route (right)	86
4.2	Looking south across Balfarg Henge interior in 2015	87
4.3	Students enjoying Balbirnie stone circle during a fieldtrip in 2013	88
4.4	The Balfarg Riding School monument reconstruction during a student fieldtrip in 2011	89
4.5	The starting point for the fieldtrip is at a parking space beside the main entrance to Balfarg Henge, here seen during a visit in 2015	91
4.6	Selection of prompt cards from the 2021 fieldtrip	92
4.7	From ritual to residual: a response to Balfarg Henge submitted as coursework in 2015	95
4.8	Scrapbook extract from the Balfarg fieldtrip, from 2021	96
5.1	Student participant using a ruler to measure elements of their phone to transcribe it to permatrace	106
5.2	Student participant drawing their phone 'freehand'	106
5.3	Drawing of a Samsung cellphone: front, back and profile view (L–R)	108
6.1	Pointing out the plaque to a tour group in Queen Square, 2022	120
6.2	The façade of the Rockefeller Building showing the repaired bomb damage, 2015	123
7.1	Webmap of New York State's county poorhouses (Beisaw 2022), with an example of the USGS map data used to generate it (United States Geological Survey 1962) and an example of how poorhouse building footprints (dashed line) can be projected on the current landscape	137
7.2	Women-owned properties in the town of Olive, taken by New York City in 1907 to construct the Ashokan Reservoir	140
8.1	A German soldier standing in front of the barracks in Vaakunakylä.	152
8.2	The hanging tree memorial with its iron rail and inscription. Antti Kaarlela is pointing to a cross engraved on the tree	153
8.3	The memorial service organized at the PoW camp in Inari	155
8.4	(a) A memorial in Varjakka harbour and (b) a work of art in the old office building on the Varjakansaari island commemorating the women and girls who drowned in the marine accident in 1907	157
8.5	Children can get acquainted with archaeology by participating in various aspects of fieldwork and research, here documenting house remains in Varjakka	159
9.1	Kilwa Kivinje mass grave	174
10.1	Second School squat, exterior of building, 2018	190

10.2	Inside an 'Our House' apartment, 2019	191
10.3	'I drew *Our House* building as a pencil because it is education'	193
11.1	This particular Transit Van	208
11.2	Tape tangle on a Bristol street	212
11.3	CRT television as overnight archaeology	213
11.4	TV script proposal and part of scatter	214
11.5	Page 25, *A Thousand Plateaus* (defaced in desperation)	218
12.1	*No one is in the garden!*, Zahedan University, 2012. From left: Mariam Naeemi, Omran Garazhian and Arman Masoudi	232
12.2	*No one is in the garden!*, Zahedan University, 2012. From left: Leila Papoli-Yazdi, Maryam Dezhamkhooy and Arman Masoudi	233

Contributors

Tiina Äikäs works as a senior researcher in archaeology at the University of Oulu, Finland. Her doctoral dissertation (2011) dealt with the ritual landscapes of Saami sacred places. In addition to the archaeology of religion, her research interests include place-bound memories, heritage studies and industrial heritage. Äikäs has led field courses for students and school children at historical sawmill sites. She is currently a PI of the project 'Smokestack Memories' (2021–3), which discusses factory smokestacks as heritage and as places of local identity.

Greg Bailey is an independent researcher and Fellow of the Royal Anthropological Institute. From 2004 to 2022 he was a columnist in *British Archaeology* magazine. Following a fifty-year career in TV and film as lab technician, sound recordist, musician and collector, producer and director, Bailey completed a certificate in archaeology at Birkbeck College (2002). In 2006 he went on to gain an MA in Archaeology for Screen Media at the University of Bristol, while still working either as director or sound recordist on TV projects both in the UK and USA. He awarded a PhD by the University of Bristol in 2017 for a thesis entitled 'Views and Soundings: Marking Boundaries for Archaeological Practice'.

April M. Beisaw is Professor of Anthropology at Vassar College, in Poughkeepsie, New York. Her research focuses on archaeological ethics, community heritage and the recent past. Beisaw is co-editor of *The Archaeology of Institutional Life* (2009) and author of *Identifying and Interpreting Animal Bones: A Manual* (2013) and *Taking Our Water for the City: The Archaeology of New York City's Watershed Communities* (2022).

Kenneth Brophy is Senior Lecturer in Archaeology at the University of Glasgow, with over twenty years of experience of teaching and doing fieldwork. His research interests include the contemporary archaeology of prehistory, from the political uses of prehistory to the social benefits of prehistoric sites in urban places. His most recent book, *Prehistoric Forteviot* (2020), was co-written with Gordon Noble. Brophy blogs as the 'Urban Prehistorian'.

William Caraher teaches in the Department of History and American Indian Studies at the University of North Dakota. He also edits the literary journal

North Dakota Quarterly and is the publisher at the Digital Press at the University of North Dakota.

Maryam Dezhamkhooy is a former Assistant Professor of Archaeology and Alexander von Humboldt fellow. She is now the affiliated researcher at the Käthe Hamburger Centre for Apocalyptic and Post-apocalyptic Studies, where she is researching waste and the women's movements in Iran. Dezhamkhooy is a specialist in the archaeology of the contemporary past. Gender, conflict, colonialism, nationalism and waste and garbage communities are her main research interests. She is a member of Gap End, Iranian engaged archaeologists, an independent circle founded with her colleagues with special interests in theory and the archaeology of contemporary past. Dezhamkhooy is also a member of the European Association of Archaeologists. Interested in gender and sexuality, she is also a member of AGE (Archaeology and Gender in Europe). She is the co-author, with Leila Papoli-Yazdi, of a monograph on gender entitled *Homogenization, Gender and Everyday Life in Pre- and Trans-modern Iran: An Archaeological Reading*.

Vesa-Pekka Herva is Professor of Archaeology at the University of Oulu, Finland. He has studied various aspects of material culture, human–environment relations, cosmology and heritage in north-eastern Europe from the Neolithic to modern times. He is the co-author, with Antti Lahelma, of *Northern Archaeology and Cosmology: A Relational View* (2019).

Rachael Kiddey is Teaching Associate in Heritage Studies in the Department of Archaeology, University of Cambridge. She previously held a British Academy postdoctoral fellowship at the School of Archaeology, University of Oxford, called 'Migrant Materialities'. Kiddey's research interests include the socio-politics of the past in the present and the role of material culture in situations of forced displacement. Her doctoral research, for which she received a PhD from the University of York in 2014, involved developing methodologies for working archaeologically with homeless people, documenting how heritage can function in transformative ways. Kiddey is the author of the monograph *Homeless Heritage* (2017).

Tuuli Matila is a postdoctoral researcher in the Department of Archaeology at the University of Oulu. Her research interests include the cultural heritage of conflicts, and especially wartime photographs. Her dissertation 'Seeing the War through a Finnish lens: Representation and Affect in the World War II Photographic Heritage' was published in 2022.

Colleen Morgan is Senior Lecturer in Digital Archaeology and Heritage in the Department of Archaeology at the University of York. She is the Director of the Digital Archaeology and Heritage Lab, the MSc in Digital Archaeology and MSc in Digital Heritage programmes. Morgan was a postdoctoral fellow for the Centre for Digital Heritage from 2015 to 2017. Her research focuses include: 1) bringing digital archaeology into conversation with current theory drawn from feminist, queer, posthuman and anarchist approaches; 2) digital embodiment, with a focus on avatars of past people; 3) and issues surrounding craft, enskillment and pedagogy in analog and digital methods in field archaeology, including photography, videography and drawing.

Gabriel Moshenska is Associate Professor in Public Archaeology at UCL Institute of Archaeology. His research and teaching focus on the public understanding of the past, the archaeology and heritage of twentieth-century conflict, and the history of archaeology and antiquarianism. Moshenska is the author of *Material Cultures of Childhood in Second World War Britain* (2019) and editor of *Key Concepts in Public Archaeology* (2017).

Leila Papoli-Yazdi is a researcher at the School of Arts and Communication (K3), Malmö University, and collaborates with the UNESCO Chair on Heritage Futures (Linnaeus University). Since 2003, she has been studying poverty, inequality and discrimination through performing field projects in the cities destroyed recently by natural disasters and through garbology research. Papoli-Yazdi has directed several projects in Pakistan, Kuwait, Iran and Sweden.

David Petts is Associate Professor in the Department of Archaeology, Durham University, where he has taught archaeology since 2007. He has an eclectic research profile, ranging widely from the early medieval period to the archaeology of the twentieth century. Major recent research projects include excavating on the early-medieval monastery of Lindisfarne (Holy Island) and exploring the impact of the Great Depression on the landscape of North-East England in the 1930s.

Nancy Rushohora is Lecturer in the Department of Archaeology and Heritage Studies of the University of Dar es Salaam, an honorary research fellow of the University of Exeter and a co-PI of the project 'Imagine the Future through Un/Archived Past'. Her research interests include the archaeology of resistance, trauma, heritage, photographs and memory.

Oula Seitsonen, Sakarin-Pentin Ilarin Oula, is an archaeologist and geographer at the University of Oulu. His research interests cover a wide temporal and geographic range, from the early pastoral livelihoods in Mongolia and East Africa to the contemporary archaeologies of modern refugee crises. His recent monograph, *Archaeologies of Hitler's Arctic War: Heritage of the Second World War German Military Presence in Finnish Lapland* (2021), is the first one in Finland to discuss the material memories of the Second World War from a theoretically informed, multidisciplinary perspective.

Antonia Thomas is Lecturer in Archaeology and the Programme Leader for the MA Contemporary Art and Archaeology at the Archaeology Institute University of the Highlands and Islands. She is currently a Co-Investigator on the RSE-funded International Network for Contemporary Archaeology in Scotland (INCAScot).

Introduction: Pedagogy in Contemporary Archaeology

Gabriel Moshenska

Introduction

Pedagogy is one of those realms of cultural practice so deeply embedded in the structures of everyday life that to stop and examine it as a 'thing' in its own right can be challenging. Simplistic understandings of pedagogy as formal, classroom-based teaching and learning have long given way to sociologically-enriched discussions of cultural reproduction, knowledge generation, the individual and the collective, and mechanisms of power, resistance and social change. The works of scholars such as Giroux, hooks, Freire and others have illuminated the mechanisms of pedagogy in this richer sense across the life course from early childhood play and socialisation, through schooling and the workplace, to the family, foodways, leisure and cultural consumption. Meanwhile, for those of us embedded in formal education structures as students and teachers, the annual cycles of curriculum-based teaching, examination and progression are a powerful habitus.

Against these different backgrounds, thinking critically about pedagogy – with love, frustration, excitement and imagination – can be both rewarding and difficult. In a recent essay (Moshenska 2021), I tried to envision possible transformations of archaeological pedagogy in higher education free, to varying degrees, from the economic and social logics of neoliberal capitalism. These imagined futures ranged from greater access to continuing education and training through Universal Basic Income, to a wholesale rearrangement of archaeological labour, training and education through networks of cooperatives modelled on existing learned societies and regional associations. Beyond the immediate aim of setting out possible pedagogical futures, the broader value of such critical, imaginative exercises is to learn how to look at the social and material dimensions of modern society as something other than natural and inevitable.

One of the distinctive elements of contemporary archaeological pedagogy is precisely this imaginative defamiliarization, learning to look at the material culture of everyday life and see it with fresh eyes as part of a global network of infrastructure, industry, economy and humanity – to see, as William Blake put it, a world in a grain of sand. One of the best accounts of practical pedagogy in contemporary archaeology, illustrating precisely this practice, is provided by Alice Gorman's book *Dr Space Junk vs The Universe* (2019). Gorman took a group of students to survey the site of the former NASA satellite tracking station at Orroral Valley near Canberra. All the structures had been removed years before: Gorman anticipated that the survey of the thickly-overgrown site would reveal a few surface artefacts and that 'it would be a nice, quick demonstration of the principles of surface survey for the students' (2019: 103). In fact, the site was far richer than anticipated: students identified more than thirty distinct artefact types including concrete fragments, wires, pipes, nails and cable ties. These apparently uniform, ubiquitous cable ties were good to think with. Closer inspection revealed a variety of lengths, widths and colours, as well as brand names and product codes. Students speculated that different gauges might correspond to different uses. The ties had been used, removed and discarded: students noted a distinction between those that had been cut, torn or melted. As Gorman put it, 'This tiny observation on a discarded piece of plastic translated into a decision and an action taken by a real person in carrying out a task. This was archaeology' (2019: 105).

Gorman encouraged the students to contemplate the cable ties. What might explain their presence? How were they associated with the site? What even *is* a cable tie, and what is its history? Students brought their own experiences and understandings of these everyday objects to the discussion, and learned more about their uses from talking to staff at a similar, working tracking station. Gorman's engaging account of contemporary archaeology pedagogy in action includes elements that appear across many of the chapters in this book: responding to unexpected discoveries; learning how to defamiliarize the everyday; and creating space for students to observe, compare, reflect and discuss modern material culture with an archaeological eye.

Aims and purposes

What is the purpose of this book? One can read about the brilliant, boundary-pushing research in contemporary archaeology in journals and books, and see it presented at conferences. While there is equally innovative and exciting teaching going on, this is harder to see: my own knowledge of this is largely drawn from conversations with colleagues, from sitting in on their courses, talking to students and seeing the work that they produce. It is time to stop selling ourselves short: as demonstrated by Gorman's account above, and by the chapters in this book, contemporary archaeology is a hive of creative pedagogy.

The first aim of this book is to bring together and share a collection of case studies in contemporary archaeological pedagogy from around the world. This is in part a celebration and recognition of this work, in part a vindication of its value, and an opportunity for those teachers and learners to critically reflect on their practices through the process of setting them down on a page. I have personally found it valuable to review more than a decade of teaching contemporary archaeology both inside and outside the classroom, and to consider what might develop or emerge from these practices. At present, as this book demonstrates, contemporary archaeological pedagogies are as methodologically inclusive, interdisciplinary and diverse as the field itself.

The second aim of this book, leading directly from this first, is to encourage and enable the teaching of contemporary archaeology, primarily within higher education but also beyond this into schools, in professional training and development and in avocational archaeology. Resources of this kind are particularly important for the development of contemporary archaeology outside of its existing 'clusters' in wealthier, Western contexts. I hope this book feels like an invitation to participate, rather than a glimpse into an exclusive club.

'Considering the vastness of the archaeological literature, it is surprising to find that so little of it concerns teaching.'

Wilk and Schiffer 1981: 15

A third aim of this book is to contribute to this peculiarly small body of literature on archaeological pedagogies in general. This is not to deny that there is some excellent work in this field: Cobb and Croucher's *Assembling Archaeology* (2020) includes reflections on this general dearth of research and writing on the topic alongside proposals for rethinking pedagogical practices in archaeology. As a contrasting example, the field of geography has a strong tradition of pedagogical research, including the almost half-century-old *Journal of Geography in Higher Education*. Naturally, every archaeological sub-discipline has its own distinctive teaching practices and traditions, including a variety of field schools, focuses on ancient languages and texts, and the lab-focused training in archaeological sciences. Contemporary archaeology is no different, but I hope that some of the practices and ideas outlined in this book will be of value to archaeologists of all periods and places.

Why now?

Writing in the summer of 2023, it feels like a very good time to be reflecting on archaeological pedagogy in general, and contemporary archaeology in particular. The past three years of global Covid-19 pandemic have seen an unprecedented level of disruption across all aspects of life, and the impacts on education – for young people in particular – are lamentable and likely to endure. Moments of rupture like this offer an opportunity to pause and to take stock, and as several of the chapters in this book demonstrate, to reflect on established practices and new approaches. Petts' account of developing contemporary archaeology teaching at Durham (see Chapter 3) includes his reflections on approaches developed to mitigate the impacts of Covid, such as new and adapted digital resources and practical exercises focused on individual rather than group work. The conventional wisdom amongst many politicians and commentators is that the move to online learning presented educators with an easier time, effectively a holiday, or at least an opportunity to slack off. Obviously this perspective is ignorant and ill-informed at best, and actively malicious at worst. The collective efforts to move teaching online, adapting materials and learning new technologies, was an extraordinary collective achievement, as Petts and others have demonstrated.

The closure of field schools and restrictions on library access and laboratory time have all impacted learning opportunities for archaeology students. Online learning has its positive and negative dimensions, depending on a multitude of factors. What is undeniable is that archaeological educators have expended enormous efforts to create new learning materials, to transform existing materials for new media, to explore new forms of accessibility, to assist students who have struggled or slipped behind and to make the best possible uses of the opportunities and resources available during the crisis. The contemporary archaeological pedagogies that emerge from the pandemic will be richer and stronger, and – if they preserve the very best of the digital platforms and resources – will be far more accessible to learners than at any point previously. Some archaeologists have also used the past two years to document and study the contemporary archaeology of the pandemic itself as a collaborative, inclusive research process, as well as one that feeds back into these new forms of teaching and learning (e.g., Geller 2020; Schofield et al. 2021).

Global pandemics aside, there is another reason why this book feels timely. Over the past two decades contemporary archaeology has developed from a small but dynamic intellectual insurgency into an established sub-field, with all the trappings of academic establishment such as formal job titles, conferences, a dedicated journal, major research grants, a growing cohort of doctoral graduates and a steadily decreasing (dying? We can but hope) number of naysayers whining that it is not 'proper' archaeology. Alongside these trappings of success, a concerted and critical eye on pedagogical practices feels both well timed and necessary for future growth. Of course, these developments have not been evenly spread: in Chapter 12, Dezhamkhooy and Papoli-Yazdi discuss the challenges of establishing contemporary archaeological practices within Iranian academia, and the strategies that they developed to circumvent these obstacles, including theatrical performances and public-facing events. Meanwhile, in Chapter 9, Rushohora reflects on the gaps in archaeological pedagogy in Tanzania, and particularly the need to embed the findings of contemporary and historical archaeologies in school curricula to enhance public understanding of the colonial eras.

Interdisciplinarity and its problems

What are the aims of a contemporary archaeological pedagogy? What knowledge, skills and abilities is it intended to pass on? To begin to answer this, we would need to consider what distinguishes contemporary archaeology as a field of practice, and in particular the methods that new practitioners might be expected to master. One significant problem here is that contemporary archaeology is distinctively – one might say flamboyantly, excessively, joyfully – interdisciplinary. The question of methods and the challenges of interdisciplinarity in contemporary archaeology are discussed in some length by Harrison and Schofield (2010) and others. Lisa Hill offers an interesting perspective on this, writing on contemporary archaeology for an audience of geographers, noting that:

> Contemporary archaeology is significant in this context for its shared methodology with human geography and its temporal proximity to matters of geographical concern ... contemporary archaeologists are trained to dig, draw, analyse and amass. For cultural geographers interested in new ways of doing, in knowledge-as-practice, archaeology offers a rich ground for collaboration and research.
>
> Hill 2015: 413; 424

But surely digging, drawing, analysing and amassing are common to most places and periods in archaeology. Where contemporary archaeology blurs, blunders or bulldozes disciplinary boundaries, we find the methods that distinguish the discipline. Distinguish it, that is, within archaeology: as Hill's observations above make clear, aspects of contemporary archaeology might seem familiar to practitioners in fields such as human geography, landscape history, urban history, material culture anthropology, heritage and memory studies, science and technology studies and others. The work of contemporary archaeologists includes ethnographies, oral histories, walks and *dérives*, photogrammetry, counter-mapping, reverse engineering, community consultations, bomb disposal, object biographies, practical necromancy, burrowing into archives, photography, breaking-and-entering and memory mapping. Some contemporary archaeologists learn or train in these methods; others work in collaborative teams that include a range of specialists from different backgrounds.

Amongst these collaborations, contemporary archaeologists often work with (and as) creative artists, producing research outputs and interventions that bridge art and archaeology. These working methods include filmmaking, photography, installations, performances, collaborative exhibitions and the co-display of artefacts and artworks. The pedagogical dimensions of this are explored in Chapter 1, the account by Antonia Thomas of developing an innovative graduate programme that combines contemporary art and contemporary archaeology. Thomas shows how this new programme draws on many years of cross-disciplinary collaborations and connections, and reflects on challenges and opportunities of a programme largely delivered online. The challenge for contemporary archaeological pedagogies is not to train students in all of the methods that they might choose to employ in their work, but rather to make them aware of the variety of existing approaches, the possibility of expanding that range, and to demonstrate and model the kinds of open, collaborative working practices that enable interdisciplinarity and creativity.

Learning how to gaze defamiliarizingly

The ability to regard the familiar and – through thought alone – render if unfamiliar, and to contemplate the meaning and outcomes of this process, is one of the central practices of contemporary archaeology, and one that students of the subject must learn to master. What does it mean to defamiliarize? Buchli and Lucas explain that 'the purpose is to create a distance from the familiar, to make the familiar unfamiliar' (2001: 13). Graves-Brown places this process at the heart of modern material culture studies (2000) and explores the connections and tensions between defamiliarization, estrangement, alienation and the Brechtian *verfremdungseffekt*: 'the things of everyday life are lifted out of the realm of the self evident' to see them in new, different, clearer perspective (quoted in Graves-Brown 2011: 135). While Graves-Brown's primary focus is the object, Edensor considers the jarring defamiliarization of places – specifically buildings and urban spaces – through processes of ruination and decay. In Chapter 6, Moshenska explores urban landscapes as palimpsests of material and immaterial memory, and the capacity of guided walking tours to highlight the traces and layers of violence in these spaces: once seen, never not noticed again.

Morgan's 'draw your phone' exercise, described in Chapter 5, is a rich and illuminating example of a contemporary archaeological approach to objects, exploring the connections with traditional archaeological image-making practices, as well as the value of object-based work in classroom teaching. The weirdness and spookiness of the defamiliarized place or object comes from seeing normal everyday things through an archaeology 'eye'. The aim is that, in stripping away familiarity, we can more clearly see the ideological, symbolic dimensions of the material. Gonzalez-Ruibal argues that this stripping away of the familiar and complacent is a moral act, a step towards seeing clearly: that we must 'do violence to things to reveal the violence that has been done to people' (2019: 64). For Harrison and Schofield, the task of making the familiar unfamiliar lies at the very heart of contemporary archaeological practice, and of its pedagogy: they describe a teaching exercise in an urban centre, a place familiar to students from its daytime and night-time economies: 'a closely familiar place but for different reasons, and lacking in obvious traces of a historic past' (2010: 183). The students divide the space into zones, map discarded objects, sketch buildings fronts and identify spots of vandalism and graffiti. These exercises are intended in part to defamiliarize the space, to enable students to see it with an archaeological 'eye', even as the tutor acknowledges that some of the activities that they are tracing might be their own.

Flinders University is home to a long-standing teaching programme in the archaeology of modern material culture, with much of the students' project work published in a series of attractive illustrated booklets.

> Students ... were charged with researching the history and social context of a selection of commonplace items. What they discovered is that often a disposable item used today might have its origins in the 19th century. Looking more closely at what seems familiar reveals their relationships to earlier non-mass produced artefacts and often contexts of use that are very different to today ... When we stop and wonder about the everyday, about how the objects that surround us came into being, we're engaging in what has come to be known as the archaeology of the contemporary past.
>
> Gorman and Wallis 2015: 5

8 *Teaching and Learning the Archaeology of the Contemporary Era*

The projects in question were part of taught modules on 'Modern Material Culture' and 'The Archaeology of Modern Society': in each case, students selected, were allocated or purchased an object that fitted within a set theme. These themes changed each year, and included 'Disposable', 'Recycle(d)', 'Road Tripping', 'Space' and 'War and Peace' (Burke et al. 2021; Gorman and Wallis 2015; Gorman et al. 2018; 2020). For the 'Loveable' theme, students purchased objects from thrift shops (Gorman and Wallis 2017), while 'Cyborg' explored the blurred boundaries between objects and the body (Wallis et al. 2022). Alongside the short essays that students researched and wrote, they were asked to create 'artistic' images based on a photograph of the object. The results are striking and the published works are fascinating, but it is also interesting to reflect on the pedagogical dimensions of this work.

The directives to look 'more closely' and to 'stop and wonder' are aimed at pushing students to the point of defamiliarization. This can be counter-intuitive: students on the 'Loveable' assignment were instructed to buy something small and cheap 'with which they had some affinity': 'What was unexpected in this regard was that some participants ... "fell in love with it"' (Gorman and Wallis 2017: 3–5). The emphasis on the visual outputs of the project is also relevant: Harrison and Schofield discuss the close affinity and synergies between contemporary archaeology and documentary photography (2010: 120–4), and the 'photo-essay' has become a relatively common and distinctive form of research output in the discipline. The openness to novel forms of assessment in contemporary archaeology is shown in several chapters in this book, including Brophy's (Chapter 4) account of field trips to 'urban prehistory' sites in Scotland. Students were encouraged to submit assessments based on artworks and creative writing: later this shifted towards a focus on scrapbooking, incorporating elements of diary, material archive and space for creativity.

Thinking autobiographically

The loved objects of the 'Loveable' project cited above highlight a slight contradiction within contemporary archaeology: despite the widely-agreed value of defamiliarization as a core concept in disciplinary thought and practice, there remains a strong strand of research, practice and teaching based around material that is often powerfully autobiographical. How on earth can one be expected to defamiliarize one's childhood teddy bear, for example, when it is probably more closely affiliated to the platonic ideal of a 'teddy bear' than it is to any concepts of the mass-produced toy?

Bailey's autobiographical account of his intellectual journey into and through contemporary archaeology (Chapter 11) highlights the strands of material connection and chance encounter that characterize much work in the field. In reflecting on his encounters with contemporary archaeology, Bailey draws together many of the themes that resonate across the chapters in this book, including a playful approach to fieldwork, a focus on the materiality of books and other media, and the personal and professional networks that continue to shape contemporary archaeology in practice.

Some of the most striking works in contemporary archaeology are those with an autobiographical dimension, exploring the relationships between people, other people and things. Christine Finn's *Leave-Home-Stay* (2013) explored the clearing out of a dead parent's home as an art-archaeology project, a topic as poignant as it is commonplace, as witnessed by John Schofield's reflections on this experience in his introduction to the book of 'Loveable', cited above:

> While undertaking this difficult yet strangely therapeutic task I recalled many of the stories associated with the objects and mementoes I was curating. I recalled the shops where things were bought, the times we were in, and the stories my mother told people about these everyday objects from around the globe ... The task was only made difficult by the sheer quantity of stuff, the fact of knowing everything held significance for her (and some for me), that she never threw anything away, and that in sorting this collection I couldn't keep everything.
>
> Schofield 2017: vii

In the midst of the Covid pandemic I reviewed student assessments restructured to take into account movement restrictions, including standing building surveys of the students' own quarantine lodgings, the feelings of claustrophobia tangible in the meagre dimensions of the plans and in the written descriptions of the spaces. This highlights another advantage of the autobiographical in contemporary archaeological pedagogy: it is close at hand (if not present at hand) and easily connected to narratives. Larry Zimmerman illustrates these aspects in his writing on two classroom exercises: the 'Excavation of the professor's wastebasket' and the 'Analysis of the professor's desk drawer' (2007: 212). Zimmerman describes how these two exercises are designed, constructed and carried out in practice, in order to teach a relatively wide range of archaeological principles. Beyond typology and stratigraphy, he points out the value of familiar, contemporary objects in context as a way to teach site formation processes and the slippery intellectual underpinnings of archaeology identifications. Zimmerman also notes that 'I personalize the exercise to myself as the Professor so they can get some insight into who I am. Looking at my trash makes them feel they know me better as a person and may show them that I have a sense of humor' (2007: 212–13).

The archaeology of the contemporary university

The links between autobiographical thinking and pedagogy in contemporary archaeology go back a long way. Gould and Schiffer's prescient 1981 publication, *Modern Material Culture: The Archaeology of Us*, contains a number of thoughtful reflections on the value of modern artefacts in the field school and the classroom. Rathje's chapter in particular, titled 'A Manifesto for Modern Material-Culture Studies', argues that:

> The most obvious contribution of modern material-culture studies is teaching archaeological principles. The main advantage of these studies is that students can do their own. Involving undergraduates as archaeological investigators of their society has a variety of unique benefits: (a) Studying an ongoing society makes students aware of the systematic relation between material culture and behavior; (b) students can easily learn the strengths and weaknesses of archaeological methods by applying them in a familiar setting; and (c) data for study are available locally in an unending supply and there is no destruction of older, scarcer sites.
>
> 1981: 53

Zimmerman's work cited above is part of a long history of contemporary archaeological teaching and training that takes the university itself as its subject, reflected also in several chapters in this book, including those by Caraher (Chapter 2), Moshenska (Chapter 6) and Petts (Chapter 3). Wilk and Schiffer's contribution to the 1981 volume focuses on the university campus as a field site for teaching archaeology and includes a reflection on Rathje's argument. They acknowledge the value of modern artefacts in teaching 'seriation, typology, and relationships between social status and possessions', but question whether it can be used to teach the full range of then-modern method and theory (1981: 16). Wilk and Schiffer go on to make the case for contemporary archaeological sites as field schools with a unique capacity to teach both theory and method, with the added advantages of accessibility and easier to locate sites to work on, and less ethically-charged materials (although I would dispute that point). Wilk and Schiffer's aim is to promote the value of archaeological field schools on and off the contemporary university campus. Their argument even draws on the themes of the familiar and the defamiliarized, outlined above:

> Surprisingly, the excitement of 'discovery', so much a part of the fieldwork experience for both student and professional, is not lost. Indeed this experience can be heightened when discoveries are made in familiar places.
>
> 1981: 19

Campus archaeology has a long history in the US in particular, much of it historical and contemporary archaeology (Camp 2022). This includes Laurie Wilkie's study of the Zeta Psi fraternity at UC Berkeley (2010); the long-running Harvard Yard Archaeology Project; and Michigan State University's Campus Archaeology Program (and see also Dufton et al. 2019). Caraher's account of campus archaeology at the University of North Dakota (Chapter 2) illustrates many of the advantages of working 'close to home' as well as its challenges. The living space of the university sees materials consumed and discarded, spaces created, transformed and abandoned, and – for students and well as teachers, in different ways – an opportunity to practice looking again at the familiar material traces of everyday life. Like Caraher, Petts (Chapter 3) showed students how to integrate archival studies of university history into their archaeological studies. The archaeology of the contemporary university is a powerful practice that creates space for defamiliarization processes, a range of pedagogical practices and experiences, and potentially for radical critiques of the neoliberal university and its histories through the lenses of gender, race, class, exclusion and violence.

Critical and radical pedagogies

Despite the relatively small amount of research and writing on archaeological pedagogies noted earlier, there is nonetheless an intellectually rich strand of work critiquing contemporary practices and exploring radical alternatives. Hamilakis' 2004 paper, *Archaeology and the Politics of Pedagogy*, is a landmark in this field, drawing on radical educationalists such as Giroux and Freire and setting out some vital waypoints for exploring the transformative power of critical pedagogy in archaeology. For my own teaching and training in the field, I have found Shanks and McGuire's *The Craft of Archaeology* (1996) and Faulkner's 'Archaeology from Below' (2000) vital to my understanding of archaeological fieldwork as – at its best – a collective learning space with a minimum of formal hierarchy and a cooperative perspective on skills sharing, mistakes, individual growth and participation. Both papers acknowledge that the current arrangements of professional and academic archaeology are inherently antagonistic to this viewpoint – themes also explored by Cobb and Croucher, again within the context of a penetrating critique of archaeological pedagogies and practices (2020, esp. Ch. 4).

There are long-standing connections between contemporary archaeology and public and community archaeology, including collaborative projects and research that includes oral history recording (e.g., Moshenska 2007; Lewis and Waites 2020). In some cases, this overlap reflects Rathje's notion that using contemporary materials for teaching and training protects 'older, scarcer sites'. In other cases, it reflects the relative abundance and accessibility of recent sites, the relative lack of legal restriction on their excavation or access, and – significantly – greater levels of public interest in sites from the recent historical past. This is explored by Äikäs et al. in Chapter 8, looking at public interactions with research and excavations on 'dark heritage' sites in Finland, and the opportunities for engagement and training that these generate for different groups and demographics. As they note, controversial and politically sensitive sites can also present distinctive pedagogical challenges and opportunities, including productive discussions around emotion, reminiscence and reconciliation. Beisaw's account of collaborative community archaeology in Chapter 7 draws on many of these same themes, examining the challenges of building landscape biographies that challenge often deep-seated historical narratives. The power of maps and collaborative map-making that Beisaw explores is another area where the methods and approaches of contemporary archaeology blur with those of human geography and other cognate disciplines, as discussed above.

There is also a growing body of radical critiques of archaeological learning from indigenous, feminist and other historically-silenced perspectives in archaeology, including case studies in collaborative field schools and other archaeological pedagogies (e.g., Gonzalez and Edwards 2020) and research into the demographics and structures of archaeological teaching and training (e.g., Supernant 2020; see also papers in Supernant et al. 2020). Cobb and Croucher draw attention to the influence of feminist thought in driving research and innovation in archaeological pedagogies from the 1990s, including important critiques of earlier radical pedagogies. Feminist, indigenous and other radical critiques of archaeological pedagogy draw attention to deep-seated structural issues with archaeology – among them, the ways that pedagogy tends to be framed as a separate sub-field, distinct and often secondary to practice. This is reflected in debates around indigenous archaeology, for example, and in discussions of how archaeologists should integrate different communities into their work – Sonya Atalay's work is particularly valuable in this regard (e.g., 2012; 2019).

There is arguably a much greater need for socially conscious pedagogies in contemporary archaeology given the frequency with which our work is entangled with living people and communities, including marginalized groups such as homeless people, refugees and people who use drugs. Alongside training in methods and teaching and learning around the intellectual frameworks of contemporary archaeology, there is a need for pedagogies that emphasize ethical praxis and meaningful engagement with stakeholders, and that create space for innovation and new collaborations. Kiddey's account of working with displaced people in Greece in Chapter 10 draws, like Caraher's in Chapter 2, on elements of anarchist pedagogies and practices. Kiddey explores the fluid categories of teacher and student in these encounters, along with other more or less marginalized identities, as well as the openness to methods and connections that often characterize radical approaches in contemporary archaeology.

Radical pedagogies such as these can create spaces for wonder, excitement, exploration and unexpected freedoms. These values are under threat in higher education worldwide, with conservative and populist governments targeting education in general, and the arts, humanities and social sciences in particular. These attacks include idiotic (but still dangerous) rhetoric, the systematic defunding of public education, censorious laws and policies, attacks on educators' employment conditions, the closure of institutions and departments, and attacks on individual scholars. All of these contribute to a climate of fear that encourages 'instrumentalist' perspectives on pedagogy as a source of measurable, monetizable value, a view criticized by Hamilakis (2004) and others. In these circumstances, radical and innovative perspectives on pedagogy are harder to pursue, just as they become more vital than ever.

Discussion

For many years the common view of contemporary archaeologies, such as Rathje's garbage project, was that their primary value lay in ethno-archaeological analogies and as a source of training in basic archaeological field techniques as well as more advanced principles in archaeological reasoning. In contrast today, with a fast-growing interest in the archaeology and heritage of the contemporary era, there is a skills gap in the field:

> This stark dichotomy between the constant increase in heritage-management responsibilities resulting from the inclusion of very recent archaeological remains, and the slowness of universities to adapt to the new situation, with the result that they are not producing enough expert staff with the appropriate training and failing to carry out enough research, is, in my opinion, one of the biggest challenges currently facing historical archaeology in Europe.
>
> Mehler 2020: 783

There is every reason to believe that contemporary archaeology will continue to grow in strength, interest and relevance worldwide, and that pedagogy in the broadest sense will expand and evolve as part of this process. The chapters in this book represent a spectrum of different approaches to contemporary archaeology pedagogies, ranging from formal learning in universities to community collaborations in the field, as well as radical, imaginative and speculative views on the present and future of our teaching and learning practices. There remains a great deal of scope for future scholarship in this area, including more explorations in interdisciplinarity, perspectives from students and community partners, and critical research method resources aimed at graduate students. It will also be interesting to see how formal teaching in contemporary archaeology continues to grow around the world. I hope that this expansion will not stifle the diversity, radicalism and general brilliance of contemporary archaeological pedagogies showcased in the chapters of this book and far beyond.

References

Atalay, S. (2012), *Community-based Archaeology: Research with, by, and for Indigenous and Local Communities*, Oakland: University of California Press.

Atalay, S. (2019), 'Can archaeology help decolonize the way institutions think? How community-based research is transforming the archaeology training toolbox and helping to transform institutions', *Archaeologies* 15 (3): 514–35.

Buchli, V. and G. Lucas, eds (2001), *Archaeologies of the Contemporary Past*, London: Routledge.

Burke, H., L. A. Wallis and A. Gorman, eds (2021a), *War and Peace: A Material Culture Study*, Brighton: Wallis Heritage Consulting.

Burke, H., L. A. Wallis and A. Gorman, eds (2021b), *Recycle(d): Objects and Their Afterlives*, Brighton: Wallis Heritage Consulting.

Camp, S. L. (2022), 'Introduction: A New Era of University Campus Archaeological Programs', *SAA Archaeological Record* 22 (2): 14–16.

Cobb, H. and K. Croucher (2020), *Assembling Archaeology: Teaching, Practice, and Research*, Oxford: Oxford University Press.

Dufton, J. A., L. R. Gosner, A. R. Knodell and C. Steidl (2019), 'Archaeology underfoot: on-campus approaches to education, outreach, and historical archaeology at Brown University', *Journal of Field Archaeology* 44 (5): 304–18.

Faulkner, N. (2000), 'Archaeology from below', *Public Archaeology* 1 (1): 21–33.

Finn, C. (2014), 'Home: an installation for living in', in I. A. Russell and A. Cochrane, eds, *Art and Archaeology: Collaborations, Conversations, Criticisms*, 115–27, New York: Springer.

Geller, P. (2020), 'The archaeology of the disposable mask, and the case for wearing one that's reusable', *Slate*, https://slate.com/technology/2020/10/disposable-masks-ocean-pollution-archaeology.html.

Gonzalez, S. L. and B. Edwards (2020), 'The intersection of Indigenous thought and archaeological practice: the field methods in Indigenous archaeology field school', *Journal of Community Archaeology & Heritage* 7 (4): 239–54.

González-Ruibal, A. (2019), *An Archaeology of the Contemporary Era*, Abingdon: Routledge.

Gorman, A. (2019), *Dr Space Junk vs the Universe: Archaeology and the Future*, Cambridge, MA: MIT Press.

Gorman, A., H. Burke, and L. Wallis, eds (2020), *Space: An Exploration of Objects*, Brighton: Wallis Heritage Consulting.

Gorman, A. and L. Wallis, eds (2015), *Disposable: The Stories Behind Everyday Objects*, Brighton: Wallis Heritage Consulting.

Gorman, A., and L. Wallis, eds (2017), *Loveable: The Stories Behind Thriftshop Objects*, Brighton: Wallis Heritage Consulting.

Gorman, A., L. Wallis, and H. Burke, eds (2018), *Road Tripping: A Journey of Artefacts*, Brighton: Wallis Heritage Consulting.

Gould, R. A. and M. B. Schiffer, eds (1981), *Modern Material Culture: The Archaeology of Us*, New York: Academic Press.

Graves-Brown, P. (2011), 'Touching from a distance: alienation, abjection, estrangement and archaeology', *Norwegian Archaeological Review* 44 (2): 131–44.

Graves-Brown, P., ed. (2000), *Matter, Materiality and Modern Culture*, London: Routledge.

Hamilakis, Y. (2004), 'Archaeology and the politics of pedagogy', *World Archaeology* 36 (2): 287–309.

Harrison, R. and J. Schofield (2010), *After Modernity: Archaeological Approaches to the Contemporary Past*, Oxford: Oxford University Press.

Hill, L. J. (2015), 'Human geography and archaeology: strange bedfellows?', *Progress in Human Geography* 39 (4): 412–31.

Lewis, C. and I. Waites (2020), 'New light on an old problem: child-related archaeological finds and the impact of the "Radburn" council estate plan', *Journal of Contemporary Archaeology* 6 (2): 245–73.

Mehler, N. (2020), 'Historical archaeology in Europe', in C. E. Orser Jr, A. Zarankin, P. Funari, S. Lawrence and J. Symonds, eds, *The Routledge Handbook of Global Historical Archaeology*, 780–97, Abingdon: Routledge.

Moshenska, G. (2007), 'Oral history in historical archaeology: excavating sites of memory', *Oral History* 35 (1): 91–9.

Moshenska, G. (2021), 'Degrowth and archaeological learning beyond the neo-liberal university', *Archaeological Dialogues* 28 (1): 19–21.

Rathje, W. (1981), 'A manifesto for modern material-culture studies', in R. A. Gould and M. B. Schiffer, eds, *Modern Material Culture: The Archaeology of Us*, 51–6, New York: Academic Press.

Schofield, J. (2017), 'Foreword', in A. Gorman and L. Wallis, eds, *Loveable: The Stories Behind Thriftshop Objects*, vii–2, Brighton: Wallis Heritage Consulting.

Schofield, J., E. Praet, K. A. Townsend and J. Vince (2021), '"COVID waste" and social media as method: an archaeology of personal protective equipment and its contribution to policy', *Antiquity* 95 (380): 435–49.

Shanks, M. and R. H. McGuire (1996), 'The craft of archaeology', *American Antiquity* 61 (1): 75–88.

Supernant, K. (2020), 'Archaeological Pedagogy, Indigenous Histories, and Reconciliation in Canada', *Journal of Archaeology and Education* 4 (3).

Supernant, K., J. E. Baxter, N. Lyons and S. Atalay, eds (2020), *Archaeologies of the Heart*, New York: Springer.

Wallis, L., H. Burke and A. Gorman, eds (2022), *Cyborg: How Humans are Becoming Machines*, Brighton: Wallis Heritage Consulting.

Wilk, R. and M. B. Schiffer (1981), 'The modern material-culture field school: teaching archaeology on the university campus', in R. A. Gould and M. B. Schiffer, eds, *Modern Material Culture: The Archaeology of Us*, 15–30, New York: Academic Press.

Wilkie, L. A. (2010), *The Lost Boys of Zeta Psi: A Historical Archaeology of Masculinity in a University Fraternity*, Berkeley: University of California Press.

Zimmerman, L. (2007), 'Simple ideas to teach big concepts: "excavating" and analyzing the professor's desk drawer and wastebasket', in H. Burke and C. Smith, eds, *Archaeology to Delight and Instruct: Active Learning in the University Classroom* , 211–22, Walnut Creek, CA: Left Coast Press.

Part One

Course and Curriculum Development

1

Contemporary Art and Archaeology: Interdisciplinary Pedagogy and Practice in the Digital University

Antonia Thomas

Introduction

This chapter considers ways of linking creative practice with contemporary archaeology in higher education. My discussion pivots around the interdisciplinary master's programme – the MA Contemporary Art and Archaeology (MA CAA) – which I lead at Orkney College, part of the University of the Highlands and Islands (UHI), Scotland, UK. Developed from professional modules and workshops in art and archaeology over the past decade, the MA was launched in September 2020. It encourages a collaborative and interdisciplinary approach which combines contemporary art theory and practice with the study of traditional archaeological subjects and themes. It is also explicitly informed by contemporary archaeology. This is presented to students as an approach to archaeological research that regards recent and contemporary societies (late twentieth- and twenty-first-century) as worthy of archaeological investigation, whilst recognizing that all pasts exist and are understood in the present.

The MA CAA is team-taught and subsequently draws on a diverse range of influences. In addition to being aligned with contemporary archaeology, much of the thinking which inspires our methodology originates with the critical ideas around art and pedagogy that emerged in Europe and the USA during the twentieth century. These include the experimental art teaching, research and practices of the Bauhaus School in Germany, from 1919 to 1933, Black Mountain College in the USA, from 1933 to 1956, and various successors including the Fluxus collective (and in particular, the influence of one of its founders, Joseph Beuys) and the Edinburgh Arts initiatives led by Richard Demarco in Scotland. I will expand a little upon these diverse influences further below, but it is important to note that they all involved interdisciplinary collaboration, 'learning through doing', and the blurring of boundaries between not only disciplines, but between teacher and student, research and practice (Allen ed. 2011; Hills 2019; Sutherland 2020).

In line with these influences, our goal with the MA CAA is not to turn artists into archaeologists, nor archaeologists into artists. Instead, we aim to allow a 'safe' space to ask questions, with these then determining what disciplinary skills and approaches might be relevant (see also Loveless 2019: 40). Art and archaeology provide reference points from which to explore wider creative engagements – across and beyond disciplines. We recognize the need for inter- and transdisciplinary thinking to embrace the complexity of the contemporary world (Braidotti and Hlavajova 2018: 10; see also Thomas et al. 2018: 127). New questions require new approaches. These require an expanded notion of what archaeology is – and what it could be – with students encouraged to think outside of their disciplinary comfort zones.

Formative and summative assessments are not limited to traditional academic formats such as written essays but can include a range of outputs such as films, sound pieces, paintings and three-dimensional artefacts in a range of artistic media. There are few restrictions on the form that assessed work may take, so long as it involves a critical investigation of the relationship between contemporary art and archaeology. Uniquely, the teaching is, and always has been, delivered largely online and through a mixture of asynchronous and synchronous learning. This allows us to challenge traditional pedagogic models for the 'hands-on' subject areas of art and archaeology, whilst expanding possibilities for participatory and conceptual practice across an internationally situated cohort of students. These aspects have highlighted critical intersections between socially engaged art, practice-as-research and contemporary archaeology. I will return to these later, but first I want to outline some of the historical background for these developments.

A (partial) history

In the early decades of the twentieth century, several avant-garde groups and movements started to emerge across Europe. Although diverse, common goals included breaking down institutional and disciplinary hierarchies around art in the academy, and integrating art practice with everyday life. The most famous was the Bauhaus School, founded in 1919 by architect Walter Gropius in Weimar and established on the idea of *Gesamtkunstwerk* or 'complete work of art' to bring all the arts together. The preliminary course at the Bauhaus, first at Weimar and then in Dessau and Berlin, was created by Johannes Itten and then developed by Josef Albers and László Moholy-Nagy. It included a wide range of practical but playful creative exercises including mirror writing, paper folding, drawing from memory, working with found objects and photography. In 1933, the Nazis closed the Bauhaus, forcing the exile of many of its teachers including Josef Albers, who was then invited to join the teaching team at the new Black Mountain College (BMC) in North Carolina, USA. The BMC's ethos was also heavily influenced by the writings of philosopher and educational reformer John Dewey, who famously considered the meaning and value of art to reside not merely in the object but in the processes that it produced and the experiences it provides (2005/1934). Dewey's belief that everyone was capable of being an artist was in turn a significant influence on Joseph Beuys, a founding figure in the Dada-inspired Fluxus movement in the early 1960s.

In 1968, Scottish artist-curator Richard Demarco met Joseph Beuys in Germany and persuaded him to make his UK debut at the Edinburgh Festival. This was the start of a long collaborative association. In 1972, partly modelled on Black Mountain College, Demarco initiated Edinburgh Arts. Between 1972 and 1980, Edinburgh Arts' summer schools deliberately blurred the boundaries between student and teacher and approached learning and teaching through art as an interdisciplinary pursuit that included ecology, architecture, archaeology and literature, as well as traditional crafts and folk culture (Sutherland 2020: 45). In 1976, the summer school involved a seventy-day, 7,500-mile journey from Malta to Orkney, where the group explored prehistoric and Norse archaeological sites, saw films by the experimental Orcadian filmmaker/poet Margaret Tait and met with contemporary photographer Gunnie Moberg and her husband, the conceptual artist and bookseller Tam MacPhail, amongst others. Demarco's syllabus deliberately combined the avant-garde with the traditional and historical, drawing 'parallels and connections with the cutting edge of contemporary art and what had gone before, often by millennia' (Sutherland 2020: 283). The Edinburgh Arts summer schools provide a key historical context for art and archaeology in Orkney.

Contemporary art and contemporary archaeology

My interest in this chapter is in the relationship between *contemporary* art and *contemporary* archaeology. Contemporary archaeology is interdisciplinary (Graves-Brown et al. 2013: 2) and can comprise, and intersect with, art history and theory, anthropology, sociology, cultural studies, heritage studies, history, geography, philosophy, politics and more. These overlaps suggest possibilities for a practice-led approach to contemporary archaeology that is not restricted to being archaeological (Bailey 2017; Thomas et al. 2018). Contemporary archaeology may be considered as having a 'special relationship' with art practice (Harrison and Schofield 2010: 107; see also Farstadvoll 2019: 4), developed through shared histories of collecting and display, visual methodologies and material engagement. The disciplinary histories of antiquarianism, archaeology and art history which emerged together in the nineteenth century have been discussed elsewhere (e.g., Russell 2013), but it is important to note that this problematic foundation provides a rich context for critical interrogation by contemporary artists (Roelstraete 2013). Contemporary archaeology, as Laura McAtackney and Krista Ryzewski note, also has the potential to operate as both 'a politically engaged cultural critique' and 'a creative practice' (2017: 5). This resonates with Doug Bailey's call for art/archaeology work to go beyond the traditional boundaries of both art and archaeology and to disrupt conventional, politically-loaded narratives of the past (2014; 2017; 2018). For Bailey, 'non-archaeologicality' is not only acceptable but encouraged (2017: 699).

And increasingly archaeologists *are* experimenting with practices such as photography, filmmaking and counter-mapping in their research, chiming with wider trends towards participatory and cross-disciplinary art practice (see, for example, contributions in Russell and Cochrane 2014; Thomas et al. 2018; Gheorgiu and Barth 2019). These art–archaeology engagements are exciting and important. But they have often seemed to exist alongside, rather than integrated with, *educational practice* in archaeology, or considered in the context of wider interdisciplinary pedagogies. Despite the awareness of the inherently political nature of knowledge production in archaeology that emerged with post-processual thinking, these insights have not generally been applied to archaeology teaching. A notable exception is the excellent recent volume by Hannah Cobb and Karina Croucher (2020), which draws heavily upon the concept of assemblage as developed by Gilles Deleuze and Felix Guattari (1987).

The non-hierarchical and unconstrained system suggested by Deleuze and Guattari's concept of the rhizome (1987: 7–9), with its potential to reframe learning as a messy, creative process that is driven by practice rather than the need to produce an end product, has also been highly influential in critical pedagogies in art. Art's 'socio-pedagogical turn' (Hill 2019) can be closely connected to the growth in socially engaged, participatory and research-based practice since the turn of the millennium (Allen 2011), and has much to offer the teaching of archaeology. But despite the growing trend for interdisciplinary projects and research outside the academy, the MA Contemporary Art and Archaeology at UHI is currently the only postgraduate course to link art *practice* with archaeology.

MA Contemporary Art and Archaeology at UHI

From the outset, the teaching on the MA Contemporary Art and Archaeology has been informed by research and practice. Although building on a long tradition of interactions between artists and archaeologists in Orkney, the MA CAA was developed out of conversations that emerged during projects over the last fifteen years. These include the Test Trenches interdisciplinary residency undertaken with the Tabula Rasa contemporary arts collective working with myself and archaeologist Daniel Lee in 2010–11 (Thomas 2014). Subsequent activities include the participatory Map Orkney Month project (Lee 2016; Lee 2018), the Archaeologists-in-Residence project by Daniel Lee and myself at the Papay Gyro Nights Contemporary Arts Festival in 2013–14 (Lee and Thomas 2013; Lee 2018; see Figure 1.1), and the Wilder Being participatory environmental art project led by artist Anne Bevan and archaeologist Jane Downes (Bevan and Downes 2018).

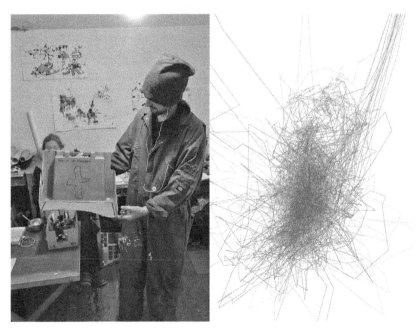

Figure 1.1 Collaborative mapping (object-studio-island) with artists Brendan Colvert and Rosey Priestman during Papay Gyro Nights Contemporary Arts Festival in 2014. Image © Daniel Lee

These projects laid the foundation for the research-led teaching in contemporary art and contemporary archaeology at UHI. In 2015, we ran the UHI's first Art and Archaeology summer school in Orkney, which combined studio-based practice in casting and printmaking with archaeological fieldtrips, outdoor drawing and informal lectures. In November 2016, the Archaeology Institute UHI hosted the annual Contemporary and Historical Archaeology in Theory (CHAT) conference in Orkney, with 'Rurality' as its main theme (CHATRurality), and a standalone 20-credit master's module in Art and Archaeology was launched in January 2017. This remains as stand-alone course for continuing professional development for artists and others, but has also been incorporated into the full MA as a compulsory component.

The MA CAA programme sits within the Creative and Cultural Industries Subject Network at UHI. Core lecturing staff are drawn from both the art and the archaeology departments, and include myself, artist Anne Bevan and archaeologist Daniel Lee, with input from guest lecturers from both art and archaeology. In the 2021–2 academic year, guest lecturers included artist Christine Borland and archaeologist Mark Edmonds, with Helen Wickstead, noted for her extensive engagements linking contemporary art and archaeology, as External Examiner. Core modules provide a theoretical and contextual background, with real-time online lectures exploring themes ranging from media archaeology to psychogeography and creative mapping, and from graffiti to space archaeology.

Running alongside the synchronous thematic lectures in the core modules are a series of 'mini-projects'. These playful visual art exercises are either undertaken in the students' own time or during break-out group sessions during online meetings, and explore archaeological techniques, concepts and material through creative and practice-led engagement with everyday objects and encounters. Students share and discuss their results on the Virtual Learning Environment, or VLE (currently Brightspace™) and in group tutorials. The preliminary mini-projects focus on drawing, in recognition of its important role in archaeological knowledge production (Morgan et al. 2021). The intention is not archaeological accuracy but is deliberately subjective and exploratory to allow an understanding of the relationship between traces and marks, gesture, scale and time (Wickstead 2013). Archaeology's particular 'way of seeing' is further explored through mini-projects in a range of topics including object studies, counter-mapping and psychogeographical *dérives*. Through their own exploratory art-based process, students learn about a range of aspects relating to contemporary archaeology, such as the subjectivity of archaeological interpretation and recording, the significance of apparently 'mundane' material culture and places, and the tension between personal and political memories.

Collaborative practice is an essential feature of creative art/archaeology work, and group working is encouraged throughout the course – even when this involves different time zones. In the second half of the teaching year, students collaborate in small groups and co-design activities and mini-projects for the rest of the cohort. This allows them to feed back into teaching, enabling reflexive, collaborative engagement in the curriculum, as the rest of the class undertake each other's mini-projects and document these in their journals. The 50 per cent weighting given to the reflective journal/sketchbook as assessment for the core modules highlights the importance of this creative experimentation, with students encouraged to see the 'thinking-through-doing' of creative practice as a form of research in itself (see also Thomas 2014). It allows a focus on process, and the 'messier' (*sensu* Law 2004) aspects of research needed for critical and creative thinking. This is important: if we are to encourage new forms of creative interdisciplinary practice, there also need to be new and innovative teaching methods and assessment criteria (Hawkins 2018: 154).

Over the course of their registration, the MA students also have to choose at least one module taken from the archaeology course catalogue (including Heritage Management, Neolithic Studies, Iron Age Scotland and Early Medieval Archaeology). This allows other subjects, periods and specialisms to be seen through a critical and creative contemporary archaeology lens, 'resisting a narrative drive that would result in setting up a "contemporary archaeology" to sit alongside "the Neolithic" or "the Iron Age"' (Piccini and Holtorf 2009: 14; see also Dixon 2009). Students must also choose at least one module in creative practice (including Art and Environment, Creative Re-use of Archive Film, Creative Writing and Acoustic Ecologies). This structure encourages critical self-reflection in the presentation, study and interpretation of the past *and* the present. It aims to highlight the intersections between art and archaeology in relation to the historical and cultural contexts of both disciplines, and how these have political implications in the contemporary world. The core and elective creative modules allow these contexts to be interrogated through *practice*. A practice-led methodology for art–archaeology engagements, as Ursula Frederick and Tracy Ireland have argued, allows us to 'move away from considering art as the *object* of investigation to an approach whereby art may also become the *means* of scrutiny' (2019: 281; original emphasis).

That scrutiny can take many forms. In her project '*An Talla*: Giving a Voice to the Voiceless', MA CAA student Aileen Ogilvie used her background in music

Figure 1.2 Aileen Ogilvie performing in the abandoned space of Perth City Hall in 2020, for her project '*An Talla*: Giving a Voice to the Voiceless'. Image © Aileen Ogilvie.

production and performance, and her expertise as a Gaelic speaker and singer-songwriter, to study Perth City Hall, which has lain empty since 2005. She used her voice as a tool of archaeological enquiry, by performing Gaelic songs in different areas of the abandoned hall to investigate the interaction between tangible and intangible heritage (see Figure 1.2). In doing so, she worked at the boundaries of both contemporary archaeology, autoethnography and creative practice-as-research.

Practice-as-research in art and archaeology

Over the last twenty years, there has been an increased focus on practice, participation and action research across a number of disciplines in the social sciences, arts and humanities (Penrhyn Jones 2019). In a higher education context, practice-as-research 'involves a research project in which practice is a key method of inquiry and where, in respect of the arts, a practice (creative writing, dance, musical score/performance, theatre/performance, visual exhibition, film or other cultural practice) is submitted as substantial evidence of a research inquiry' (Nelson 2013: 8–9).

The growth of art practice-as-research within the academy can be related to both the 'socio-pedagogical turn' in contemporary art (in part influenced by the experimental art approaches of the BMC, Fluxus and others in the twentieth century) and the increasing influence of critical interdisciplinarity, as part of a wider rise in poststructuralist, feminist, queer and critical race theoretical approaches (Loveless 2019: 40). These emerged alongside developments in critical pedagogy and the work of theorists such as Paolo Freire, who famously critiqued the dominant model of teaching as a unilinear process of banking, where the 'active' teacher banks knowledge with a 'passive' student (1979). Following Freire (and Stuart Hall), Henry Giroux conceived public pedagogy as part of 'a critical practice designed to understand the social context of everyday life as lived relations of power' (Giroux 2011/2000: 49). There is a clear alignment here with various developments within post-processual archaeology from the 1990s, which also emphasized self-reflexivity, individual agency and historical contingency (Cobb and Croucher 2020: 28). These firmly situated archaeology as a 'craft', which takes place in the present as a cultural and political practice, and in which research is inalienable from pedagogy (Shanks and McGuire 1996).

As Angela Piccini notes, there is an important relationship between archaeological practice and practice-as-research in art, with both archaeology and creative practice employing 'a combination of lab/studio- and field-based practices with material storytelling' (Piccini and Holtorf 2009: 12–13). Outside of the art department, archaeology is arguably one of the most visually oriented subjects within the university. Archaeologists make use of an incredible range of visual media produced by both analogue and digital technologies, and including freehand sketches, laser scans, CAD drawings, archive maps and historical photographs, at a range of scales from microscopy to satellite imagery (Kavanagh 2007: 151). Helen Wickstead has discussed how archaeology draws within an 'expanded field' (*sensu* Krauss 1979) and suggests that activities such as excavation, surveying and geophysics can be considered as drawing (2013: 552). Despite this, archaeological teaching tends not to stray too far from 'objective' visual methods. Why, for example, are students in archaeology not ordinarily encouraged to keep a sketchbook which supports and feeds into their studies? Why do traditional archaeology degrees not usually permit students to submit a film instead of an essay? It is widely accepted that archaeology is a visual discipline, and that this visuality is not neutral (González-Ruibal 2020), but only rarely is that visuality interrogated critically and creatively within the *teaching* of archaeology.

Many of our mini-projects are explicitly inspired by pedagogical exercises developed by the twentieth-century avant-garde artist groups and institutions described earlier. These provide models for exploratory practice that can be used to interrogate visual methods in archaeology, through their application to contemporary subjects and sites. In other cases, these mini-projects form the springboard for more advanced explorations, such as Eòghann MacColl's compass-point drawing, made as a psychogeography project and submitted as coursework. This was given additional relevance and meaning as it was undertaken during lockdown in the Covid-19 pandemic. Restricted to his farm, MacColl made live drawings whilst walking to four cardinal compass points at the farm's boundaries, with the drawings left on the art piece installed at each point (see Figure 1.3). He later repeated this exercise live over Zoom™ as part of the FestivalCHAT conference in November 2020, in an innovative performance combining analogue and digital creative practice.[1]

Figure 1.3 Live drawing by Eòghann MacColl: '(Re)mapping the way: psychogeography in a rural place'. Undertaken as part of the MA Contemporary Art and Archaeology and later presented at FestivalCHAT in 2020. Image © Eòghann MacColl.

Art practice-as-research, as noted by Natalie Loveless, demands 'an inter- or trans-disciplinary perspective that, while marshalling the insights of emerging and developing fine arts methodologies, exceeds the fine arts proper' (2019: 7). It has clear overlaps with critical interdisciplinarity, which involves 'a process of disruption, a search for ambiguity, and an act of provocation' (Condee 2006: 21). This definition chimes with Doug Bailey's call for a deliberately provocative art/archaeology that 'disarticulates, repurposes and disrupts' (2017). Practice-as-research therefore has political as well as pedagogical potential. It can destabilize the traditional division of labour where artists are seen as producers of art, whilst academics talk and write about art as part of their research (Malterud 2012: 3). In archaeology, it is equally true that the way we teach and learn has fundamental sociopolitical dimensions (Cobb and Croucher 2020: 17), yet the potential for practice-as-research within conventional archaeology teaching and learning remains to be realized.

Creative practice in the digital university

The UHI comprises thirteen semi-autonomous partner colleges and research institutions geographically spread over an area that is roughly the size of Belgium. The hybrid and online delivery models used in many of its courses means that students join not only from the Highlands and Islands of Scotland, but from every inhabited continent in the world. Past and present MA CAA students include practitioners from a range of creative and academic disciplines, and are based in the USA, Canada, Italy, France, Ireland and the UK. Within such a distributed university, participation and collaboration can be challenging, requiring full use of blended learning approaches.

The MA CAA is based in Orkney and builds on the archipelago's rich history of art and archaeology interactions. But from the outset, it was designed for online delivery. Synchronous, 'real-time' seminars and tutorials take place over the VLE, which is linked to course content, reading lists and library hyperlinks, web resources, online forums and discussion boards, supplemented by asynchronous learning in the form of pre-recorded lectures and self-guided 'mini-projects'. Analogue exercises done outside the classroom are photographed or scanned and shared digitally. Students meet in small groups outside the timetabled sessions and undertake distance collaborations using digital platforms of their own choice. Our 'flipped' classroom then uses scheduled lecture slots for interaction and discussion, aiming to avoid the unilinear outpouring of knowledge from lecturer to student (e.g., Freire's 'banking' model). The student becomes the active agent in their digital learning.

Media theorist David Gauntlett has argued that the internet – and by extension digital teaching and learning – can be an empowering creative space for people 'who like to make things, share ideas, and learn together' (Gauntlett 2014). There is a radical potential here to exploit the creative opportunities afforded by digital technologies whilst practising a critical archaeology (Gartski 2022). The shift from 'spade-work' to 'screen-work' in archaeological practice (Edgeworth 2015) and the recent growth in digital art–archaeology engagements (e.g., Tringham 2016; Danis 2019; Reilly et al. 2020; Dawson et al. 2022) suggest some exciting future directions for student work. One example can be seen in the innovative co-designed virtual fieldtrips to Dumbarton Rock led by the interdisciplinary art–archaeology team of Gina Wall and Alex Hale as a response to the Covid-19 pandemic (Wall and Hale 2020). These disrupted and reimagined the digitally accessible archives of Historic Environment Scotland to create new critical readings of sites and landscapes. Their work showed that rather than being an inferior substitute for in-person teaching, digital teaching allows possibilities for social engagement and critical practice that might not otherwise be possible. Teaching and learning contemporary archaeology, through art practice, in a digital university can generate 'different imaginative expectation(s)' (Wall 2015: 9). This can be seen in Rebecca Lambert's ongoing 'Underpasses are Liminal Places' project,[2] initiated as part of her coursework for the Art and Archaeology module (see Figure 1.4). This has since developed into a multimedia, participatory project using a range of social media platforms and an ongoing, crowdfunded website, and has been presented to several international audiences including at the FestivalCHAT in 2020.

Gina Wall has argued for the radical and democratizing potential of digital teaching. In her discussion of her previous role teaching fine art by distance learning at the UHI, she drew parallels with projects such as the Collège Internationale de Philosophie and the Copenhagen Free University. Wall notes that this model requires us 'to constantly rethink the *site* of the university' (2015: 6). Within the digital university, or *trans*versity as she calls it, 'learning and teaching do not happen in place but between places, in the textured learning space facilitated by technology' (Wall 2015: 8).

By opening up possibilities for *where* pedagogy happens, we can challenge the dominant power structures which support the neoliberal university system (Schick and Timperley 2021: 4). We need to recognize, however, that the digital technologies which allow these interactions have themselves been created as part

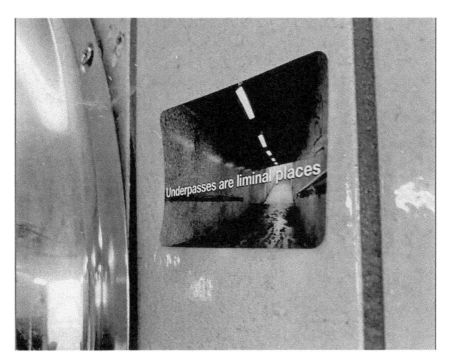

Figure 1.4 Still from Rebecca Lambert's multimedia 'Underpasses are Liminal Spaces' project. Image © Rebecca Lambert.

of the political economy of late capitalist knowledge production (Braidotti 2018). There is always the danger that remote digital learning could simply reverse the banking model (Cobb and Croucher 2020: 135). To some extent this can be mitigated through the encouragement of collaborative group work, and overall, my experience of distance delivery has been that so far, the benefits outweigh any potential risks. By flattening the social hierarchies between student and teacher (Wall 2015: 8), it makes education possible for a range of students, many of whom might not be able to study otherwise because of health inequalities or caring responsibilities. Digital delivery brings the sociopolitical conditions of learning and teaching to the forefront of our considerations and pedagogical practice.

Art-as-social practice-as-contemporary archaeology?

The MA Contemporary Art and Archaeology is currently one of two taught postgraduate programmes within the Visual Arts at UHI, the other being the MA Art and Social Practice (MA ASP) led by Roxane Permar from the Centre for Island Creativity, Shetland College UHI. Established in 2017, the MA Art and Social Practice at UHI was the first course of its nature to be delivered online and from a rural setting. Designed for practitioners who are committed to socially engaged art practice within their communities, its digital delivery allows for a disruption to conventional ideas about where art practices are located and how work is disseminated. This MA provided a framework for the delivery and direction of the MA Contemporary Art and Archaeology. From the outset, modules and extracurricular events such as guest seminars have been shared between the two programmes. Several MA CAA students elect to take modules within the MA ASP diet, and students enrolled on the MA ASP (and MSc Archaeological Practice students) can elect a module in Contemporary Art and Archaeology.

In delivery and structure, the MA CAA has been aligned with the MA Art and Social Practice from the beginning, but as the courses have grown in parallel, a number of synergies between socially engaged art and contemporary archaeology have also emerged. The digital delivery of both MAs means that many students are part-time and are professional practitioners working within their communities in a range of roles (including community archaeologists, art teachers, educational psychologists and social workers). Their experiences make a critical contribution. For example, drawing on her work as a community archaeologist working on the CITiZAN (Coastal and Intertidal Zone Archaeological Network) and inspired by Wall and Hale's call to reimagine archives (2020), MA CAA student Lara Band created the film-based installation 'Lines of Rupture, Lines of Flight' for the Creative Re-Use of Archive Film module. It uses archive moving image, layered with contemporary sound to explore memory and the multi-temporal post-industrial landscape of Pegwell Bay Hoverport, Kent, England. It is an excellent example of creative practice-as-research and filmmaking as contemporary archaeology (see Figure 1.5).

A participatory approach is taken by MA CAA student Carmel Brennan, whose remarkable ongoing project 'Letters to the Earth: Between Despair and Hope' involves more than fifty international collaborators in the UK, Europe, Canada and the USA, each of whom have created an artwork or essay responding to the climate crisis. Her sensitive work demonstrates the necessity for interdisciplinary work, particularly when it is practice-led, to respond to our unprecedented environmental situation (see also Braidotti and Hlavajova 2018: 10). It is scheduled to be exhibited in Canada in 2023.

Socially engaged art practice involves people as the central artistic focus, medium or material and often serves to challenge the conventional modes of

Figure 1.5 Still from the 'Lines of Rupture, Lines of Flight (Pegwell Bay)' film installation by Lara Band, 2022. Image © Lara Band.

artistic production and consumption under capitalism (Bishop 2012: 2). There are clear synergies with recent contemporary archaeology projects which have combined theoretical and methodological approaches to focus on and collaborate with marginalized people. Examples include Rachael Kiddey's groundbreaking collaborative heritage work with homeless colleagues, which she describes as 'an explicit form of therapeutic social intervention' (2017: 167), and Laura McAtackney's explorations of imprisonment and dark heritage (2014). In highlighting the need for constructive social and political change, these archaeologies mirror socially-engaged art. They have, as James Dixon has noted, the potential to do much more than try to understand the past, 'namely, to understand ourselves and use our perspective on the relationship between people and things to consider how we think and act in the present' (2009: 26). These considerations lie at the heart of the MA Contemporary Art and Archaeology.

Conclusions

The MA Contemporary Art and Archaeology at UHI welcomed its third cohort of students at the start of the academic year in September 2022. With each year, the student cohort has involved practitioners from different disciplinary, social and geographical backgrounds. These shifts affect the focus and directions that our conversations take, and the course content and outputs evolve accordingly.

Although it builds on several years of teaching and practice linking art and archaeology at Orkney College UHI, as a full taught postgraduate programme it is still relatively young and in a process of becoming. Launched in September 2020, as the UK was still under restrictions relating to the Covid-19 pandemic, the MA has been delivered during exceptional times for both the creative industries and higher education. Despite these challenges, the quality, range and originality of the work produced by students is extraordinary and truly crosses boundaries between contemporary art and contemporary archaeology.

The MA CAA's position within Visual Arts, rather than Archaeology, is fundamental. The ability to submit sound pieces, or films, or a series of paintings or drawings, for example, rather than being constrained by a rigid essay format, allows for a flexibility and creativity that is essential to explore contemporary archaeology. In her critical review of inter- and trans-disciplinarity in archaeology, Liv Nilsson Stutz makes a plea for 'a collaborative transdisciplinary archaeology that truly integrates multiple perspectives to understand the past, and that insists on problematizing it – and our contemporary world – not on simplifying it' (Nilsson Stutz 2018: 55). These multiple perspectives must include the adoption of new methodologies beyond the restrictive formats of traditional university archaeology teaching, including those borrowed from visual arts practice.

On a personal level, the interdisciplinary dialogues with the rest of teaching team, the guest lecturers and of course the student-practitioners have allowed me to reflect upon my own work linking art and archaeology. My experience leading the MA has made me think about my professional identity and question what form my own 'practice' takes, as an archaeologist, teaching art practice-as-research, within a digital university. I have been introduced to radical new interpretations of archaeological evidence and topics by the students and have come to appreciate the importance of my teaching and collaboration as forms of socially engaged art practice in their own right.

In this chapter, I have discussed the MA Contemporary Art and Archaeology at UHI within the wider context of developments in socially engaged practice, critical interdisciplinarity and art practice-as-research. In their shared concerns with breaking down disciplinary and social barriers, these find common ground with contemporary archaeology. Digital teaching plays a key role in realizing the radical creative and social potential of these developments. In combining these factors, the MA Contemporary Art and Archaeology at UHI is demonstrating the potential to integrate practice-as-research with critical interdisciplinary pedagogies and forge a new *transdisciplinary* direction for applied Contemporary

Art and Archaeology work. This direction can be socially engaged, inclusive and radical in both its ethos and the creative practice it generates.

Acknowledgements

This chapter is dedicated to the staff and especially the students on the MA Contemporary Art and Archaeology at UHI, for their inspirational input over the last few years – thank you so much for everything you've taught me. I am particularly grateful to Lara Band, Rebecca Lambert, Eòghann MacColl and Aileen Ogilvie for sharing elements of their coursework and artistic output. Thanks also to Daniel Lee and Rachael Kiddey for reading and commenting on earlier drafts of this chapter.

Notes

1 https://festivalchat2020.wordpress.com/2020/10/15/psychogeography-in-a-rural-place/.
2 http://www.liminalworlds.org/liminal-underpasses/.

References

Allen, F., ed. (2011), *Education (Documents of Contemporary Art)*, London and Cambridge, MA: Whitechapel Gallery/MIT Press.
Bailey, D. (2014), 'Art // Archaeology // Art: letting-go beyond', in I. A. Russell and A. Cochrane, eds, *Art and Archaeology: Collaborations, Conversations, Criticisms*, 231–50, New York: Springer-Kluwer, DOI: 10.1007/978-1-4614-8990-0_15.
Bailey, D. (2017), 'Disarticulate–Repurpose–Disrupt: Art/Archaeology', *Cambridge Archaeological Journal* 27 (4): 691–701, DOI:10.1017/S0959774317000713.
Bailey, D. (2018), 'Art/Archaeology: What Value Artistic–Archaeological Collaboration?', *Journal of Contemporary Archaeology* 4 (2): 246–56, DOI: 10.1558/jca.34116.
Bevan, E. A. and J. Downes (2018), 'Thinking Place: A Creative Exploration of Coastal Erosion', *Journal of Contemporary Archaeology* 4 (2): 229–37, DOI: 10.1558/jca.32394
Bishop, C. (2012), *Artificial Hells: Participatory Art and the Politics of Spectatorship*, London: Verso.
Braidotti, R. (2018), 'Foreword', in V. Bozalek, R. Braidotti, T. Shefer and M. Zembylas, eds, *Socially Just Pedagogies: Posthumanist, Feminist and Materialist Perspectives in Higher Education*, xiii–xxviii, London: Bloomsbury Academic.

Braidotti, R. and M. Hlavajova (2018), 'Introduction', in R. Braidotti and M. Hlavajova, eds, *Posthuman Glossary*, 1–14, London: Bloomsbury Academic.

Cobb, H. and K. Croucher (2020), *Assembling Archaeology: Teaching, Practice, and Research*, Oxford: Oxford University Press, DOI: 10.1093/oso/9780198784258.001.0001.

Condee, W. (2006), 'The Interdisciplinary Turn in the Arts and Humanities', *Issues in Interdisciplinary Studies* 34: 12–29.

Danis, A. (2019), 'Augmented, Hyper-mediated, IRL', *European Journal of Archaeology* 22 (3): 386–97.

Dawson, I., A. M. Jones, L. Minkin and P. Reilly, eds (2022), *Diffracting Digital Images: Archaeology, Art Practice and Cultural Heritage*, London: Routledge.

Deleuze, G. and F. Guattari (1987), *A Thousand Plateaus: Capitalism and Schizophrenia*, trans. Brian Massumi, London: Continuum.

Dewey, J. (2005/1934), *Art as Experience*, London: Penguin Books.

Dixon, J. (2009), 'An Archaeological Avant-Garde', in A. Horning and M. Palmer, eds, *Engaging the Recent Past: Public, Political, Post-Medieval Archaeology*, 101–10, SPMA Monograph no. 5, Leeds: Maney.

Edgeworth, M. (2015), 'From spadework to screenwork: new forms of archaeological discovery in digital space', in A. Carusi, A. S. Hoel, T. Webmoor and S. Woolgar, eds, *Visualization in the Age of Computerization*, 40–58, London: Routledge.

Farstadvoll, S. (2019), 'Vestigial Matters: Contemporary Archaeology and Hyperart', *Norwegian Archaeological Review* 52 (1): 1–19, DOI: 10.1080/00293652.2019.1577913.

Frederick, U. and T. Ireland (2019), '"Last drinks at the Hibernian": practice-led research into art and archaeology', *Australian Archaeology* 85 (3): 279–94.

Freire, P. (1979), *The Pedagogy of the Oppressed*, London: Penguin.

Gartski, K. (2022), 'Challenges of a Critical Archaeology in the Modern World', in K. Gartski, ed., *Critical Archaeology in the Digital Age: Proceedings of the 12th IEMA Visiting Scholar's Conference*, 1–10, Los Angeles: Cotsen Institute of Archaeology Press.

Gauntlett, D. (2014), 'The internet is ancient, small steps are important, and four other theses about making things in a digital world', in N. Zagalo and P. Branco, eds, *Creative Technologies: Create and Engage Using Art and Play*, 17–33, London: Springer.

Gheorgiu, D. and T. Barth, eds (2019), *Artistic Practices and Archaeological Research*, Oxford: Archaeopress.

Giroux, H. (2011/2000), 'Public Pedagogy as Cultural Politics', in F. Allen, ed., *Education (Documents of Contemporary Art)*, 48–51, London and Cambridge, MA: Whitechapel Gallery/MIT Press.

González-Ruibal, A. (2020), 'Visual Archaeologies: Editorial Introduction', *Journal of Contemporary Archaeology* 7 (1): 1–3, DOI: 10.1558/jca.42565.

Graves-Brown, P., R. Harrison and A. Piccini (2013), 'Introduction', in P. Graves-Brown, R. Harrison and A. Piccini, eds, *The Oxford Handbook of Archaeology of the Contemporary World*, 1–26, Oxford: Oxford University Press, DOI: 10.1093/oxfordhb/9780199602001.001.0001.

Harrison, R. and J. Schofield (2010), *After Modernity: Archaeological Approaches to the Contemporary Past*, Oxford: Oxford University Press.

Hawkins, H. (2018), 'To Talk of Turns . . .: Three Cross-Disciplinary Provocations for Creative Turns', *Journal of Contemporary Archaeology* 4 (2): 147–56, DOI: 10.1558/jca.32399.

Hills, W. (2019), 'Education Through Participation: The Contemporary Terrain of Socio-pedagogic Art', in H. Mathews, ed., *Shapes of Knowledge*, 15–31, Melbourne: Monash University Museum of Art.

Holtorf, C. and A. Piccini, eds (2009), *Contemporary Archaeologies: Excavating Now*, Frankfurt am Main: Peter Lang.

Kavanagh, H. (2007), 'The Repertoire of Archaeological Images', in J. Elkins, ed., *Visual Practices Across the University*, 140–51, Leiden: Brill, DOI: 10.30965 /9783846743737_016.

Kiddey, R. (2017), *Homeless Heritage: Collaborative Social Archaeology as Therapeutic Practice*, Oxford: Oxford University Press.

Krauss, R. (1979), 'Sculpture in the Expanded Field', *October* 8: 30–44, DOI: 10.2307 /778224.

Law, J. (2004), *After Method: Mess in Social Science Research*, London: Routledge.

Lee, D. H. J. (2016), 'Map Orkney Month: imagining archaeological mappings', *Livingmaps Review* 1.

Lee, D. H. J. (2018), 'Experimental mapping in archaeology: process, practice and archaeologies of the moment', in M. Gillings, P. Haciguzeller and G. Lock, eds, *Re-Mapping Archaeology: Critical Perspectives, Alternative Mappings*, 43–176, London: Routledge.

Lee, D. and A. Thomas (2013), 'Archaeologists in Residence at Papay Gyro Nights: experience, expectations and folklore-in-the-making'. Paper presented at CHAT Conference, 2013, UCL London, https://archaeologistsinresidence.wordpress. com/2013/11/16/archaeologists-in-residence-at-papay-gyro-nights-experience-expectations-and-folklore-in-the-making/.

Loveless, N. (2019), *How to Make Art at the End of the World: A Manifesto for Research-Creation*, Durham, NC: Duke University Press.

Malterud, N. (2012), 'Artistic research – necessary and challenging', *InFormation: Nordic Journal of Art and Research* 1, https://www.ninamalterud.no/pdf/tekster_kunstutd/ Malterud_Artistic_Research_2012.pdf.

McAtackney, L. (2014), *An Archaeology of the Troubles: The Dark Heritage of Long Kesh/ Maze Prison*, Oxford: Oxford University Press.

McAtackney, L. and K. Ryjewski (2017), *Contemporary Archaeology and the City: Creativity, Ruination and Political Action*, Oxford: Oxford University Press.

Morgan, C., H. Petrie, H. Wright and J. S. Taylor (2021), 'Drawing and Knowledge Construction in Archaeology: The Aide Mémoire Project', *Journal of Field Archaeology* 46 (8): 614–28, DOI: 10.1080/00934690.2021.1985304.

Nelson, R. (2013), *Practice as Research in the Arts: Principles, Protocols, Pedagogies, Resistances*, Basingstoke: Palgrave Macmillan.

Nilsson Stutz, L. (2018), 'A Future for Archaeology: In Defense of an Intellectually Engaged, Collaborative and Confident Archaeology', *Norwegian Archaeological Review* 51 (1–2): 48–56, DOI: 10.1080/00293652.2018.1544168.

Penrhyn Jones, S. (2019), 'A Crisis Discipline: Broadening Understanding of Environmental Communication Through Theory and Practice', *International Journal for Creative Media Research* 2, DOI: 10.33008/IJCMR.2019.16.

Piccini, A. and C. Holtorf (2009), 'Introduction: Fragments from a Conversation about Contemporary Archaeologies', in C. Holtorf and A. Piccini, eds, *Contemporary Archaeologies: Excavating Now*, 9–29, Frankfurt am Main: Peter Lang.

Reilly, P., S. Callery, I. Dawson and S. Gant (2021), 'Provenance Illusions and Elusive Paradata: When Archaeology and Art/Archaeological Practice Meets the Phygital', *Open Archaeology* 7 (1): 454–81, DOI: 10.1515/opar-2020-0143.

Roelstraete, D., ed. (2013), *The Way of the Shovel: On the Archaeological Imaginary in Art*, Chicago and London: Museum of Contemporary Art, Chicago, and University of Chicago Press.

Russell, I. A. (2013), 'The Art of the Past: Before and After Archaeology', in D. Roelstraete, ed., *The Way of the Shovel: On the Archaeological Imaginary in Art*, 296–313, Chicago and London: Museum of Contemporary Art, Chicago, and University of Chicago Press.

Russell, I. A. and A. Cochrane, eds (2014), *Art and Archaeology: Collaborations, Conversations, Criticisms*, New York: Springer-Kluwer.

Schick, K. and C. Timperley (2021), 'Subversive Pedagogues', in K. Schick and C. Timperley, eds, *Subversive Pedagogies: Radical Possibility in the Academy*, 1–19, London: Routledge, DOI: 10.4324/9781003217183-1.

Shanks, M. and R. H. McGuire (1996), 'The Craft of Archaeology', *American Antiquity* 61 (1): 75–88.

Sutherland, G. (2020), 'On the Road to Meikle Seggie: Richard Demarco's Edinburgh Arts Journeys 1972–80', PhD thesis, University of Dundee.

Thomas, A. (2014), 'Creating Contexts: Between the Archaeological Site and Art Gallery', in I. A. Russell and A. Cochrane, eds, *Art and Archaeology: Collaborations, Conversations, Criticisms*, 141–55, New York: Springer-Kluwer, DOI: 10.1007/978-1-4614-8990-0_11.

Thomas, A., D. Lee, U. Frederick and C. White (2018), 'Beyond Art/Archaeology: Research and Practice after the "Creative Turn"', *Journal of Contemporary Archaeology* 4 (2): 121–9, DOI: 10.1558/jca.33150.

Tringham, R. (2016), 'Chapter 16. Ruth Tringham with Michael Shanks and Christopher Witmore', in W. Rathje, M. Shanks and C. Witmore, eds, *Archaeology in the Making: Conversations Through a Discipline*, 308–34, Abingdon: Routledge.

Wall, G. (2015), 'Future thinking: imaginative expectations for the leaky university', *Journal of Perspectives in Applied Academic Practice* 3 (1): 6–10, DOI: 10.14297/jpaap.v3i1.153.

Wall, G. and A. Hale (2020), 'Art and Archaeology: Uncomfortable Archival Landscapes', *International Journal of Art and Design Education* 39 (4): 770–87.

Wickstead, H. (2013), 'Between the Lines: Drawing Archaeology', in P. Graves-Brown, R. Harrison and A. Piccini, eds, *The Oxford Handbook of Archaeology of the Contemporary World*, 549–64, Oxford: Oxford University Press, DOI: 10.1093/oxfordhb/9780199602001.013.012.

2

Documenting Wesley College: A Mildly Anarchist Teaching Encounter[1]

William Caraher

Introduction

In an American context, the teaching and study of the archaeology of the contemporary world have always existed together. Schiffer and Gould's seminal *Modern Material Culture* (1981) featured an article by Schiffer and Wilk titled 'The Modern Material-Culture Field School: Teaching Archaeology on the University Campus', which used the material culture of the University of Arizona campus as a context for teaching archaeological methods and interpretation (Schiffer and Wilk 1981). At the same institution, Bill Rathje's contemporary 'Garbage Project' grew out of his efforts to introduce undergraduates both to sampling and behavioural archaeology through the systematic study of domestic trash collected from Tucson neighbourhoods (see Rathje and Murphy 1992 for a summary of the project). Laurie Wilkie based her brilliant archaeology textbook, *Strung Out on Archaeology*, on the study of contemporary Mardi Gras beads (Wilkie 2014).

The last forty years have seen a steady stream of studies that demonstrate how the contemporary university campus can provide a compelling site for teaching archaeology (e.g. Skowronek and Lewis 2010). Most of these campus projects focused on using contemporary material and contexts to instruct students in the systematic practices associated with traditional archaeology: sampling, surface collection, mapping, recording and stratigraphic excavation. It is notable that despite this attention to modern material on campus (e.g., Miller 2017; Camp 2010), most published efforts appear to have avoided engaging fully with conversations in the field of archaeology of the contemporary world. For example, many do not emphasize the growing role that time-based media, particularly video and audio recordings, have come to play in the archaeology of the contemporary world (although see Webmoor 2014). While recent discussions about campus archaeology have emphasized its potential to engage with a wider range of campus and community stakeholders (Klein et al. 2018), these discussions have nevertheless tended to focus on promoting the value of this work for training students in archaeological methods rather than efforts to diversify the voices associated with campus life. Of course, training students is a noble aim and consistent with the educational role of the university, but such training-oriented forms of teaching privilege outcomes, educational or otherwise, over the thoughtful engagement with campus spaces and life. In fact, the emphasis on systematic methods, practices and procedures as part of most campus archaeology courses reinforces the kinds of modern structures that archaeology of the contemporary world has sometimes sought to critique or even subvert. The course that I taught in the spring of 2018 sought to address the tendency to see teaching and archaeology as the pursuit focused narrowly on assessable outcomes and fungible products. Instead, the course featured open-ended documentation practices and experiential learning that blossomed into archival research, public outreach and performance that commemorated a group of historic campus buildings slated for demolition.

The focus of the course was on two pairs of buildings on the University of North Dakota (UND) campus: Corwin/Larimore Hall and Robertson/Sayre Hall. These buildings were demolished in the early summer of 2018 (see Figure 2.1).

Figure 2.1 Wesley College Campus from the east. Corwin/Larimore Hall in the foreground and Robertson/Sayre Hall in the background.

They were built between 1909 and 1929 in the Beaux Arts style as the main buildings for an institution called Wesley College, which relocated to Grand Forks, ND, in 1905. Wesley College was a Methodist institution that taught music, religion and elocution and offered housing to students in two dormitories: Sayre Hall for men and Larimore Hall for women. Students taking classes at Wesley College would also enrol at UND, a public four-year institution, from which they received their degrees. In 1965, UND purchased and absorbed Wesley College after the institution endured decades of declining financial fortunes. For the next fifty years, the two pairs of buildings served variously as dorms, offices, classrooms, laboratories and the home of UND's honours programme. By the twenty-first century, the buildings had acquired considerable deferred maintenance debt and the administration ordered their demolition as part of a general effort to reduce and refresh the campus footprint.

The course involved exploring and documenting these buildings between their abandonment as active campus structures and their final demolition. As the buildings represented some of the oldest structures on campus, the university administration treated their destruction with some seriousness. They employed a local contractor to prepare a Historic American Buildings Survey (HABS) Type 2 report on the buildings and had the demolition contractor prepare high-resolution exterior laser scans. This level of documentation ensured that the buildings received formal architectural recording worthy of their place in the history of the campus. It also left room for less formal efforts focused on documenting the numerous interventions which occurred over their lifetimes and the detritus associated with their use and recent abandonment. The status of buildings after abandonment has long attracted the interest of archaeologists. Recent work by archaeologists of the contemporary world has explored buildings' transition from functional structures to ruins at sites not recognized as worthy of preservation (see the various studies in Olsen and Pétursdottir 2014 and Desilvey 2017). Thus, the class on these buildings focused initially on the building's liminal situation between use and demolition.

Understanding how the course developed requires a bit of curricular context. The course ran as a 1-credit addition to a rather unusual 3-credit class that focused on the university budget. After decades of regular budget and enrolment increases, the University of North Dakota was enduring a painful period of contraction, which resulted in both high-profile programme cuts and layoffs. At the same time, the university was implementing a new internal budgeting model that bore the brunt of campus-wide frustrations regarding the distribution of resources. Instability in administrative leadership, the increasingly populist and often anti-intellectual political culture of the state, and challenges associated with communicating effectively across a wide range of campus stakeholders contributed to confusion and at times anger toward the university administration (see, e.g., Liming 2019). My course on the university budget created an opportunity to engage with the changes on our campus in a way informed by a more detailed and accurate understanding of the actual mechanisms of funding, the national conversation about higher education in the US, and the particular historical developments on our campus. It also motivated student interest in the ongoing physical changes happening on our campus and this, in turn, prompted me to offer a course on the Wesley College buildings.

There were two issues that made planning the course and fieldwork challenging. First, I only became aware of the timetable for the buildings' demolition after the semester had already started. This meant that we only had a small window of time to enter the buildings and document them before the destruction associated with asbestos mitigation began. Thus, unlike some projects documented in this volume, we did not have the time to plan thoroughly in advance of our fieldwork. In fact, the only planning that I did prior to opening the course for enrolment was securing access to the buildings. The circumstances surrounding the creation of this course made any formal structure both difficult to implement and unnecessary, as an outside contractor would follow formal documentation standards. I offered the course for 1 academic credit, which is the lowest academic value possible for a course on our campus. Its spontaneity and low academic stakes allowed the course to operate at the very fringes of the panoptic perspectives of campus administrators. It both eluded the gaze of the technocrats, whose authority rests on structures associated with assessment, and fell outside the purview of the faculty committees who also seek to establish authority in the contested space of the American college classroom. In this way the class existed in a bureaucratic blind spot which contributed to its 'mildly anarchic' character. In some way, the self-congratulatory tone noted in this chapter by one of the reviewers speaks to my effort to turn the necessity of approaching these buildings in an improvised way into the virtue of an experience-oriented course.

The timing of this class allowed us to enter the buildings while they occupied a liminal status on campus in the narrow time between abandonment and their final destruction. The university had turned off all but emergency utilities, locked the outside doors of the buildings, and faculty and staff had removed all the objects from the building that could be reused or repurposed on campus. This further contributed to a sense of subversive access, as the students had free rein within the buildings, and the university facilities staff was only too eager to work with students to explore what was under the carpeting, behind walls and above false ceilings. A liminal class that existed in a liminal space seem ideally suited to approaches that embraced both the archaeology of the contemporary world and an anarchist opportunity to explore a building outside administrative oversight. Whatever the course lacked in preparation, it embraced in equal measure the spirit of contemporaneity by locating the development of our methods in the same moment as the spaces and material it sought to document and interpret.

The class

The class began with a brief introduction to the buildings, their history and the archaeology of the contemporary world. We then explored the buildings armed with notebooks, a few cameras scavenged from departmental and personal supplies, measuring tapes and mobile phones. Since the class commenced without much advanced notice, we had no idea what we would find in the buildings. On the one hand, this situation made it difficult to institute recording methods or to prepare formal recording forms. On the other hand, students found intriguing the level of access that we had to the building. They could enter faculty offices, laboratory spaces, classrooms and maintenance spaces that often had access restriction in active buildings on campus. The ability to move through a building without any barriers is something that most faculty take more or less for granted, although we usually refrain from barrelling into a colleague's office or laboratory uninvited. For students, however, these spaces were far less familiar and stimulated a sense of transgressing traditional campus boundaries.

The movement through the buildings exposed us to a wide range of movable and non-moveable objects left behind by the previous occupants (cf. Schofield 2009). Because we had not arranged for any storage space or secure study area, we could not systematically collect artefacts from the building. As a result, we had to describe the objects in situ in our notebooks. We also decided to take photos and videos of the rooms in the buildings as we went. We developed these methods on the fly and, through discussions, developed priorities that would help us to adapt our approaches to new situations as we explored the spaces. In fact, after working in Corwin/Larimore Hall for about two weeks, we shifted our attention to Robertson/Sayer Hall in response to deadlines for asbestos mitigation which would limit our access to the buildings and involve the removal of walls.

At the start of work in Corwin/Larimore Hall, we encountered rooms with massive numbers of artefacts left behind. These ranged from office and classroom furniture to psychology laboratories with tangles of cables, outdated computers and specialized equipment utterly foreign to the students (see Figure 2.2). In some cases, offices appeared to be frozen in time. A single late-twentieth-century Apple iMac computer stood on a desk as it might have appeared in the year 2000 (see Figure 2.3). In other cases, offices and laboratories look like they had been tossed during a burglary. Other rooms initially appeared carefully abandoned only to reveal during documentation some kind of intimate trace that connected the empty office to its earlier occupant (see Figure 2.4). The situations in these

Figure 2.2 Abandoned laboratory space in Corwin/Larimore Hall.

Documenting Wesley College　　47

Figure 2.3 Abandoned iMac dating to around the year 2000 still stands on its table nearly twenty years later.

Figure 2.4 Intimate traces of the building's past life lingered on after abandonment. Photo by Wyatt Atcheley.

offices, labs and classroom enticed students to delve more deeply into the contents of rooms. They looked inside desk drawers, documented the patterns of adhesive tape left on the back of doors and explored the spaces above acoustic ceiling tiles. One student, Wyatt Atchley, an avid photographer, prepared a photo essay that drew out the traces of the building's recent past and connected it with recent discussions of austerity that we were having in the sister course on the university budget (Atchley 2018; Caraher, Wittgraf and Atchley 2021). The intimacy of Atchley's photographs reflected the growing commitment that the students felt not only toward this course but also toward these buildings.

As they did this work, the students started to notice various construction scars and began to piece together the history of these buildings' adaptations over time. One of the challenges that we faced in studying these buildings is that we lacked the original blueprints. As we tried to make sense of the complex histories in the material record, we decamped to the University Archives where we pored over various collections in an effort to find evidence connected to the changes made to the buildings over time. This was not guided by a kind of archival fundamentalism, but by our ongoing time in the space of the Corwin/Larimore and Robertson/Sayre Halls. Questions that emerged through the students' exploration of the spaces triggered their interest in comparing the material changes with photographs, technical plans and any other sources of information that might reveal their histories. A more systematic and well-planned approach would perhaps have prioritized archival research. Our unusual circumstances required that the buildings themselves take the lead and perhaps our willingness to embrace necessity convinced us that they obliged.

For example, the low arched ceiling of a large classroom in Corwin Hall announced its former life as the recital hall of Wesley College's music programme (see Figure 2.5). When UND acquired and modified the building to accommodate offices and classrooms, they truncated the room's north side, where the proscenium would have stood, and replaced it with a wall and chalk boards. Despite its modified condition, the students understood the potential of recording in the acoustics of this space as both a gesture to the room's history as a performance space and as a chance to document the building's acoustic signature. We have published the results of this work in collaboration with some of Atchley's photographs in the journal *Epoiesen* (Caraher, Wittgraf and Atchley 2021).

In Sayre Hall, a drop ceiling hid a strange pattern of wood slats affixed to the ceiling of a room (see Figure 2.6). These wood slats once supported a coffered ceiling that distinguished the room as the formal sitting room of the Sayre Hall dormitory. The photographs that the students found in the University Archives

Figure 2.5 The north wall of the Corwin Hall recital room, preserving the shape of the proscenium arch.

Figure 2.6 Sayre Hall ceiling reveals evidence for the former coffering.

Figure 2.7 A photo from the 1920s of the Sayre Hall sitting room showing the coffered ceilings. From the University Archives at UND.

revealed turn-of-the-century space worthy of the 'jazz age' tastes of pre-Depression America, complete with potted ferns, an elaborate fireplace, and terrazzo floor with mosaic inlays (see Figure 2.7). A return visit to the room led us to remove the institutional wall-to-wall carpeting to reveal the more elegant terrazzo and mosaic flooring beneath.

Despite our commitment to spending time in the buildings themselves, it was our time in the archives that led the students to perhaps the most spectacular find associated with the Wesley College buildings. Amid the various records associated with the soliciting of funds from donors and the construction of the buildings was a folder associated with the relationship between the Sayre family and the long-serving president of Wesley College, Edward P. Robertson. These papers contained the story of A. J. Sayre's son, Harold Holt Sayre, who had died in the First World War. In 1918, Robertson honoured the request of A. J. Sayre and changed the name of Sayre Hall to Harold H. Sayre Hall as a memorial to his son's sacrifice. Included in the folder associated with this correspondence was a four-page poem, *At the Grave of a Dead Gunner*, written by Horace Shidler. Sayre was the gunner in the plane that Shidler had piloted (see Caraher, Wittgraf and Atchley 2021 for the text of this poem). This tribute affected the class deeply and transformed the process of documenting these buildings from one driven

Figure 2.8 Names of former students carved into the window of Sayre Hall.

by curiosity to one driven by a sense of respect not only for Sayre's memory but for the students, faculty, administrators and staff who had passed through these buildings. Later that week, students discovered names carved into a pane of window glass in 1910, 1911, 1913 and 1914 (see Figure 2.8). These students lived in rooms in Sayre Hall before going on to careers in the law, higher education and business. One of the students, however, died in France in the First World War and, like Shidler's poem, connected this building to centennial reflections marking the conclusion of the Great War.

Students made all these discoveries and we became increasingly motivated that our work do more than simply document these buildings in their abandoned state. Through ongoing conversations both in the buildings and in the University Archives, we recognized that the ongoing use of these buildings served to keep the memories of Sayre and Wesley College students evergreen and that the demolition of the buildings would break the connections between the lived space of campus and the Great War. To mark this transformation the students helped coordinate a final event for the buildings and invited the university president, representatives of the city of Grand Forks, the campus Reserve Officers Training Corp and, perhaps most importantly, the commanding officer of the Grand Forks Air Force Base to speak at a ceremony recognizing the loss that these buildings will mean for campus memory. A colleague in the Department of History provided a brief historical survey of the Great War and a colleague from the Department of English played the bagpipes to reinforce the solemnity of the occasion. The weather cooperated, and on a brilliant spring day, we recognized the buildings and those whom they honoured.

Reflections and discussion

The unusual circumstances in which this class developed meant that I privileged the opportunity over any particular outcome. As a result, there was no measure against which I could assess the success or failure of the course. Indeed, the absence of any anticipated outcome as an objective undercut the need for a particularly explicit pedagogy or even field methodology. The understanding that the buildings would receive formal documentation by a contractor further allowed us to avoid the need to produce a product dictated by disciplinary parameters or professional standards. The technology at our disposal (notebooks, cameras and our phones) and access to the building constrained our work. The students allowed their curiosity to dictate their approach to knowledge making. They did this on their own, energized as much by the lack of formal responsibilities or obligations as the transgressive character of the work. This informality encouraged the students to follow the lead of the objects and buildings themselves to the archives, and their observations and discoveries reflected a pedagogical experience anchored in a form of free inquiry structured by the spaces and objects that the students encountered. While the students were enrolled in a formal class and there was a power differential between my status as faculty and their status as students, there was also a sense that we were working together. This collegiality contributed to what I have termed a 'mildly anarchic' approach that deliberately eschewed many standards encouraged by bureaucratic expectations of the contemporary university, while still operating within its institutional constraints. The reflections in the following section derive from hindsight, but this retroactive approach to understand the character of the course may well offer some salient points for future efforts in constructing distinctive possible pedagogies for the archaeology of and in the contemporary world.

An approach to teaching that eschews narrowly defined or content-oriented outcomes is hardly revolutionary. Paolo Friere's oft-cited critique of the 'banking model of education', for example, offered a learning model where learners and teachers created new knowledge together through dialogue (Friere 1970). Friere's scepticism toward contemporary education resonated in part with Paul Goodman's call to abolish most educational institutions (Goodman 1964) and Ivan Illich's notion of 'deschooling' (Illich 1971). Friere, Goodman and Illich regarded most contemporary schooling as a mechanism for social and economic control and championed more anarchist-inflected propositions that encouraged open-ended, collaborative and hands-on approaches as a means of unlocking the emancipatory potential of education (Haworth 2012). In more recent years, a steady stream of scholars has sought to reconcile the institutional constraints on higher education with the desire for more emancipatory or even transgressive learning (e.g., hooks 1994; Gannon 2020). In fact, as higher education has become increasingly associated with workforce development and shaped by private capital (e.g., Dorn 2017; Newfield 2016), the need to imagine alternatives that work to challenge existing systems of learning has become more urgent. Recent calls for ungrading, for example, stress the role that grading plays in sorting and ranking students (e.g., Blum 2020). Thus, grading not only reinforces the role of education in determining the value of students in the market, but also exerts an outsized impact on student experience where grades become the goal rather than learning. Dispensing with grades, as I did in this course, often coincides with efforts to critique marketplace models of education that require or least imply winners and losers (e.g., Menand 2010; Caraher 2018). While efforts to imagine alternatives to current approaches to higher education often seek to challenge the influence of markets and capital (e.g., Staley 2019), sustained external pressures from a wide range of stakeholders continue to push institutions to adopt the practices of the private sector with their concern for efficiency, competition and economy. The lack of grades in my class shifted the focus from students working to attain something, to the class working together to construct goals over the course of our fieldwork.

In the course on the university budget, students and I discussed the rise of incentive-based budget models and the arguments that these models reward efficient production of outcomes and results (Hearn et al. 2006). This emphasis on efficiency informed some of the ideas that I was simultaneously developing associated with the concept of 'slow archaeology' (Caraher 2016; Caraher 2019). Slow archaeology in its various forms emphasizes the value of a sustained engagement with spaces and objects and the use of less structured recording methods alongside more formal and digital field techniques. In this way, slow archaeology seeks to critique the role that efficiency has come to play both in archaeological methodology and across contemporary society (Alexander 2008). This has become all the more visible in the late twentieth and early twenty-first century, as the modern economy, shaped by the 'great acceleration' (McNeil and Engelke 2016), has stressed the need for speed and efficiency in archaeology not only to keep pace with development (Zorin 2015; Ryzewski 2022) but also to document the transformations wrought by rising sea levels and climate change

(Anderson et al. 2017; Cook, Johnston and Selby 2021; Boger, Perdikaris and Rivera-Collazo 2019). In this regard, our work has echoes of James Flexner's recent calls for 'degrowth' in archaeology that rejects development-driven approaches to documenting the past and encourages practices designed to foreground a shared interest between practitioners and the public, as a way of subverting outcome-oriented approaches to fieldwork both in academia and the private sector (Flexner 2020).

By allowing student interests to start with the objects and spaces that they encountered in these buildings, the class anticipated some of the approaches modelled by Christopher Witmore in his 'chorography' of the landscape of the north-eastern Peloponnesus (Witmore 2020). Witmore's chorography foregrounded the role of objects, places and space as opposed to practices, methods and institutions in producing the freedom for new kinds of knowledge. In much the same way that Witmore modelled in his book, the students and I walked through, talked about and worked together to understand the spaces and objects present in these buildings. We followed leads, debated theories and used this time together to create and share our distinct experiences. This time in buildings also produced some material outcomes: a photo essay (Atchley 2018), a musical composition, publications (Caraher, Wittgraf and Atchley 2021) and events. These outcomes, however, represented only a narrow window into our time in the buildings. It is tempting to see Atchley's often melancholic photographs as a commentary on the loss of these historic buildings and the erasure of the memories that their walls preserved. It is likewise appealing to see the insistent and angry sounds and video that characterize Michael Wittgraf's 'Hearing Corwin Hall' as a commentary on the campus-wide frustrations. The discoveries in the archive, the photographs, videos and descriptions taken to document the buildings, and even the public events associated with their demolition, drew attention to the buildings and the changing character of campus. It would be easy to see these products of our work as testimonies to its value, but I would contend that privileging visible outcomes runs the risk of undermining the less tangible but no less important experiences of the group during their time in the buildings. In other words, emphasizing outcomes should not supplant the irreducible experience of spending time in these buildings. Spending time in the Wesley College buildings led the students to develop a greater sensitivity toward the changing economic realities facing campus, the history that the Wesley College buildings embodied and the ease with which they could be erased from both the campus plan and memory. Our experiences in the Wesley College buildings produced outcomes that resisted being reduced to the documentation that could stand in as the economic, political or historical equivalent of the structures themselves.

Our reluctance to engage in the kind of formal documentation practices associated with heritage management and compliance created space for us to emphasize and celebrate the ambiguous state of these buildings between abandonment and destruction. This, in turn, amplified the class's interest in engaging with the materiality of the university of campus in transgressive ways. Just as the buildings stood between use and destruction, students came to recognize their middle ground between being insiders to the college campus and outsiders to the inner workings of the university. They also brought to bear on campus views of the world characteristic of their own efforts to negotiate adulthood and social, economic and political roles in contemporary society, as Laurie Wilkie has demonstrated in her excavations of a fraternity on the University of California campus (Wilkie 2010). In fact, students' eagerness to transgress the traditional limits of student movement on campus drove the class forward and encouraged them to enter spaces typically reserved for faculty offices and laboratories. Students explored the buildings in far more physical ways than was possible elsewhere on campus, where the administration would discourage tearing up carpets and punching holes in walls. In fact, their interest in the physical form of the buildings also brought them into contact with individuals associated with the maintenance, upkeep and management of these buildings whom they might never have otherwise encountered. The entire class revelled in watching a maintenance worker from campus facilities take a sledgehammer to the walls of Sayre Hall in search of a lost fireplace and listened attentively to a specialist on campus floor coverings explain the different layers of carpet in the Corwin Hall recital room. The collegial introduction to the building's plumbing, heating and cooling systems offered by the campus engineer demonstrated how the Wesley College buildings were integrated with the rest of campus in ways that were not always readily visible.

The students were also able to transgress boundaries often established by university administrators and faculty to control student movement. In some cases, this involved small-scale barriers which delineated faculty offices where students might occasionally venture, but rarely stay for long, from classroom and public spaces where campus authorities encouraged students to gather. Campuses also contain numerous spaces accessed only by administrators, maintenance and facilities personnel, housing and dining staffs and other specialized employees whose collective work to keep campus warm, safe, clean and functional was kept out of public view. Students' efforts to document spaces associated with service areas, faculty, staff and departmental offices, and laboratories provided a kind of material analogue to more bureaucratic and procedural discussions that we were having in the course on the university budget. Their encounters with maintenance personnel, evidence left behind by past students and the intimate traces remaining in faculty offices expanded their perspectives and its story.

In a general way, offering students access to buildings that were caught between abandonment and demolition, and spaces that were both part of campus and often hidden from their view, supported the unstructured pedagogy of the course and our collective decisions to eschew formal standards of archaeological documentation. The class deliberately operated at the edges of archaeological methods, expected pedagogical practices and the history of campus itself. These conditions allowed us to understand how archaeology of the contemporary world could engage active sites, politically fraught spaces, and approaches that push the discipline of archaeology itself to reflect more deliberately on its political and economic commitments. Of particular significance was how our class provided an opportunity to produce a plan that not only adapted to the character of the buildings but also the interests of the students. This allowed for priorities to develop on the fly and for the students to shift their interest seamlessly from the materiality of the buildings to the archives. Experiences took the place of compliance or outcome-driven processes.

Conclusion

Archaeology of the contemporary world represents a hybrid field within the broader discipline of archaeology. Not only have efforts to document contemporary society reinforced the potential of methods, practices and procedures developed by archaeologists to study earlier periods, but the field has also revealed the limits of these approaches critiquing the modern world from which they derived. If the former ensures that archaeology of the contemporary world provides an approach for teaching archaeological methods on campus, the latter coincides with trends in teaching and learning that seek to subvert the economic, political and social drivers behind higher education in the late twentieth and early twenty-first century. Many of these approaches to teaching share certain anarchist tendencies in that they resist outcomes dictated by the needs of industry and capital, and in this way, they parallel recent critiques of development-driven archaeological practices. At the same time, I recognize that my course existed within institutional constraints. As a result, the self-congratulatory tone of this chapter serves as an awkward mask for the institutional realities of salaries, tuition, credit hours, expertise and professional authority that inescapably functioned in the background.

By facilitating student access to buildings between abandonment and demolition – itself a display of professional authority – the class leveraged the liminal character of students' roles on campus with the ambiguous place of Wesley College. As a result, students found ways to transgress both traditional barriers of access in buildings, as well as their status within the educational process. It goes without saying that classes like this were possible only because of a distinctive set of situations, opportunities and students. As such, this chapter may not present a model that another faculty member could easily implement or adapt to their own institution. At the same time, my hope is that creating open-ended opportunities for students to document and explore their material surroundings both reveals and amplifies the subversive potential of archaeology in and of the contemporary world.

Notes

1 This is an inadvertent reference to the Banksy mural in Bristol called 'The Mild Mild West' (https://en.wikipedia.org/wiki/The_Mild_Mild_West). Thanks to Rachael Kiddey for this observation and reference.

References

Alexander, J. K. (2008), *The Mantra of Efficiency from Waterwheel to Social Control*, Baltimore, MD: Johns Hopkins University Press.

Anderson, D. G., T. G. Bissett, S. J. Yerka, J. J. Wells, E. C. Kansa, S. W. Kansa and K. N. Myers (2017), 'Sea-Level Rise and Archaeological Site Destruction: An Example from the Southeastern United States using DINAA (Digital Index of North American Archaeology)', *PLOS ONE* 12 (11): e0188142.

Atcheley, W. (2018), 'Images of Austerity', *North Dakota Quarterly* 85: 124–6.

Blum, S. D., ed. (2020), *Ungrading: Why Rating Students Undermines Learning (and What to Do Instead)*, Morgantown: West Virginia University Press.

Boger, R., S. Perdikaris and I. Rivera-Collazo (2019), 'Cultural Heritage and Local Ecological Knowledge under Threat: Two Caribbean Examples from Barbuda and Puerto Rico', *Journal of Anthropology and Archaeology* 7 (2): 1–14.

Caraher, W. R. (2016), 'Slow Archaeology: Technology, Efficiency, and Archaeological Work', in E. Averett, D. Counts and J. Gordon, eds, *Mobilizing the Past for a Digital*

Future: The Potential of Digital Archaeology, 421–41, Grand Forks: Digital Press at the University of North Dakota.

Caraher, W. R. (2018), 'Humanities in the Age of Austerity: A Case Study from the University of North Dakota', *North Dakota Quarterly* 85: 208–21.

Caraher, W. R. (2019), 'Slow Archaeology, Punk Archaeology, and the Archaeology of Care', *European Journal of Archaeology* 22 (3): 372–85.

Caraher, W. R., M. Wittgraf and W. Atchley (2021), 'Hearing Corwin Hall: The Archaeology of Anxiety on an American University Campus', *Epoiesen* 4, http://dx.doi.org/10.22215/epoiesen/2021.1.

Cook, I., R. Johnston and K. Selby (2021), 'Climate Change and Cultural Heritage: A Landscape Vulnerability Framework', *Journal of Island and Coastal Archaeology* 16: 1–19, https://doi.org/10.1080/15564894.2019.1605430.

DeSilvey, C. (2017), *Curated Decay: Heritage Beyond Saving*, Minneapolis: University of Minnesota Press.

Dorn, C. (2017), *For the Common Good: A New History of Higher Education in America*, Ithaca, NY: Cornell University Press.

Estes, N. (2019), *Our History Is the Future: Standing Rock versus the Dakota Access Pipeline, and the Long Tradition of Indigenous Resistance*, London: Verso.

Flexner, J. (2020), 'Degrowth and a sustainable future for archaeology', *Archaeological Dialogues* 27 (2): 159–71, DOI:10.1017/S1380203820000203.

Friere, P. (1970), *Pedagogy of the Oppressed*, trans. M. B. Ramos, New York: Herder and Herder.

Gannon, K. M. (2020), *Radical Hope: A Teaching Manifesto*, Morgantown: West Virginia University Press.

González-Ruibal, A. (2008), 'Time to destroy: an archaeology of supermodernity', *Current Anthropology* 49 (2): 247–79.

González-Ruibal, A. (2018), 'Beyond the Anthropocene: Defining the Age of Destruction', *Norwegian Archaeological Review* 51 (1–2): 10–21, DOI: 10.1080/00293652.2018.1544169.

Goodman, P. (1964), *Compulsory Miseducation*, Harmondsworth: Penguin.

Haworth, R. H. (2012), *Anarchist Pedagogies: Collective Actions, Theories, and Critical Reflections on Education*, Oakland, CA: PM Press.

Hearn, J. C., D. R. Lewis, L. Kallsen, J. M. Holdsworth and L. M. Jones (2006), 'Incentives for Managed Growth: A Case Study of Incentives-Based Planning and Budgeting in a Large Public Research University', *Journal of Higher Education* 77 (2): 286–316, DOI: 10.1080/00221546.2006.11778927.

hooks, b. (1994), *Teaching to Transgress: Education as the Practice of Freedom*, London: Routledge.

Illich, I. (1971), *Deschooling Society*, New York: Harper and Row.

Kaufman, N. (2019), 'Conclusion: Moving Forward: Futures for a Preservation Movement', in R. Mason and M. Page, eds, *Giving Preservation a History: Histories of Historic Preservation in the United States*, 2nd edn, 232–42, London: Routledge.

Klein, T. H., L. Goldstein, D. Gangloff, W. B. Lees, K. Ryzewski, B. W. Styles and A. P. Wright (2018), 'The future of American archaeology: engage the voting public or kiss your research goodbye!', *Advances in Archaeological Practice* 6 (1): 1–18.

Liming, S. (2019), 'My University Is Dying: And Soon Yours Will Be, Too', *The Review: Chronicle of Higher Education*, 25 September 2019, https://www.chronicle.com/article/my-university-is-dying/.

McNeil, J. R. and P. Engelke (2016), *The Great Acceleration: An Environmental History of the Anthropocene since 1945*, Cambridge, MA: Harvard University Press.

Menand, L. (2010), *The Marketplace of Ideas: Reform and Resistance in the American University*, New York: Norton.

Miller, G. L. (2017), 'No Smoking Please? Campus Cigarette Butt Collection as an Archaeological Field Exercise', *Journal of Archaeology and Education* 1 (2): 1–17.

Newfield, C. (2018), *The Great Mistake: How We Wrecked Public Universities and How We Can Fix Them*, Baltimore, MD: Johns Hopkins University Press.

Olsen, B. and Þ. Pétursdóttir, eds (2014), *Ruin Memories: Materialities, Aesthetics and the Archaeology of the Recent Past*, London: Routledge.

Rathje, W. and C. Murphy (1992), *Rubbish! The Archaeology of Garbage*, New York: HarperCollins.

Ryzewski, K. (2022), *Detroit Remains: Archaeology and Community Histories of Six Legendary Places*, Tuscaloosa: University of Alabama Press.

Schiffer, M. B. and R. Wilk (1981), 'The Modern Material-Culture Field School: Teaching Archaeology on the University Campus', in R. Gould and M. B. Schiffer, eds, *Modern Material Culture: The Archaeology of Us*, 15–30, New York: Academic Press.

Schofield, J. (2009), 'Office cultures and corporate memory: some archaeological perspectives', *Archaeologies* 5 (2): 293–305.

Skowronek, R. K. and K. E. Lewis, eds (2010), *Beneath the Ivory Tower: The Archaeology of Academia*, Gainesville: University Press of Florida.

Staley, D. J. (2019), *Alternative Universities: Speculative Design for Innovation in Higher Education*, Baltimore, MD: Johns Hopkins University Press.

Webmoor, T. (2014), 'Object-oriented metrologies of care and the proximate ruin of Building 500', in B. Olsen and Þ. Pétursdóttir, eds, *Ruin Memories: Materialities, Aesthetics and the Archaeology of the Recent Past*, 462–85, London: Routledge.

Wilkie, L. (2010), *The Lost Boys of Zeta Psi: A Historical Archaeology of Masculinity in a University Fraternity*, Berkeley: University of California Press.

Wilkie, L. (2014), *Strung Out on Archaeology: An Introduction to Archaeological Research*, Walnut Creek, CA: Left Coast Press.

Witmore, C. (2020), *Old Lands: A Chorography of the Eastern Peloponnese*, London: Routledge.

Zorzin, N. (2015), 'Dystopian archaeologies: the implementation of the logic of capital in heritage management', in C. Gnecco and A. Dias, eds, *Disentangling Contract Archaeology*, special issue of *International Journal of Historical Archaeology* 19 (4): 791–809.

3

Teaching Contemporary Archaeology: The Durham Experience

David Petts

Introduction

Contemporary archaeology has a complex 'prehistory' and it has only coalesced as a defined sub-field relatively recently (for reviews of the topic's development, see Harrison and Breithoff 2017; Harrison and Schofield 2010; McAtackney and Penrose 2016; key earlier interventions include Buchli and Lucas 2001; Beck et al. 2007; Finn 2001; Gonzalez-Ruibal 2006; and Hall 2000). As a result, the teaching of contemporary archaeology is still in its infancy, and faces a range of practical and theoretical challenges. This chapter explores an attempt to develop new modes of teaching and assessing contemporary archaeology within the context of a British Department of Archaeology.

In British universities, undergraduate curricula are circumscribed by the demands of the QAA Benchmarking Statements, which highlight the key areas which an archaeological degree should cover (Subject Benchmark Statement 2014). This requires that all archaeology degrees are founded on an engagement with four key contexts: the historical and social, the ethical and professional, the theoretical and the scientific. It does not, however, prescribe the coverage of specific areas or chronological boundaries. This also needs to be set against the context of relatively limited research into the pedagogy of archaeology and cultural heritage studies (although see Bender and Messenger; Cobb and Croucher 2014, 2016; Croucher and Romer 2007; Hamilakis 2004).

Many UK university archaeology degrees are also accredited by the Chartered Institute for Archaeologists and Universities Archaeology UK, placing emphasis on professional and vocational training for students planning a career within the archaeology and heritage sector (Welham, Cummings and Geary 2018). This grew out of the recognition of some of the structural challenges existing within the need to provide professional training as the start of a training journey that will subsequently continue through both advanced degrees and Continued Professional Development programmes (cf. Bradley, Geary and Sutcliffe 2015; Everill 2015; Everill, Finneran and Flatman 2015; Flatman 2015).

Initially, it may not be apparent how contemporary archaeology as a field can contribute towards skilling-up professional archaeology. However, increasingly, commercial archaeology needs to record and understand aspects of the contemporary and recent past, as archaeological curators and the wider sector are recognizing the importance of this period. For example, the national curatorial body Historic England undertook a major research project into the post-Second World War landscapes of Britain (Penrose 2010), building on a range of earlier projects on specific post-war monument types (e.g., Cocroft 2006; Cocroft and Thomas 2003).

Contemporary and twentieth-century archaeology has also become embedded in regional research priorities (e.g., Petts and Gerrard 2006: 189–96; Medleycott 2011; Ransley et al. 2013: 72–80), although often implicitly as a facet of a broader post-medieval agenda. This increased value placed on the recent past has resulted in a burgeoning published and 'grey' literature (e.g., Annis 2019, 2020; Dwyer 2007). It is not only within the field of commercial archaeology that there has been an increased engagement with the recent past. Increasingly, community archaeology has intersected with the field (e.g., Nevell and Brogan 2021). Museums have also accelerated their interest, with an increase in the collection of contemporary material culture – with proactive programmes of recording the material aspect of current events. This is most obvious in the collection of material related to Covid-19, but is also evident in engagement with phenomena such as public and political protest (e.g., Gledhill 2012; Laurenson, Robertson and Goggins 2020; Patterson and Friend 2021; Spenneman 2022). It is clear that the study of contemporary archaeology is no longer an idiosyncratic niche within the wider discipline, but one that has clear and direct wider commercial and public interest, as well as an academic relevance.

Thus, it is not hard to build a pedagogical and vocational justification for the inclusion of contemporary archaeology within a modern curriculum. However, formal and sectorial guidelines all ensure consistency within and between taught archaeology programmes in the UK, but equally, impose limitations on the autonomy of the individual lecturer to take decisions about content, mode of delivery and assessment when teaching contemporary archaeology. This means that the scope for a more radical form of pedagogy that builds on the political, disruptive potential of contemporary archaeology is often held in check by the pragmatics of external bureaucratic constraints. The Department of Archaeology at Durham University has a strong track record of teaching and researching the archaeology of the post-medieval period, but until recently very little engagement with archaeology of the twentieth or twenty-first century. Though there were certainly no informal barriers to the notion of extending our chronological coverage, there were inevitable pragmatic constraints.

Even within a relatively large archaeological department, there were practical limits on curriculum development, particularly pressures on timetabling and staffing. There are also other emerging sub-fields jostling for space within a crowded teaching space. The emergence of other fields, the development of new methodological techniques and the pressure to expand global coverage all meant that contemporary archaeology was faced with challenges in finding space within the programme. In purely pragmatic terms, then, the teaching of contemporary archaeology faces basic problems in inserting itself into an already pressured and resource-constrained curriculum, with often limited expertise within the existing teaching staff.

There are also conceptual challenges in the teaching of contemporary archaeology. As a field, it is conspicuously theoretically eclectic, drawing on a range of intellectual traditions, both from within archaeology, but also from geography, sociology, anthropology and social theory. Whilst an explicit engagement with archaeological theory is a thread running through many aspects of archaeology, the conceptual underpinnings of contemporary archaeology are often much more explicitly embedded within the basic disciplinary framework. Even key introductory texts (e.g., Harrison and Schofield 2010; Gonzalez-Ruibal 2018) place social theory front and centre in the basic exposition in a way not found for other periods, where synthetic period overviews often background theory and prioritize discussions of basic chronological frameworks and the basic repertoire of sites and material culture (contrast, for example, chapters in Hunter and Ralston 2009 or Scarre 2005). This can cause problems in introducing contemporary archaeology, with a perceived 'steep learning-curve' need to engage with the key theoretical debates often being a deterrent to student engagement. Relatively few UK universities now have core 'theoretical archaeology' courses, with elements of theory instead being embedded within period teaching on a relatively ad hoc basis.

Contemporary archaeology is also methodologically eclectic. Although traditional archaeological techniques – building recording, artefact study, geophysical survey, excavation – are skills needed in contemporary archaeology, they are often approached with a different sensibility to that which governs traditional 'objective' recording (e.g., Godbout 2018; Shapland 2020). The discipline also engages in more novel ways with the material (and increasingly digital) record

– including oral history, auto-ethnography and 'deep mapping' (Casella 2012; Marshall, Roseneil and Armstrong 2009; Nida et al. 2015; Mashedder-Rigby 2014). As researchers are often exploring the archaeology of their own society, there is also a greater engagement with the challenges of reflexivity, and the blurring of subject and object (e.g., Chadwick 2003; Dixon 2017). Other binary oppositions are also challenged, with creative and artistic practice often coming to the fore as both research tool and end product, confounding the distinction between methodology and output (Thomas et al. 2015; see also Thomas, this volume).

Consequently, there are both practical and conceptual issues with introducing the teaching of contemporary archaeology within a UK university context, including a crowded curriculum, limited teaching staff and the perceived barrier of entry that the field's explicit engagement with theory provokes.

The Durham context

The Department of Archaeology at Durham University is a well-established centre of archaeological research. Founded in 1956, it has emerged as a major player in archaeological teaching and research. It has a relatively large faculty (a total of thirty-four FTE academic staff in January 2022) and substantial undergraduate, postgrad-taught and postgrad-research cohorts. However, until 2020 there was only one staff member with post-medieval historical archaeology as a disciplinary specialism. Nonetheless, there were enough staff (primarily medievalists) whose research interests did extend into the post-medieval period to provide a solid base for teaching this field at undergraduate level and supervising research at postgraduate level.

However, it was becoming increasingly apparent to me that students were keen to engage with archaeology of the more recent past, particularly the nineteenth and twentieth century. This was visible in requests for supervision of dissertation topics in these fields. In particular, proposals for research into industrial archaeology, twentieth-century military archaeology and nineteenth-/twentieth-century burial archaeology were common. In addition, through informal conversations with students it was clear that they were open to using archaeology to study the recent past and the present. In response, I began to find space to introduce contemporary archaeological topics within existing courses. I was involved in teaching two of our key first-year courses – 'Archaeology of Britain' (AIB) and 'Medieval to the Modern World' (MMW) – both of which were team taught and relatively traditional in structure, with the bulk of teaching dominated by lectures supplemented by tutorials and fieldtrips. The major challenge with introducing new topics was the limited space – in both courses, only a single lecture was available to tackle some of these issues. This meant that it was only possible to introduce two topics. There was no scope to provide anything resembling a broad synoptic overview of the archaeology of the modern world. For MMW, the two key topics addressed were the archaeology of the Great Depression in England and an examination of connectivity and shipping in the modern world (inspired by Graves-Brown 2013). The Great Depression topic was chosen as it was the subject of a research project I was leading at the time (Petts, O'Donnell and Armstrong 2021). It allowed us to embed research-led teaching, and in practical terms, allowed me to demonstrate the applicability of such traditional techniques as field-walking, geophysical survey and building survey.

AIB also had limited space and again only two topics were introduced. First, the Home Front in Britain during the Second World War covered issues such as defensive structures, the impact of bombing and evidence from graffiti. The second topic was the archaeology of modern streetscapes. This included a brief mention of 'desire lines', the tension between car and pedestrian, hostile architecture and CCTV surveillance. This provided an opportunity to introduce some classic contemporary archaeology projects (e.g., Bailey et al. 2009; Crea et al. 2014). Large teaching groups and short teaching slots made interactivity difficult beyond the usual opportunity for student questions. One of the biggest challenges was that at the point in the academic year when both lectures were delivered, the first-year students had yet to engage with our relatively limited teaching on theoretical archaeology (as broadly understood). This meant that it was not easy to situate the topics covered within larger debates about the relationship between archaeology, material culture and the modern world.

Developing pedagogy at Level Two

Initially, options for developing Level 2 teaching in this area seemed limited. There was a lack of obvious space within the curriculum, and pressure on my own teaching time. However, a new space did open up within our Level 2 'Advanced Skills' course. This was a practical, methodology-focused course that aimed at providing a range of core professional skills through short specialist options focusing on topics such as ceramics, small finds, building recording and geophysical survey. These were designed to be hands-on, taught in small groups with a practical focus. With increasing student numbers there was a need to create new options, with staff encouraged to suggest ideas. This led me to propose a new topic entitled 'Adventures in Contemporary Archaeology'.

The ambition of this course was to work with students to collaboratively develop a small research project on a contemporary subject over a course of ten weeks. The course started with a two-hour discussion of contemporary archaeology and its emergence as a discipline before moving on to the practical elements of the course. This initial opening session provided an opportunity to 'smuggle in' theoretical issues, although the practical focus of the overarching course did require a wider emphasis on methodology over conceptual issues. The initial aim was that the subject of the research project would be entirely defined by the students themselves. However, it was soon clear that there were some issues around this point. First, the timetable meant that there was relatively little time for the student group to define their research topic if the project was to be fully designed, carried out and reported on within the ten-week timetable. Second, there was a nervousness from the students themselves about what would form a suitable subject, and what was practical within the constraints of our schedule. This meant I had to rapidly pivot from an entirely unstructured approach to one that offered the students some form of basic armature around which they could develop their ideas. As a result, I decided to focus the project on our Student Union building at Durham. The building, Dunelm House, is a classic example of concrete Brutalist architecture completed in 1966 (Roberts 2021: 336; see Figure 3.1). It had long been a controversial structure – its stark

Figure 3.1 Dunelm House, Durham University, used as the Durham Student Union building and focus for the 'Adventures in Contemporary Archaeology' recording project, 2018. © David Petts.

looks dividing opinion both inside and outside the university. In 2016 the university unveiled plans to demolish it and had requested a formal certificate giving it immunity from Listing by Historic England (Moore 2017). This resulted in some considerable controversy; the building was finally given a Grade II Listing in 2021 ('Listing Success' 2021). Dunelm House had the advantage of being a building the students all knew to a greater or lesser extent, and which already had issues for debate and discussion attached to it.

We started off with a 'fieldtrip' to the building. This was not 'lecturer-led' but rather a free-form exploration of the building. We looked at architectural form, landscape setting and how the use of space had changed over time. For example, access routes had changed, former public spaces were now used for storage, key external and internal views and sight-lines blocked, and evidence of additions and deletions of internal features such as bars and dance floors were noted. This loose structure allowed students to contribute personal memories about using the building, and particular topics of interest, such as the evolving patterns of disabled access, were drawn out. Following the initial visit, students were encouraged to think about the end point of the project and their assessment. Again, the initial aim had been for students to come up with their own assessment structure.

I was keen to get the students to think creatively about what the final assessed piece of work might consist of; I encouraged them to think about using art, multimedia approaches and posters, and to go beyond the traditional essay report they were familiar with. Despite my initial ambitions, I again encountered a hesitancy on the part of the students about going beyond what they were familiar with in terms of structure, and in the end all of them submitted very traditional linear reports. If the aim to introduce diversity and creativity in assessment form perhaps failed, there was more success in coming up with underlying research topics. Subjects for their reports included looking at the way in which the building had been used as a music venue, the way in which the space was used by people with disabilities, evolving social space and its landscape context. The best reports were those which drew on a real personal engagement with the site.

The research for the project drew on a range of sources – simple fieldwork (mainly photographic), archives, personal interviews and questionnaires. Students were supported in their archival work through a structured visit to the university archives. These holdings included both formal documentation about the use and management of the building and a range of ephemera (e.g., posters for gigs; programmes from events; student pamphlets which shed a helpful 'student eye' view on the site, etc.). Students also worked on a collaborative bibliography and resource base. I was able to oversee this and where necessary fill in gaps and provide useful practical resources, such as a complete set of floor plans for the building obtained via our Estates and Buildings Department.

Overall, this resulted in some excellent student coursework and positive student feedback. However, it was clear that there was a need for me to make tweaks to the overall structure. The biggest challenges were around my initial ambitions for the project to be student-driven and freeform in aim and structure. Whilst these were laudable aims, it was clear that for pragmatic reasons (in particular around timetabling) I needed to provide more structure. Even though we, as a department, had been working hard on diversifying forms of assessment, there was a still a reluctance from the students about being unconventional in their final product.

These challenges were taken into account the second time the course was run; although, as will be seen, the issues were still not entirely satisfactorily dealt with. This second iteration of teaching commenced with a field site already selected by me: in this case, the former University Observatory (see Figure 3.2). This time I ensured more structure in the fieldwork. Floor plans were once again obtained from the university authorities, and these were used as a basis for a

Figure 3.2 Durham University Observatory, focus for the 'Adventures in Contemporary Archaeology' recording project, 2019. © David Petts.

more formal photographic survey of the building. Although many rooms were empty, students were able to draw out plenty of detail concerning the use of space within the structure. Multiple phasing of wiring and electrics were recorded, changing patterns of circulation identified and even the former location of a dart board noted by a circular penumbra of dart holes in a wooden wall! External survey recorded changes in fenestration on the main building and phases of repair and painting on the brick shed, while also identifying the footprint of a former garage or storage structure.

This survey work was supplemented by additional archival and desk-based work. From a teaching perspective this was helpful, as the former garage that had been identified through fieldwork was not shown on any mapping, allowing a discussion of the strengths/weakness of even relatively recent documentary sources. This also produced evidence for the function of the brick storage shed, which had in fact been built to house a piece of scientific equipment, as well as to tie down specific dates for periods of repair through the invoices from builders and other tradesmen. Once again, a collaborative bibliography was developed directing students to relevant materials.

This time I was more conservative in expectations about the final output, with a more prescribed and traditional format for the assessed work. Students were still encouraged to come up with their own topic within these constraints, and once again they were able to embrace this and produced a range of different ideas for their work.

Impact of Covid-19

As I looked towards the third cycle of this course, I was increasingly comfortable with the format, and had selected the site for the next cohort of students to study. However, the advent of Covid-19 resulted in the need to radically reappraise how the course could be delivered, and we had to move from face-to-face teaching (including any fieldwork) to a programme that had to be delivered remotely. Whilst a 'flipped' model of teaching had long been advocated within UK higher education, it took a global pandemic for this model to be embraced on a large scale within the sector (Lage, Platt and Treglia 2000; Walkeden et al. 2021).

The fundamental premise of a collaborative field-based project was clearly not possible. This required a rethink about how to run the course; whilst not ideal, this did provide the opportunity to step back and address some of the underlying challenges I had been struggling with. My major disappointment had been the perceived reluctance of students to take the opportunity I had provided to embrace alternative modes of assessment. From the perspective of the teacher, I had seen the chance for students to frame their own assessments in modes beyond the traditional written report as an exciting one, an opportunity for students to exercise creativity. However, it was clear that for students, what I had seen as an opportunity was seen by them as a risk. At Durham, we distinguish between *formative* and *summative* assessment. Formative assessments are used to provide an opportunity to explore a topic or assessment type and receive feedback, with the marks not contributing towards their final degree marks. They are an opportunity to experiment in a relatively risk-free context and for staff to identify strengths and weaknesses in student performance. *Summative* assessment differs in that the marks are used for the final degree assessment. It was becoming clear that if students were going to be asked to embrace novel assessment forms there was a need to embed formative stages to allow them to 'sand-box' their approaches. Crucially, due to the structure of this particular course, there was no formal formative assessment component. The requirement to restructure the course in the light of Covid-19 constraints, however, offered me the opportunity to integrate formative components into the course structure.

Building a new course structure, I aimed to embed small formative assessments. This had the advantage that students were exposed to a range of different ways of approaching and reporting on contemporary archaeology. Since they were not assessed, students were encouraged and enabled to experiment without risk. As students reported back on their activities to the group, they were exposed to alternative approaches and techniques in a safe, non-judgemental context.

The course was broken into six thematic blocks: 'What is Contemporary Archaeology?'; 'Deep- and Counter-mapping'; 'Psycho-geography/*dérives/* drifts'; 'Matter out of place'; 'Means and Ends: Practice and Output in Contemporary Archaeology'; and 'The Contemporary Archaeology of Disease'. Each topic was explored in a series of short pre-recorded lectures. Students were then briefed on a practical task each week and required to present the results of this practical work the following week. These tasks included a 'deep mapping' exercise for Durham City Centre; carrying out a dérive/drift across the same area (either self-led or using the *Dérive* phone app – https://deriveapp.com/); carrying out an artefact biography; and a simple garbology project (drawing on influences from Schofield et al. 2020; Moreu and Gomez 2019). These activities were structured to encourage the use of a range of feedback techniques – inevitably traditional PowerPoint presentations featured strongly, but Google Earth Tours were a key element of the mapping projects.

For the final assessment, I was searching for a compromise that would encourage students to express methodological creativity whilst eliminating the perceived risk from the student perspective. I homed in on the notion of running a short Twitter conference: a public, online event on Twitter at which papers are presented through a short sequence of Tweets – usually with images. These would be timetabled in the same way as presentations at a traditional workshop or conference would be. I had seen Twitter conferences in action before and had been particularly inspired by the 'Public Archaeology Twitter Conference' (https://publicarchaeologyconference.wordpress.com/; Delgado-Anés, Romero Pellitero and Richardson 2017).

Students were asked to give a short presentation via Twitter, comprising a maximum of ten Tweets. They were then asked to submit a report which included the text of the Tweets (around 500 words), a 1,000-word description of the project and a 500-word reflective commentary on the conference experience. The decision to assess a written report rather than the Twitter presentation itself was in order to filter out the direct impact of external variables beyond direct student control, such as technical problems or problematic public responses.

In terms of presentation content, the students were given the option of developing one of the formative presentations they had already carried out or developing something new. In the end, there was a roughly 50–50 split between developing earlier work and submitting entirely new topics. Presentation topics include an exploration of the packaging and context of a bottle of chili sauce; an exercise in auto-garbology; and a series of dérive, psychography and 'deep-mapping' projects based on Durham and villages in the local area. The conference itself was very effective. Publicity both within the department and more widely via social media ensured that there was a public audience for the presentations themselves. This meant that each student had the opportunity to field questions about their work and respond to queries. As the 'chair' of the session, I was able to moderate, ask questions myself and cue and coordinate feedback. As the student cohort was small, the whole event only lasted two hours, which was the right length to ensure full engagement from the student cohort and the audience. Crucially, all the students had some basic level of familiarity with Twitter and only one did not have their own Twitter account. This meant that in general, they were able to navigate some of the basic technical issues, such as effectively creating a thread, integrating images and answering questions.

Reception and reflection

Feedback from students was incredibly positive – they relished the opportunity to try something a little different from the usual assessed activities, whilst they found the final text-based reflective commentary familiar enough to avoid undue worries about submitting this work at the end of the process. The formal module evaluation resulted in exceptionally good feedback. Positive feedback was also received from other staff and students who engaged as the virtual 'audience'. As a teacher and lecturer, I found the process one of the most engaging and positive teaching experiences I have been involved in. I could see the see the students developing their research skills and embracing the opportunities to explore an aspect of archaeology that was very different from their previous experiences. The nature of the structured activities before the final conference had allowed them to build up confidence in working outside the normal structures of archaeology, and crucially, engaging with the notions of reflection and personal engagement with their contemporary surroundings that is such an important aspect of much modern contemporary archaeological endeavour (cf. Ayers, Bryant and Missimer 2020).

As we move away from the limitations imposed by the lockdowns, I am faced with new pedagogical challenges. I am now able to return to more hands-on site and object-based engagement with the raw materials of contemporary archaeology, and I find this return to materiality attractive, personally and pedagogically. Despite the success of the digitally delivered format, there were aspects of my original vision for the course that did not work. In particular, I had intended the course to foreground collaborative research – with the student cohort working together to develop and evolve a research project, with an emphasis on consensus and teamwork. However, the digital delivery in the time of Covid-19 resulted in individual, personalized research projects. Although these were grounded in impressive personal engagement with their topics, the sharing came at the point of delivery and dissemination rather than at the research stage. I am faced with a pedagogical challenge: how to build on the personal engagement students felt with individual projects, which resulted in impressive exercises in auto-ethnography and personal reflection, in combination with the more cooperative and consensual modes of working provoked by the need to work within a large team. Both approaches are important from an intellectual, pedagogical and vocational perspective, but is it possible to move beyond a zero-sum game and to nurture the individual output within the context of a wider group-based approach?

It is also tempting to build on the work previous cohorts of students had done, and using the campus as a learning and teaching resource has many attractions (cf.

Dufton et al. 2019). It offers a shared landscape which all students have some level of personal engagement with and understanding of. On a purely practical level, it is easy, safe and cheap to access – dull, but important factors that any teacher inevitably has to take into account. As I look towards the next cycle of teaching this course, these are decisions that will need to be made. Inevitably, this will be an iterative process – all repeat teaching is a reflective process, building on successes, getting feedback from students and colleagues, tackling challenges and hedging against risk, constantly balancing a pedagogical ideal with the raw pragmatics of teaching in a modern Higher Education context. For me the greatest success of all versions of the course has been that by exploring contemporary archaeology from an approach that prioritized practice and material engagement with the raw stuff of the field, it has been possible to see a real student engagement with the topic. In the process of all the work we did together, I could see students suddenly 'getting' how archaeological methods and sensibilities might be used to engage with the contemporary world, with a significant proportion of students taking this forward as dissertation subjects. It has also been as much of a learning experience for me as for the students – building on ideas and approaches that I perhaps initially did not feel comfortable with, and I have to recognize the impact of Covid-19 in pushing me into taking pedagogical approaches I am not sure I would otherwise have developed.

Finally, the internal landscape within the department has changed since the initial forays in teaching contemporary archaeology described above. The appointment of Rui Gomes-Coelho brings intellectual and disciplinary heft to our teaching, as a specialist in the archaeology of the more recent past. Student engagement at undergraduate and postgraduate level in the field has also continued to burgeon: recent dissertation topics include twenty-first-century fishing landscapes; the police phone-box as heritage; and archaeological approaches to the International Space Station. Most recently, funding was secured for a PhD project jointly supervised by the Museum of London Archaeology exploring the archaeology of the welfare state in London. It is clear that contemporary archaeology and its teaching is now well established at Durham, and the exploration of new ways of teaching the field is showing ever greater potential.

References

Annis, R. G. (2019), *Former Electricity Substation, Merryoaks, Durham City: Archaeological Building Recording*, Durham: Archaeological Services, Durham University, https://doi.org/10.5284/1054484.

Annis, R. G. (2020), *Darlington Fire Station, Darlington: Archaeological Building Recording*, Durham: Archaeological Services, Durham University, https://doi.org/10.5284/1076482.

Ayers, J., J. Bryant and M. Missimer (2020), 'The Use of Reflective Pedagogies in Sustainability Leadership Education – A Case Study', *Sustainability* 12 (17), https://doi.org/10.3390/su12176726.

Bailey, G., C. Newland, A. Nilsson and J. Schofield (2009), 'Transit, transition: excavating J641 VUJ', *Cambridge Archaeological Journal* 19: 1–27.

Beck C. M., H. Drollinger and J. Schofield (2007), 'Archaeology of dissent: landscape and symbolism at the Nevada Peace Camp', in J. Schofield and W. Cocroft, eds, *A Fearsome Heritage: Diverse Legacies of the Cold War*, 297–320, London and New York: Routledge.

Bender, S. J. and P. M. Messenger (2019), *Pedagogy and Practice in Heritage Studies*, Gainesville: University Press of Florida.

Bradley, A., K. Geary and T. Sutcliffe (2015), 'Two roads: developing routes to professional archaeological practice', *The Historic Environment: Policy and Practice* 6 (2): 98–109.

Buchli, V. and G. Lucas, eds (2001), *Archaeologies of the Contemporary Past*, London: Routledge.

Casella, E. C. (2012), '"That's just a family thing, you know": memory, community kinship, and social belonging in the Hagg cottages of Cheshire, northwest England', *International Journal of Historical Archaeology* 16: 284–9.

Chadwick, A. (2003), 'Post-processualism, professionalisation and archaeological methodologies: towards reflective and radical practice', *Archaeological Dialogues* 10: 97–117.

Cobb, H. and K. Croucher (2014), 'Assembling archaeological pedagogy: a theoretical framework for valuing pedagogy in archaeological interpretation and practice', *Archaeological Dialogues* 21 (2): 197–216.

Cobb, H., and K. Croucher (2016), 'Personal, Political, Pedagogic: Challenging the Binary Bind in Archaeological Teaching, Learning and Fieldwork', *Journal of Archaeological Method and Theory* 23: 949–69.

Cocroft, W. (2006), *War Art: Murals and Graffiti: Military Life, Power and Subversion*, York: Council for British Archaeology.

Cocroft, W. and R. Thomas (2003), *Cold War: Building for Nuclear Confrontation 1946–1989*, Swindon: English Heritage.

Colley, S. (2004), 'University-based archaeology teaching and learning and professionalism in Australia', *World Archaeology* 36 (2): 189–202.

Crea, G., A. Dafnis, J. Hallam, R. Kiddey and J. Schofield (2014), 'Turbo Island, Bristol: excavating a contemporary homeless place', *Post-Medieval Archaeology* 48 (1): 133–50.

Croucher, K. and W. Romer (2007), *Inclusivity in Teaching Practice and the Curriculum*, Guides for Teaching and Learning in Archaeology 6. Higher Education Academy, https://www.heacademy.ac.uk/system/files/Number6_Teaching_and_Learning_Guide_Inclusivity.pdf.

Delgado-Anés, L., P. Romero Pellitero and L. J. Richardson (2017), 'Virtual archaeology through social networks: the case of the I Public Archaeology Twitter Conference', in N. Rodríguez Ortega, ed., *III Congreso de la Sociedad Internacional Humanidades Digitales Hispánicas*, 293–98, Malaga: n.p.

Dixon, J. (2017), 'Buildings Archaeology Without Recording', *Journal of Contemporary Archaeology* 4 (2): 213–20.

Dufton, A. J., L. R. Gosner, A. R. Knodell and C. Steidl (2019), 'Archaeology underfoot: on-campus approaches to education, outreach, and historical archaeology at Brown University', *Journal of Field Archaeology* 44 (5): 304–18.

Dwyer, E. (2007), *Overhead Power Transmission Lines and Associated Structures in the Lower Lea Valley*, London: Museum of London Archaeology, https://doi.org/10.5284/1016337.

Everill, P. (2015), 'Pedagogy and practice: the provision and assessment of archaeological training in UK higher education', *The Historic Environment: Policy and Practice* 6 (2): 122–41.

Everill, P., N. Finneran and J. Flatman (2015), 'Training and teaching in the historic environment', *The Historic Environment: Policy and Practice* 6 (2): 93–7.

Finn, C. A. (2001), *Artifacts: An Archaeologist's Year in Silicon Valley*, Cambridge, MA: MIT Press.

Flatman, J. (2015), '"A slight degree of tension": training the archaeologists of the future', *The Historic Environment: Policy and Practice* 6 (2): 142–55.

Gledhill, J. (2012), 'Collecting Occupy London: public collecting institutions and social protest movements in the 21st century', *Social Movement Studies* 11 (3–4): 342–8.

Godbout, G. (2018), 'The Junk Drawer Project: Field Photography and the Construction of Assemblage', *Journal of Contemporary Archaeology* 4 (2): 177–83.

Gonzalez-Ruibal, A. (2006), 'The past is tomorrow: towards an archaeology of the vanishing present', *Norwegian Archaeological Review* 39: 110–25.

Gonzalez-Ruibal, A. (2018), *An Archaeology of the Contemporary Era*, London: Routledge.

Graves-Brown, P. (2013), 'The box and the Encinal Terminal: an archaeology of globalization', *Post-Medieval Archaeology* 47 (1): 252–9.

Hall, M. (2000), *Archaeology and the Modern World: Colonial Transcripts in South Africa and the Chesapeake*, London and New York: Routledge.

Hamilakis, Y. (2004), 'Archaeology and the politics of pedagogy', *World Archaeology* 36 (2): 287–309.

Harrison, R. and E. Breithoff (2017), 'Archaeologies of the contemporary world', *Annual Review of Anthropology* 46: 203–21.

Harrison, R. and J. Schofield (2010), *After Modernity: Archaeological Approaches to the Contemporary Past*, Oxford: Oxford University Press.

Hunter, J. and I. Ralston (2009), *The Archaeology of Britain: An Introduction from Earliest Times to the Twenty-first Century*, London: Routledge.

Lage, M. J., G. J. Platt and M. Treglia (2000), 'Inverting the classroom: a gateway to creating an inclusive learning environment', *Journal of Economic Education* 31: 30–43.

Laurenson, S., C. Robertson and S. Goggins (2020), 'Collecting COVID-19 at National Museums Scotland', *Museum and Society* 18 (3): 334–6.

'Listing Success for Durham's Magnificent Dunelm House' (2021), *Twentieth Century Society*, https://c20society.org.uk/news/listing-success-for-durhams-magnificent-dunelm-house.

Marshall, Y., S. Roseneil and K. Armstrong (2009), 'Situating the Greenham Archaeology: An Autoethnography of a Feminist Project', *Public Archaeology* 8 (2–3): 225–45.

Massheder-Rigby, K. (2014), 'Digging up memories: collaborations between archaeology and oral history to investigate the industrial housing experience', *AP: Online Journal in Public Archaeology* 4 (2): 61–75.

McAtackney, L. and S. Penrose (2016), 'The contemporary in post-medieval archaeology', *Post-Medieval Archaeology* 50 (1): 148–58.

Medleycott, M., ed. (2011), *Research and Archaeology Revisited: A Revised Framework for the East of England*, Norwich: Scole Archaeological Committee for East Anglia.

Moore, R. (2017), 'Save Dunelm House from the wrecking ball', *The Observer*, 12 February 2017, https://www.theguardian.com/artanddesign/2017/feb/12/durham-university-dunelm-house-threat-of-demolition-brutalism.

Moreu, B. C. and D. L. Goméz (2019), 'Intimate with your junk! A waste management experiment for the material world', *The Sociological Review Monographs* 67: 318–39.

Nida, B., T. Harris, A. R. Williams and L. Martin (2018), 'What Did the Miners See? Archaeology, Deep Mapping, and the Battle of Blair Mountain', *West Virginia History: A Journal of Regional Studies* 12 (1): 97–120.

Nevell, M. and L. Brogan (2021), 'Community archaeology, identity and the excavation of Manchester's Reno Nightclub', in L. Maloney and J. Schofield, eds, *Music and Heritage: New Perspectives on Place-making and Sonic Identity*, 150–9, London: Routledge.

Patterson, M. E. and R. Friend (2021), 'Beyond Window Rainbows: Collecting Children's Culture in the COVID Crisis', *Collections* 17 (2): 167–78.

Penrose, S. (2010), *Images of Change: An Archaeology of England's Contemporary Landscape*, Swindon: English Heritage.

Petts, D. with C. Gerrard (2006), *Shared Visions: Regional Research Framework for North-East England*, Durham: Durham County Council.

Petts, D., R. O'Donnell and K. Armstrong (2021), 'Material Responses to the Great Depression in Northeast England', *International Journal of Historical Archaeology* 25 (4): 1165–93.

Ransley, J., F. Sturt, J. Dix, J. Adams and L. Blue, eds (2013), *People and the Sea: A Maritime Archaeological Research Agenda for England*, York: Council for British Archaeology.

Roberts, M. (2021), *Buildings of England: County Durham*, London: Yale University Press.

Scarre, C. (2005), *The Human Past: World Prehistory and the Development of Human Societies*, London: Thames and Hudson.

Schofield, J., K. Wyles, S. Doherty, A. Donnelly, J. Jones and A. Porter (2020), 'Object narratives as a methodology for mitigating marine plastic pollution: multidisciplinary investigations in Galápagos', *Antiquity* 94 (373): 228–44.

Shapland, M. (2020), 'Capturing the Spirit of Singular Places: A Biographical Approach to Historic Building Recording', *Post-Medieval Archaeology* 54 (1): 18–41.

Spennemann, D. (2022), 'Curating the Contemporary: A Case for National and Local COVID-19 Collections', *Curator: The Museum Journal* 65 (1): 27–42.

Subject Benchmark Statement: Archaeology (2014), London: Quality Assurance Agency.

Thomas, A., D. Lee, U. Frederick and C. White (2019), 'Beyond art/archaeology: research and practice after the creative turn', *Journal of Contemporary Archaeology* 4 (2): 121–9.

Walkeden, I., M. Crombie, M. Teschendorff, M. Rajkuma, E. Scorsini, L. O'Riley, T. McLean, I. Claringbold and R. Kurpiel (2021), 'Learning archaeology online: student perspectives on the most effective activities and resources delivered remotely', *Excavations, Surveys and Heritage Management in Victoria* 10: 133–42.

Welham, K., V. Cummings and K. Geary (2018), 'Accrediting degree courses in archaeology', *The Archaeologist* 103: 12–13.

Part Two

Pedagogical Practices

4

The Henge with a Postcode: The Benefits of Contemporary Archaeology Fieldtrips

Kenneth Brophy

Introduction

Contemporary archaeology can be a challenging fieldtrip target because of student expectations (they want to see old stuff!) and the sheer everydayness of most of the sites visited (why have you brought us to this industrial estate?!). Yet student engagements with the contemporary can also be amongst the most rewarding for the same reasons if done well. In this chapter I want to argue that the 'archaeology of now' can be an effective and creative target for fieldtrips at a time when there is more pressure than ever to cut back on such activities in the UK.

Contemporary archaeology has a relatively short history compared to many other aspects of the discipline (see Harrison and Schofield 2009), but in one form or another has been taught at Higher Education level for half a century in some places. Indeed, it could be argued that the intellectual roots of contemporary archaeology emerged from a teaching context, with the seminal Tucson Garbage Project beginning life as a student teaching and training exercise in 1973 (Rathje 1979; Rathje and Murray 2001). At my own institution, the University of Glasgow, historical archaeology has a rich tradition going back four decades. The Centre of Battlefield Archaeology was established in 2000, and twentieth-century Scotland has been covered in select lectures and seminars for about a decade, but explicit teaching of contemporary archaeology only really began in the 2019–20 academic year with my module 'Contemporary and future archaeologies'. Despite being increasingly taught as part of archaeology degree programmes across the UK and beyond, there remains a limited body of literature on the pedagogical methods related to, and opportunities of, teaching contemporary archaeology.

In this chapter I would like to share my own practice of research-led contemporary archaeology teaching in relation to fieldtrips. For twenty years I have led a fieldtrip to a complex of reconstructed prehistoric monuments in suburban Glenrothes, Fife, with the express objective of provoking dialogue with and amongst students about the past in the present; the juxtaposition of prehistoric sites within an urban context works very well for this purpose. This fits well with the contemporary archaeology of prehistory, a major strand of my research, which focuses on the ways that prehistory remains relevant today, in terms of how it is perceived, valued, used and deployed, and how this can benefit communities (see Brophy 2004, 2018; Barclay and Brophy 2020). This research utilizes various theoretical methodologies including phenomenology and psychogeography, and other creative practices (Brophy 2019). The most public forum for this research is my blog, *The Urban Prehistorian*, which has been active since 2012.

In this chapter the format of the fieldtrip, student expectations and opinions, and assessment types will be discussed. It will also reflect on the intellectual challenges and opportunities of fieldtrips that focus on, in this case, the contemporary setting of replicas and reconstructions of prehistoric monuments that date back to the 1970s and 1980s, focusing on practice during the fieldtrip, the teaching context and the creative assessment methods that have been developed around various incarnations of this trip. I will argue that contemporary archaeology offers an opportunity to refresh the student fieldtrip experience, and that experiential and creative approaches can be used to elevate these experiences beyond mere passive visits.

Fieldtrip pedagogy

There is no extensive body of literature about fieldtrips within archaeology as learning tools. Regardless of what they are called – fieldtrips, excursions or visits (Holtorf 2001: 81) – they are generally regarded as *a good thing*, and an essential part of the undergraduate degree programme by colleagues I have spoken to about this. Yet this is not reflected in much depth in the *Subject Benchmark Statement for Archaeology*. The previous version (QAA 2014) had little to say on this matter and situated 'field visits' within the broader area of fieldwork. This version of the benchmark statement noted that 'field experience constitutes an essential aspect of the engagement with professional practice and is therefore part of any programme' (QAA 2014: section 5.5). One suggested method by which the degree could be delivered is 'field visits to appropriate monuments, structures and collections' (QAA 2014: section 5.7.ii). The most recent version, dating to March 2022 (QAA 2022) places fieldtrips more centrally, with 'visits' seen as one of the 'principal learning and teaching methods that an Archaeology student may experience' (QAA 2022: section 2.20) in the form of 'in-person or virtual visits to appropriate monuments, structures and collections for direct experience of material covered by the course' (QAA 2022: section 2.20).

Nonetheless both versions of the benchmark statements, I would argue, enshrine 'active' forms of fieldwork (excavation, survey, etc.) as the preferred option, rather than fieldtrips which might be regarded as more closely representing a 'passive fieldtrip trope' (Wall and Hale 2020: 780) within the discipline. Holtorf (2001: 81–2) is especially critical of the traditional 'passive' model of fieldtrips and site visits, noting problems as diverse as the amount of time spent on the bus, poor timekeeping, the patchy quality of preparation for participants, and the fieldtrip experience often being lecture-like and lacking interaction. However, I would argue that the act of getting out of the classroom and visiting sites and monuments to look at them is such an essential part of the learning journey and the process of becoming an archaeologist (with the proviso that this might not work or be possible for everyone) that it is worth facing such challenges. There are many benefits to field visits and daytrips to see local sites, including the opportunity to spend time together, as well as the activities and tasks carried out during some fieldtrips, such as worksheets, journals, note-taking, sketching and photography, which can deliver transferable skills even if not being assessed. Holtorf emphasizes 'a change from the ordinary' and encounters with 'the Other' as additional benefits (2001: 83). As Jones and Washko (2021: 10) note, 'learning on field trips stems from the pedagogy embedded in them – including active learning, co-creation of knowledge, peer-instructor feedback, and strong sense of place'. Visits can also create memories, often formative experiences (e.g., Shanks 1992: 5, 106), a trait they share with other types of fieldwork (Henson 2012: 200–1), while we should not downplay the benefits of fun and conviviality. The almost complete absence of fieldtrips during the Covid-19 pandemic restrictions (impacting on most of 2020 to 2022 in the UK) was a vivid demonstration of the negative connotations for the student learning and social experience when fieldtrips are rendered impossible or wholly virtual.

Perhaps the clearest statement on the role of fieldtrips within education in archaeology is Holtorf's exploration of fieldtrip theory (2001). He notes the positive development of 'task-orientated' fieldtrips in the UK since 1990, but also bemoans the generally uncritical view of fieldtrips as teaching aids, compared with, for instance, geography, which has a long tradition of self-reflection.

Innovations in fieldtrip theory and practice suggested by Holtorf include concentrating on themes, not sites; a 'focus on the sensual and bodily experiences which can be gained during visits of archaeological sites' (Holtorf 2001: 84); and appropriate non-traditional assessment methods. These aspirations have very much underpinned my own fieldtrips as set out in this chapter and I will elaborate on this as we go on.

There are of course other disadvantages to running fieldtrips in archaeology, and these amount to more than just standing about in the cold and the rain (Johnson 2010: 1), a feeling that I am very familiar with. Consideration must be given to the carbon footprint and environmental impact of fieldtrips, from diesel-guzzling buses to endless paper handouts that are often left on the bus or in rucksacks. Fieldtrips can be exclusionary in various ways, from the financial cost of participation to issues around ableism, access and the over-representation of some groups of students. The current benchmark statement for archaeology is clear that fieldwork and field visits are areas where a particular effort has to be made to avoid exclusion and discrimination: 'all practical efforts should be made to ensure equal access to extracurricular activities such as field trips' (QAA 2022: section 2.21). In this respect, the Covid-19 pandemic that began in 2020 has hastened the development of virtual options for archaeology students that may help overcome issues around cost, participation and environmental impact. Digital technology is a route to facilitating augmented and virtual fieldtrip experiences of increasing quality, and may offset some of the less carbon neutral ways of running trips.

Taken together, traditional and virtual means of excursion delivery can ensure these often pleasurable, and usually educational, trips remain part of the archaeology curriculum even at a time of increased pressure on costs (Jones and Washko 2021: 10). In this sense, contemporary archaeology may well offer additional learning opportunities, with, for instance, trips potentially requiring less travel at a lower cost (financial and environmental) than famous rural sites some distance from educational institutes. On balance, then, fieldtrips offer a valuable student learning experience but need to be planned with some care both in terms of logistics and the benefits to participants.

The Balfarg fieldtrip

I have been running fieldtrips to Balfarg from the University of Glasgow since the early 2000s. The fieldtrips have run as part of Honours courses (years 3 and 4 in a Scottish undergraduate degree programme) and taught postgraduate modules. In early years the trip was part of a course called 'Landscape archaeologies past and present', where the fieldtrip was a bridging element between two halves of this course – prehistoric and post-medieval landscapes. More recently, this course has been replaced by 'Contemporary and future archaeologies', which reflects my own development as a researcher, this course being wholly concerned with the archaeology of the twentieth and twenty-first centuries. In this context, prehistoric sites offer an opportunity to engage with concepts such as deep time in the present, archaeological replicas, authenticity, and tensions around heritage and development. This fieldtrip has therefore evolved to deliver several of Holtorf's suggested themes for proactive archaeology fieldtrips, notably 'accessing the past in the present', 'the visitor experience' and 'experiencing monumentality' (2001: 85–6). Central to this fieldtrip has always been that the students are not visiting prehistoric monuments dating back 4,000 to 5,000 years, but reconstructions and replicas that were created in the 1970s and 1980s, a distinction that is made very clear to them in advance.

The fieldtrips are generally with small groups of students, numbering no more than twenty, and take place on Saturdays, usually finishing in the early afternoon. At times, Balfarg has been the only focus, while on other occasions additional sites have been on the itinerary, such as Huly Hill Bronze Age cairn and standing stones beside a major road interchange at Newbridge, Edinburgh, or Wilsontown, an abandoned ironworks and associated village in South Lanarkshire. The trip involves about two and a half hours of travel time on a minibus, with a toilet stop built in, and so in this respect is not carbon neutral.

One of the benefits of repeat visits to this site over two decades is that it has been possible to monitor changes, use and the decline of the monuments (Brophy 2004, 2015). To give two examples of change, there has been the installation of new noticeboards to replace the 1990s' originals at both Balfarg Henge and Balbirnie stone circle, and considerable urban development has impacted on the route and setting of the field visit. As such, the trips form an important part of an ongoing long-term research project of mine to document how these monuments are used and valued, which includes engaging with the local community and researching the modern biographies of these monuments. This monitoring conforms to another of Holtorf's fieldtrip themes, 'the aesthetics of decay' (2001: 85).

The Balfarg complex background

The Balfarg complex is one of the most remarkable prehistoric monument complexes in Scotland, not only because of the richness of the prehistoric

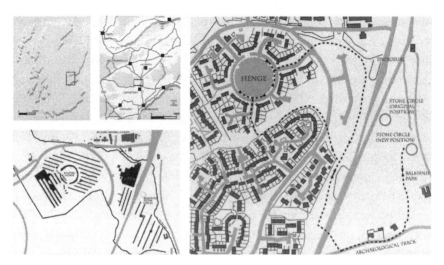

Figure 4.1 Location map showing Balfarg's position (left) and the Archaeology Trail route (right). Source: Barclay 1993.

archaeology but also because of the modern biography of the three monuments that comprise the complex (Barclay 1993; Brophy 2004). Balfarg sits within a suburb on the northern side of Glenrothes, Fife (see Figure 4.1), a New Town established in the 1950s (Levitt 1997). The monument complex is accessible via the A92 road, which has links to the M90 motorway to the south and the A91 to the north. There are three main components to the complex – Balfarg Henge, Balfarg Riding School enclosure and Balbirnie stone circle – all of which date back to the Neolithic period, but which were radically reworked in the 1970s and 1980s to their present forms.

The largest monument is Balfarg Henge (see Figure 4.2), which was initially recorded from the air as a cropmark in the 1940s (Atkinson 1952). The threat of the development of housing in the 1970s led to an invitation from the Scottish Development Department (Ancient Monuments Branch) to Roger Mercer to carry out a complete 'rescue excavation' of the monument. This work was carried out in alternating bone dry and completely rain-soaked conditions across 1977 and 1978 (Mercer 1981). The excavation revealed a complex monument, including up to six concentric timber circles that were subsequently enclosed by a henge earthwork 60m in diameter in the third millennium BCE. Standing stones were erected at the single entranceway. In the Bronze Age, several burials were inserted in this monument's interior, including one of a teenage male buried with a handled beaker and flint knife in the centre of the henge (Mercer 1981; Barclay 1993).

Figure 4.2 Looking south across Balfarg Henge interior in 2015. Photo by K. Brophy.

During the excavations, discussions with Glenrothes Development Corporation led to the idea that the henge could be incorporated into the new housing estate that was planned for this location, rather than being built over (Roger Mercer pers. comm.). Therefore, in the years after the excavations were completed, the monument was grassed over with the henge ditch left open, the standing stones reinstated, wooden markers added to show where one of the timber circles had stood and a slab left in place to mark the location of the central beaker burial. (The external bank had been ploughed flat and no attempt was made to replicate this.) Noticeboards were also designed and added to the site as it became enclosed by housing and a suburban street called The Henge.

Balbirnie stone circle (see Figure 4.3) was initially located 200m from the henge. It was excavated in 1970–1 by Graham Ritchie in advance of road upgrade work (Ritchie 1974; Gibson 2011). The stone circle, ten stones in a setting 15m in diameter, was constructed in the late Neolithic. Cremated human bone, mostly the remains of adult females, was found in some of the stone-holes, as were sherds of Neolithic pottery (Gibson 2011). After a hiatus of several centuries, renewed funerary activity occurred, including the insertion of cists in the monument and its conversion to a cairn (Ritchie 1974; Barclay 1993).

Figure 4.3 Students enjoying Balbirnie stone circle during a fieldtrip in 2013. Photo by K. Brophy.

The reason for the excavation of the stone circle was the widening of the A92 road; a decision was taken by the Department for the Environment for a total excavation, followed by removal and reconstruction stone by stone in a location 125m to the south-east (Ritchie 1974: 1). The cup-marked capstone of a cist was taken to the National Museum of Scotland and a replica put in situ. The remarkable decision to move the stone circle need not have been made, as in the end the stone circle location was bypassed by the road due to a change in plans. This had the effect of moving the circle from a fairly prominent ridge position to a less visible location in a hollow; Ritchie (pers. comm.) described the new incarnation of the stone circle to me as a 'rather quaint garden feature'.

Balfarg Riding School is situated between Balfarg Henge and Balbirnie (for relative locations, see Figure 4.1). The monument was first identified as a cropmark in 1978 and, at the time of its discovery, had already been partially destroyed by roadworks on the A92. The site subsequently came under threat from further road and housing development and was fully excavated between 1983 and 1985 under the direction of Gordon Barclay and Chris Russell-White (1994). This was a complex monument with Neolithic phases of activity, including the construction of two timber rectangular structures, putative

Figure 4.4 The Balfarg Riding School monument reconstruction during a student fieldtrip in 2011. Photo by K. Brophy.

excarnation structures for the exposure of the dead (Barclay and Russell-White 1994: 178ff.). Once these structures fell out of use, a henge-like earthwork enclosure was constructed here, with a diameter of around 40m. A ring-cairn and other burial structures were added to the complex in the Bronze Age; some of these features were disturbed by a medieval mill-lade (Barclay 1993).

At the end of the excavation, the decision was taken to build on work already done here to present the site to the public. Gordon Barclay (pers. comm.) oversaw the construction of a replica of one the Neolithic timber structures using cut-down telegraph poles, and surviving elements of the shallow ditch of the henge were left open (see Figure 4.4). This site sits in grass on the edge of the A92, overlooked on two sides by houses.

In the late 1980s, Fife Council Archaeologist Peter Yeoman saw an opportunity to connect these three reconstructed monuments, and with the cooperation of the excavators of all three sites an Archaeological Trail was proposed and established (Peter Yeoman pers. comm.; for route, see Figure 4.1). A series of noticeboards was commissioned for the trail: two each at Balbirnie and Balfarg, and one at Balfarg Riding School. These related to the sites but also the monument complex context. Yeoman also commissioned Barclay to write an accessible guide to the archaeology of Balfarg to accompany the walking trail (Barclay

1993). This colourful booklet was available to purchase at council buildings and local tourist information centres throughout the 1990s.

This innovative initiative was well intentioned and allowed the prehistoric monument replicas to become a visually prominent aspect of the landscape for the local community, and in my own work with the community there remains a high level of awareness of the significance of these reconstructions and the deep time of this place. Since around 2000 I have been monitoring aspects of the use of the replica monuments, key observations being that the sites are used for dog walking, games and sports, and a good deal of littering goes on. Instances of 'anti-social' behaviour are also evident, for example graffiti, paint thrown onto stones, broken garden gnome deposition and fireworks; and on one visit I noted the noticeboard for Balfarg Riding School had in the very recent past been set on fire and thrown into the henge ditch (Brophy 2004, 2015, 2019).

The noticeboards that were originally put in place were extremely tired by the 2010s (those that had avoided being set on fire), in some cases not even legible and certainly outdated in terms of interpretation; all were replaced with new boards in 2015–16. Urban expansion since the establishment of the Trail has made the walking route less and less legible, with housing developments on the east side of the A92 engulfing Balbirnie stone circle, changing the nature of the setting, which is now less quaint than it used to be. On the other hand, relatively new traffic lights and road crossings have made the transfer across the A92 – initially a perilous feature of the walking trail and a perennial focus of my risk-assessment paperwork – much safer.

The fieldtrip and activities

The format of every Balfarg trip is similar and although there have been modifications due to road improvements and housing development it has always worked on the principle that the students can to an extent explore with minimal guidance from me, taking the form of a semi-structured walk. Generally, the starting point and introduction to the experience is at the noticeboard location on the north side of Balfarg Henge on The Henge (see Figure 4.5). From there we head to the Balfarg Riding School monument reconstruction, and then finish at Balbirnie stone circle, before walking back in a loop to the minibus, the actual route evolving as housing has expanded and road crossing-points have changed. The walk aspires to follow the route of the Archaeological Trail, but this has become difficult to follow due to development. During this walk, I introduce various aspects of the history and prehistory of the places we visit and prompt

Figure 4.5 The starting point for the fieldtrip is at a parking space beside the main entrance to Balfarg Henge, here seen during a visit in 2015. Photo by K. Brophy.

discussion, engagement and note-taking. I also allow the students time to explore on their own, and they always have tasks to work on.

Various themes are tackled on each trip, in the form of prompts, some embedded in a rudimentary handout that students are provided with beforehand. Key ideas that we explore start from two quotes that are always included in the handout:

> 'A megalith in an urban environment does not seem to work.'
>
> Tilley 1996: 195

> 'I personally like to take fieldtrips to the site as a good example of development pressure on archaeology ... it's also a great place to discuss approaches to managing the competing demands of modern development pressure and the historic environment ... and to comment on the success or otherwise of the strategy employed at this site ... relocating stone circles etc and the precedence this sets in planning terms.'
>
> Douglas Speirs, Fife Council archaeologist, pers. comm.

Issues around prehistoric sites in an urban environment, and the planning challenges that caused each site to have such a distinctive modern biography, are thus important talking points. Students are also challenged to think about issues such as authenticity (at Balbirnie we discuss 'what is more important – material or location authenticity?'), the contemporary archaeology of the monuments and how the local community might use and understand the reconstructions.

In the 2021 version of the trip, I introduced prompt cards (see Figure 4.6) that were randomly handed out to the students when we arrived on site; they were asked to either write or draw a response or carry out some action during the trip. Examples include:

- Make a list of stuff lying about at the stone circle.
- Take a selfie with a timber post.
- Sum up Balfarg Henge in three words.
- Balbirnie stone circle isn't archaeology: discuss.
- How do the houses round the henge make you feel?

The prompt cards were meant to be a fun way to encourage the students to engage with the tensions and complex issues around the contemporary archaeology of this suburban landscape, and students engaged very well with the exercise, producing thoughtful and creative responses, which were aligned with

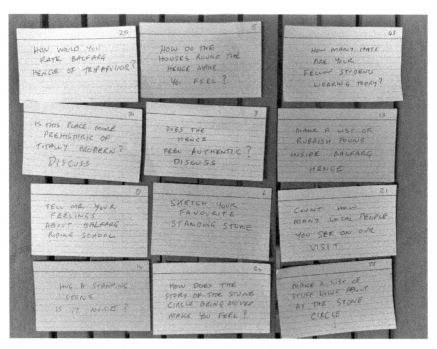

Figure 4.6 Selection of prompt cards from the 2021 fieldtrip.

the fieldtrip themes and sometimes actions ('hug a standing stone'). In response to the card prompt, 'How do the cracks on the henge standing stone make you feel?', one student wrote that they were 'amazed at how it can still be seen . . . even with damage. It is still able to present a story.' In another instance, the prompt 'How do the graves at the stone circle make you feel?', a student answered, 'The road was very disorientating.' Awareness was shown of the modernity of the sites: Balbirnie stone circle was adjudged by one student to be 'a product of archaeology'.

Some students chose to keep their prompt cards and stick them into their scrapbook (see below for more on assessment). In most years, the fieldtrip is followed by a seminar where issues raised during the trip can be discussed in the classroom, and answers and responses to the prompt cards helped shape discussion that time around.

Assessment

This fieldtrip has always been the focus of coursework and again this has changed through time. Initially I challenged the students to submit a report on their site visit in whatever format suited them, but more recently assessment has moved to a scrapbook format. In each case the percentage value of the assessment has remained low to encourage risk-taking and creativity. In both cases, creative approaches have been given primacy with a certain amount of flexibility in terms of how the coursework might be completed and graded.

The first iteration of this was a report that asked the students to capture the experience of exploring Balfarg on foot. This exercise encouraged the students to take a creative response to the weirdness of spending time at Balfarg, my experience being that some students found the temporal and architectural juxtapositions unsettling. The brief for the report was as follows:

> These experiences will form the basis of a short paper based on the landscape visited. This should be about 1000 words long, and include all relevant sketches, photographs, observations and references – you may also want to submit notes taken on-site. This is an informal piece of work . . . This is an opportunity for you to recount your experiences of a particular landscape, a true palimpsest.

Additional guidance was given in the fieldtrip handout itself, including:

> [Y]ou should be observing but also participating in thinking about the landscape and the monuments . . . I encourage you to take any approach you want . . . possible options could be a prehistoric narrative, a phenomenological description, a dialogue with locals, a travelogue, a guide to the trail or a straight piece of academic writing.

This piece of coursework was aligned with the course's intended learning outcomes (ILOs), including to 'be aware of the problems of management and conservation of historic and prehistoric landscapes' and to 'understand the potential meaning and power of landscape, space and place today, and how this is relevant to the study of the past'. The reports that I marked over the course of a decade provided a wonderful range of pieces of creative work: reports came in the form of poems, comic strips, drama scripts, dialogues, text message conversation, travelogues, press cuttings, drawings and so on. My feedback was generally given in the same format as the report, which was challenging and hard work, but worth it for the level of student engagement with the feedback. In one example in which a report was submitted in the form of a poem, my feedback was:

> This is an effective combination
> And I like the fact that this is
> One of those poems that don't always rhyme
> (A near rhyme poem is not a crime)
> There are also colourful images sprinkled like stardust on ice
> And the fact you use a lovely font makes it all look nice.
> But for, some reason, there are misplaced commas,
> although this punctuation situation is far from a horror –
> It relates to performance and pace
> But at times, they, look, all, over, the, place.
> The fragmentation of Balfarg has little justification
> Which you emphasise by the use of imaginative, er, justification.

In 2015 a student submitted an A3 artwork as his response to the fieldtrip, which perfectly encapsulated the temporary confusion that Balfarg can create for visitors (see Figure 4.7). This piece is called 'From ritual to residual' and I have no doubt that it received an excellent grade, showing a level of engagement and insight into the fieldtrip experience that goes beyond words. The format of this element of coursework and my feedback methodology were subsequently shared with colleagues in the College of Arts as an example of best practice and innovation in assessment.

More recently, when the trip became part of my contemporary archaeology course, scrapbooks became the most common form of assessment. These are literal scrapbooks given to the students at the start of the course to be completed based on three walking tours that happen during this course, including Balfarg. The following information is given to students:

Figure 4.7 From ritual to residual: a response to Balfarg Henge submitted as coursework in 2015.

You will be provided with an actual physical scrapbook at the start of the course which you should use to document your fieldtrip experiences. The scrapbook is your means to creatively engage with the experience on the fieldtrips and you are encouraged to be imaginative in how you interpret these guidelines. This is more than just a journal and you should include not just notes on what you do and see, but also additional supporting images and information e.g. photos, sketches, creative mapping, found items, materials associated with the trip e.g. receipts, travel tickets. Furthermore, your notes should do more than describe the trip; they should also include critical reflection on your own personal subjective experiences. You are not necessarily expected to take notes directly into the scrapbook while outside; you are encouraged to add notes and additional information after the event as well as sticking things into the scrapbook. This will encourage reflection and the collection of supporting material, print photos and so on. The scrapbook is intended to offer a visual and alternative narrative to capture the fieldtrips and your experiences on them and to capture your engagement with contemporary archaeology.

A formative support seminar runs between walks where past examples are shown to students and they are encouraged to reflect on their own efforts to date by sharing their scrapbooks with others in the class.

Again, this exercise aligns with course ILOs, such as 'Employ creativity to engage with contemporary experiences of historic and prehistoric sites and monuments.' The scrapbook encourages creativity but does not get assessed on artistic quality, and this is emphasized to students as some are nervous about design at the expense of content. There is an increasing use of digital scrapbooks in Higher Education settings, but analogue versions remain common in schools. However, both formats have common benefits: for example, they 'make concepts more tangible and help students better retain them' and 'encourage thinking at the higher levels . . . specifically synthesis and evaluation' (MacNeil 2020). In my experience this method also benefits students who do less well in more traditional assessments, such as essays, and tests a different range of skills from most of our standard assessment tools.

The scrapbooks that are produced are generally a delight to read (see Figure 4.8) but challenging to grade, as there is a tendency for the marker to be more positive about content that has a lot of detail or looks fantastic, whereas the secret of a successful scrapbook is the connections made between experiences and evidence for insight over and above a simple description of the walk. Scrapbooks typically include photos, sketches, maps showing our walks, commentary or text, but some have other elements, including 'found objects' such as leaves, cuttings

Figure 4.8 Scrapbook extract from the Balfarg fieldtrip, from 2021.

from relevant publications, original artwork, and pop-up elements. Content frequently focuses on juxtaposition. One student wrote beside a picture of Balfarg Henge that it is 'more of a playground / jungle gym than a Neolithic henge'. Another included a collage of images showing miniature eco-systems thriving on top of the decaying replica timber posts at the Riding School site. There is always a general focus on discarded food and drink packaging within the monuments and graffiti in the spaces in between in photos, sketches and notes.

Reactions from students suggests that the combination of fieldtrip and scrapbook is effective. Feedback comments from recent cohorts included observations that the 'scrapbook form of assessment was also great fun, and I found an excellent way to reflect on the course. The field trips also allowed for hands-on application of theory, which is something I usually find very difficult'; that the 'fieldtrip was a good way of learning in an engaging way'; and that the scrapbook 'was a great alternative to worksheets'.

There is an emphasis in my guidance and on fieldtrips on the experiential aspect of being at Balfarg, with 'the parameters of the experience . . . the material perception and the imagination' (Shanks 1992: 154). These are rarely simple narratives or descriptions of a field experience but rather something much more immersive, giving primacy to things like scale, aesthetics, perception and impact (Holtorf 2001: 85) of these monuments and the spaces in between.

Conclusion

Contemporary archaeology is increasingly becoming part of the syllabus in UK university departments, and my experiences at Glasgow suggest that fieldtrips offer an opportunity for students to creatively engage with the archaeology of the contemporary. Over two decades the Balfarg fieldtrip has evolved through various incarnations in terms of the course it has been situated in, and assessment and teaching methods, with more than 150 students involved. Positive feedback from participants suggests to me that they value the opportunity to be creative with their engagements on site and in their coursework, and that they benefit from experiencing 'the Other', which in this case is a visit to the kind of place that they were not expecting an archaeology trip to feature and a chance to meet people they might not have expected to meet.

Fieldtrips will presumably be an enduring element of degree courses for many years to come, but this is not without its challenges. There will be a temptation to cut back and scale down aspirations and costs or give in to the excesses of paperwork required for such trips nowadays. Therefore, a strong case will have to be made for such trips to continue due to challenges in terms of pedagogical value, accessibility, financial constraints and environmental factors. Making use of unusual or non-traditional destinations for fieldtrips, of the kind offered by contemporary archaeology; foregrounding active participation rather than passive consumption; innovative assessment methods; and creating the opportunity for immersive and memorable experiences may all be means to make the case for fieldtrips to retain a core place in the learning journey of our students. As archaeologists we know the fundamental value of leaving the classroom and visiting sites; it is time we more strongly articulated these values.

Acknowledgements

I would like to thank Gordon Barclay, Peter Yeoman and the late Roger Mercer for allowing me to interview them about their work at Balfarg. I am also very grateful to the many students who accompanied me on this fieldtrip and for their creativity and enthusiasm, especially those whose work features in this chapter with permission: Ian Perry and Imogen Bell. Thanks to Lorraine McEwan for help with the illustrations.

References

Atkinson, R. J. C. (1952), 'Four New "Henge" Monuments in Scotland and Northumberland', *Proceedings of the Society of Antiquaries of Scotland* 84: 57–66.

Barclay, G. J. (1993), *Balfarg: The Prehistoric Ceremonial Complex*, Fife: Historic Scotland and Fife Council.

Barclay, G. J. and K. Brophy (2020), '"A veritable chauvinism of prehistory"? The Late Neolithic Brexit Myth', *Archaeological Journal* 178 (2): 330–60.

Barclay, G. J. and C. Russell-White (1994), 'Excavations in the ceremonial complex of the fourth to second millennium BC at Balfarg and Balbirnie, Glenrothes, Fife', *Proceedings of the Society of Antiquaries of Scotland* 123: 43–110.

Brophy, K. (2004), 'Ruins in the landscape: modern monuments', in G. J. Barclay and I. A. G. Shepherd, eds, *Scotland in Ancient Europe: The Neolithic and Early Bronze Age of Scotland in their European context*, 143–54, Edinburgh: Society of Antiquaries of Scotland.

Brophy, K. (2015), 'A tale of two trails', *Urban Prehistorian blog*, January 2015, https://theurbanprehistorian.wordpress.com/2015/01/28/a-tale-of-two-trails/.

Brophy, K, (2018), '"The finest set of cup and ring marks in existence": the story of the Cochno Stone, West Dunbartonshire', *Scottish Archaeological Journal* 40: 1–23.

Brophy, K. (2019), 'Urban prehistoric enclosures: empty spaces / busy places', in C. Campbell, A. Giovine and J. Keating, eds, *Empty Spaces: Confronting Emptiness in National, Cultural and Urban History*, 181–203, London: Institute of Historical Research.

Gibson, A. (2011), 'Dating Balbirnie: recent radiocarbon dates from the stone circle and cairn at Balbirnie, Fife, and a review of its place in the overall Balfarg/Balbirnie site sequence', *Proceedings of the Society of Antiquaries of Scotland* 140: 51–77.

Harrison, R. and J. Schofield (2009), 'Archaeo-ethnography, auto-archaeology: introducing archaeologies of the contemporary past', *Archaeologies* 5 (2): 185–209.

Henson, D. (2012), *Doing Archaeology: A Subject Guide for Students*, London: Routledge.

Holtorf, C. (2001), 'Fieldtrip theory: towards archaeological ways of seeing', in P. Rainbird and Y. Hamilakis, eds, *Interrogating Pedagogies: Archaeology in Higher Education*, 81–7, Oxford: BAR.

Johnson, M. (2010), *Archaeological Theory: An introduction*, 2nd edn, London: Wiley-Blackwell.

Jones, J. C. and S. Washko (2021), 'More than fun in the sun: the pedagogy of field trips improves student learning in higher education', *Journal of Geoscience Education* 70 (3): 292–305.

Levitt, I. (1997), 'New Towns, new Scotland, new ideology 1937–57', *Scottish Historical Review* 76 (202): 222–38.

MacNeil, S. (2020), 'Academic digital scrapbooking', https://www.profweb.ca/en/publications/articles/academic-digital-scrapbooking.

Mercer, R. (1981), 'The excavation of a late Neolithic henge-type enclosure at Balfarg, Markinch, Fife, Scotland', *Proceedings of the Society of Antiquaries of Scotland* 111: 63–171.

QAA (2014), *Subject Benchmark Statement: Archaeology*.

QAA (2022), *Subject Benchmark Statement: Archaeology*, https://www.qaa.ac.uk/quality-code/subject-benchmark-statements/archaeology.

Rathje, W. L. (1979), 'Modern material culture studies', *Advances in Archaeological Method and Theory* 2: 1–37.

Rathje, W. L. and C. Murphy (2001), *Rubbish! The Archaeology of Garbage*, Tucson: University of Arizona Press.

Ritchie, J. N. G. (1974), 'Excavation of the stone circle and cairn at Balbirnie, Fife', *Archaeological Journal* 131: 1–32.

Shanks, M. (1992), *Experiencing the Past: On the Character of Archaeology*, London: Routledge.

Tilley, C. (1993), 'Art, architecture, landscape [Neolithic Sweden]', in B. Bender, ed., *Landscape: Politics and Perspectives*, 49–84, Oxford: Berg.

Wall, G. and A. Hale (2020), 'Art and archaeology: uncomfortable archival landscapes', *International Journal of Art and Design Education* 39 (4): 770–87.

5

Draw Your Phone: The Cellphone as an Intimate, Everyday Artefact

Colleen Morgan

Introduction

First, as Ingold (2007) entreats us to find and drown a rock in water before reading about materiality, I would ask you to draw your cellphone. Put it on the table in front of you and draw it to the best of your ability, and however you wish to represent it. You might as well, you look at it all day, right? And you may find that it is the best 30–40 minutes that you spend while on your phone.

Cellphones mediate, augment, translate and dictate our daily lives in complex ways that are largely unexamined by archaeologists. As personal media devices, they are both highly visible, in that we stare at them all day, but also increasingly invisible, as we use them to transmit and transport us to the internet. Certainly, cellphones are a ubiquitous and transformative personal artefact. Their inclusion and status within daily life is taken for granted; professing a lack of a smartphone is a subversive venture into nearly subhuman Luddism. This ubiquity, in/visibility and utility makes them perfect pedagogical devices to understand archaeological recording and reasoning. While there has been increasing attention toward other artefacts of late-stage global capitalism amongst archaeologists, studies of cellphones are relatively limited. Yet they provide a perfect entry into questions that are central to archaeological thought: how do we understand the symbolic or emotive qualities of artefacts? What do we record as pertinent information, and what is omitted? How is archaeology relevant to current thinking about materiality and technology?

In this chapter I describe an exercise during which I have asked undergraduate, postgraduate and developer-led archaeologists to engage in an apparently ludicrous exercise: to draw their cellphone according to archaeological standards.

In general, I have found in previous research (Morgan et al. 2021) that while students are drawing, they closely observe an object that is in their hands, and learn archaeological 'professional vision' (Goodwin 1994) while interacting with these artefacts. Further, drawing cellphones also promotes innovative thinking about how to understand and document the tangible and intangible aspects of contemporary artefacts. I investigate drawing cellphones in terms of 1) archaeological investigations of digital things; 2) as part of ongoing research on drawing and archaeological knowledge construction; and 3) as a meditation on our most intimate and problematic talisman.

A (digital) contemporary archaeology

The digital presents a worthy challenge for contemporary archaeology and to studies of material culture in general. Digital assemblages threaten the perceived boundaries of material culture as associated technologies are considered to be lightweight, 'in the cloud' and occasionally completely immaterial. This belies the experience of most digital archaeologists who know the weight of carrying equipment around while teaching or conducting fieldwork or traversing the overwhelming expanse of digital archives. This materiality is relatively well established within contemporary archaeology. Christine Finn's early work on Silicon Valley (2002) and her discussion of computer collections (2003) is formative in examining computing materials as an archaeologist. Later, Moshenska's (2014) excavation of a USB drive examined an assortment of digital files related to schoolwork as well as adult content. Schofield and colleagues (2018) examined the computer mouse, while Sara Perry and I (2015) excavated a hard drive, during which time I found the intriguing absurdity of applying archaeological methods to digital materials quite playful and illuminating.

Cellphones have been of particular use to archaeologists. Archaeologists have been using smartphones and tablets for fieldwork since the early experimental work by Dominic Powlesland (1986), who used a Sharp PC-1500 in 1984 to record primary context and object data (see also Wright 2011). Likewise, there have been extensive investigations of apps to support heritage interpretation and access to archaeological data (e.g., Jeater 2012). The cellphone itself came under examination as an archaeological artefact in Cassie Newland's (2004) MA dissertation on the archaeology of mobile phones. She documented the cultural context of cellphones, with case studies including a protest over the construction of a cellphone mast. Robb (2021) creatively discusses the investigation of the materiality of cellphones through a fictional plenary address to a futuristic Material Culture conference. Though not archaeologists, Maxwell and Milligan (2013) examine the contemporary material culture of cellphones through utopian and dystopian lenses, with a particular focus on the destructive environmental consequences of their production and disposal. Likewise, material culture specialist and anthropologist Miller and colleagues (2021) conducted a brilliant and extensive ethnographic investigation of smartphones, finding both global commonalities and highly specific contextual use. Amongst the many useful considerations of the smartphone, they investigate it as a material object, through the internal and external personalization such as 'wallpaper', dangling charms and cases, and track its movements between owners and through space (Miller et al. 2021). Finally, Miller and colleagues discuss the cellphone as a 'transportal home', arguing that the 'smartphone is best understood not just as a device through which we communicate, but also as a place within which we now live' (2021: 219).

These investigations of digital technology in general and of cellphones in particular reflect the broad shift toward their use in everyday life, and within archaeological practice. Digital methods have proliferated in archaeology, at first unexamined, but it is becoming increasingly obvious that moving from knowledge production through analogue media recording to digital is different in fundamental ways that are impacting our understanding of the artefacts and landscapes we are recording. The changes most pertinent to this chapter surround the use of drawing for archaeological recording. In an exhaustive review, we discussed the historical context of drawing in archaeology, current conventions, and the affordances of digital drawing with questions regarding its impact (Morgan and Wright 2018). With an expanded team, funding and a new name – the 'Aide Memoire Project' – we subsequently devised a series of investigations drawing from qualitative and quantitative methods used in user-interface design studies and we demonstrated key differences in the perception of drawing and the inadequacy of digital surrogates in supporting learning in students (Morgan et al. 2021). Specifically, we found that drawing artefacts and archaeological remains supported the creation of mental models that are important in archaeological knowledge production, and this resonated with research in cognitive psychology on learning outcomes (e.g., Van Meter and Firetto 2013). Further, we noted that drawing should still be taught in the context of field recording and more widely integrated into archaeological pedagogy of all kinds and at all levels.

Alongside this background research, I introduced an exercise that called for students to illustrate an unexpected artefact: their own cellphones. I led a course titled 'Communicating Archaeology' for all of the second-year undergraduates on the archaeology degree at the University of York, usually between 80 and 100 students at a time. Lectures were complemented by workshops – small group teaching – wherein students learned the basics of archaeological illustration, photography, videography and mapmaking. This was in part a response to a perceived lack of visualization skills amongst students in archaeology (James 2015) and a focus within Archaeology at York on media literacy and critical digital pedagogy (Perry et al. 2022). When the lectures were in person, I brought in practical elements to focus the discussion. For example, at the outset of the mapmaking lecture, I asked students to draw a map of their route to the lecture hall. During the week on illustration, I asked them to take their phones out and put them on the desk. Instead of asking them to turn them off or put them away, I asked them to draw their phones. This exercise had three purposes: 1) to introduce an element of play into the lecture; 2) to spur discussion on the purpose and content of archaeological drawing; and 3) to demonstrate professional vision, as previously discussed. The exercise was extemporaneous and preceded their more formal workshop where they would draw sherds, flint and coins. The initial exercise was received relatively well, and prompted questions about the content and scale of the drawing. As such, I repeated the exercise until the Covid-19 pandemic disrupted in-person teaching and the lectures were all pre-recorded and moved online.

Inspired by the relative success and fun I had with undergraduate students drawing phones, I decided to try it again with taught postgraduate students as a guest lecturer for Archaeology of the Modern World at University College London. During this instance, Sefryn Penrose, the module organizer, provided drawing film, pencils, rubbers, graph paper and drawing boards, which considerably formalized the exercise. Like the undergraduates, these students had relatively little experience in using archaeological conventions for drawing. They had more experience in discussing critical theory and materiality, which changed the context and tenor of the exercise yet again. Finally, Sara Perry and I led a workshop attended by academics and very experienced archaeologists wherein we used the exercise as part of a reimagining of context sheets. These archaeologists were all extensively experienced in archaeological drawing conventions, but had not deployed them to record their phones. This decentring was intended to introduce playfulness to discussions that could quickly turn into rote recitations of received knowledge regarding archaeological recording. The uptake on the drawing was varied, with some finishing quickly – generally those who did not incorporate the user interface into their drawing – and others recording their cellphones with intricate detail. These varied approaches were later reflected in the more structured exercise I describe below. The exercise was successful in opening up participants to playful methods and in encouraging conversation amongst a group who did not all know each other. Overall, discussions during each instance were different, but each still produced productive explorations of materiality and engaging group discussions regarding the construction of archaeological knowledge.

The cellphone drawing exercise

While these previous exercises were fun and engaging, they were informal compared to the more controlled investigations carried out during the Aide Memoire Project. To understand the impact of drawing cellphones more fully, I asked for student volunteers with some basic archaeological drawing experience and recreated the conditions described as part of the in-lab investigations during the Aide Memoire Project (Morgan et al. 2021). Four students engaged with the exercise, a small sample, but enough for one researcher to effectively manage given the parameters of the investigation.

I sat the students at Covid-secure workstations with drawing materials, introduced them to the research more generally, including discussing the ethics of the exercise, and had them fill out a questionnaire describing their background experience in illustration. This pre-drawing questionnaire also asks for a written description of the artefact, which is key to evaluating their engagement with the exercise. Then I asked the students to take their phones out, describe the 'artefact' and then begin to draw.

As the students began drawing, I took photographs of their progress. This phase of the investigation was very quiet as the students were immersed in their task (see Figure 5.1). I intentionally tried to leave it to the students regarding their choices as to what to include or exclude from their illustration. One student was measuring all of the sides of the phone with great care and translating those measurements to their drawing. The others traced the outline of their phone, much like some methods of archaeological illustration, before filling in the details in the middle (see Figure 5.2). One student, the most experienced in archaeological practice and media generation, drew three 'views': the front, back and profile, and elements of the user interface. The other three did not draw the user interface; we will return to more discussion of this below.

Figure 5.1 Student participant using a ruler to measure elements of their phone to transcribe it to permatrace. Photo by author. CC-BY Colleen Morgan.

Figure 5.2 Student participant drawing their phone 'freehand'. Photo by author. CC-BY Colleen Morgan.

After forty minutes of silent drawing, all the participants were finished. I asked them to fill out a post-illustration questionnaire and then conducted a loosely structured focus group discussion. Though this was limited in duration, and outside of the usual setting of a class, this structured investigation allowed me to record and evaluate the student interaction with this exercise in a way that further supports its implementation as a useful and insightful endeavour.

The questionnaires the students completed allowed me to evaluate 1) their relative experience in archaeology; 2) their experience with archaeological illustration; and 3) record their observations of the cellphone before and after the exercise. Their observations were commensurate with what we had found in our previous Aide Memoire investigations: initial observations were somewhat superficial whereas after drawing the cellphone their descriptions became considerably more detailed, in one case noting fingerprints on the screen surface and detailed descriptions of the holes and buttons in the cellphone. In previous investigations, there was some anxiety regarding writing descriptions when we used archaeological objects – there could be a 'wrong' answer regarding medieval potsherds or flint tools. This anxiety did not manifest in the cellphone drawing exercise, as the students knew their cellphones intimately, such as its make, model, age and general condition – yet they still learned more about the cellphone through drawing. We also asked participants if they understood the 'archaeological object' differently after recording the cellphone, and each answered in the affirmative, one student adding that 'I've never really looked at it as a static object before and it was interesting to really notice how an old break in the case affects the visuals.' This detailed observation elicited by drawing aligned with our findings during previous research on archaeological drawing.

After completing the drawings, I led a focus group through a loosely structured discussion of the exercise. Students discussed their individual drawings and I asked if they learned anything new about their phones after drawing them. One student replied at relative length:

> Yes. Well, now I know the dimensions of it; how big the little hole on the top is for the microphone. I know where the scratches are. So, yeah, I used it every day for a year and looked at it for six hours a day, according to screen time ... I've seen it about 100,000 times, but this was the first time, I actually *actually* looked at it.

Beyond gaining a more acute sense of the physical attributes of the phone, the discussion delved into the nature of the connection students have with the artefact and interface. As previously mentioned, one student drew the front,

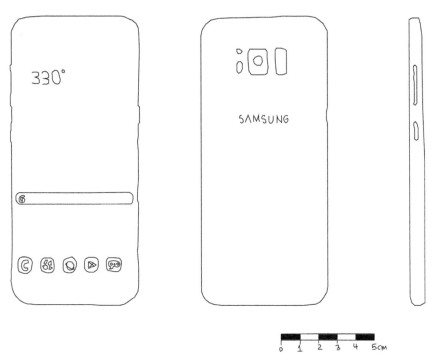

Figure 5.3 Drawing of a Samsung cellphone: front, back and profile view (L–R). Drawing by student participant; digitization by Colleen Morgan.

reverse and profile of the phone (see Figure 5.3) along with details of the user interface. This student also kept a leaf from an excavation as a keepsake inside the clear encasement. There was some discussion of the choices in cases and what they may reveal about the person's connection to the phone, but primary interest was in the contents of the user interface. One student suggested that it might be worthwhile to switch phones to draw them, an idea that was treated with horror by the other students. The deeply personal aspects of the contents of the phone were discussed; even the configuration of the apps could be subject to scrutiny regarding dating apps or emergency contacts. Indeed, most had silenced notifications and so therefore kept their screens blank for the drawing exercise. One mentioned that this was to make the task easier, as the 'screen would be changing all the time' and therefore difficult to draw. That the students may receive a sensitive text during observation was not considered during the ethics application and would need careful attention if the exercise is repeated. Finally, students found the exercise calming, one stating, 'I find that kind of observational drawing quite therapeutic', and the others agreed. It may be that drawing the physical object could be one of the best uses of a cellphone.

Conclusions

Drawing phones is absurd, risky and worthwhile. Our previous research during the Aide Memoire project delved into the wealth of educational literature that supports drawing as an effective way to learn in many different disciplines (Morgan et al. 2021). As such, expanding the engagement with drawing from the relatively isolated and rare instances that it is taught within archaeology – field schools and specialist media creation modules – into a more general pedagogical toolkit is a worthy objective. As previously noted, drawing is a 'forcing function' in that the student must fully understand the scrutinized subject through meta-cognitive awareness and control to complete their drawing (Van Meter and Firetto 2013: 259, cited in Morgan et al. 2021). With regard to contemporary archaeology, drawing a familiar artefact evoked the frisson and alienation described by Buchli and Lucas: 'archaeological method takes us further away, distances us from any attachment to the objects and the material world we encounter' (2001: 9). Making the everyday alien through archaeological methods feels delightfully transgressive, but is also a comment on our encounters with non-contemporary archaeological artefacts. Was the bone awl as intimate of an object as a cellphone? What emotional and experiential worlds do artefacts contain?

Furthermore, another way to expand this exercise might be to follow technological supply chains as part of digital object biographies. There is a considerable literature regarding the anthropology and materiality of cellphones (e.g., Bell et al. 2018; Miller et al. 2021), including research on the rare earth materials (Mantz 2018), that can help contextualize both the cellphone as an intimate artefact and more broadly characterize digital archaeology and its technologies within supply-chain capitalism (e.g., Tsing 2009). A lesson plan that traced the lineage of cellphones and the extraction of rare earth materials as well as examining the intimate attachment we have to our objects (e.g., Bell and Spikins 2018; see also Robb 2021) alongside the drawing activity as described would be a worthwhile intervention in many classrooms.

Finally, this exercise allows further exploration of digital artefacts: can the user interface of a cellphone be recorded through archaeological methods? Is an app a deposit or a site? Are archaeological analogies even useful for understanding how we interact with the 'bag of holding' interiority of cellphones? Miller and colleagues' (2021) characterization of the smartphone as a 'transportal home' might be a useful metaphor for further exploration and understanding. Alongside a drawing of the physical object, there might be a 'memory map' that regards the smartphone as stationary, while other places and contexts spin and converge around it (Miller et al. 2021: 221). I have productively investigated this phenomenon as 'telepresence' or 'interstitial spaces' before (Morgan 2009; 2019), and archaeological explorations of digital technology benefit from translations of traditional methods into metaphors to think with. Therefore, a 'household archaeology' of the cellphone, one that investigates digital dwelling, microstratigraphy, social relations and embodiment (*sensu* Tringham 2012), might be a generative approach to understanding this slippery device.

References

Bell, J. A., B. Kobak, J. Kuipers and A. Kemble (2018), 'Introduction – Unseen Connections: The Materiality of Cell Phones', *Anthropological Quarterly* 91 (2): 465–84.

Bell, T. and P. Spikins (2018), 'The object of my affection: attachment security and material culture', *Time and Mind* 11 (1): 23–39.

Burridge, J. M., B. M. Collins, B. N. Galton, A. R. Halbert, T. R. Heywood, W. H. Latham, R. W. Phippen, P. Quarendon, P. Reilly, M. W. Ricketts, J. Simmons, S. J. P. Todd, A. G. N. Walter and J. R. Woodwark (1989), 'The WINSOM solid modeller and its application to data visualization', *IBM Systems Journal* 28 (4): 548–68.

Finn, C. (2002), *Artifacts: An Archaeologist's Year in Silicon Valley*, Cambridge, MA: MIT Press.

Finn, C. (2003), 'Bits and Pieces: A Mini Survey of Computer Collecting', *Industrial Archaeology Review* 25 (2), 119–28.

Goodwin, C. (1994), 'Professional Vision', *American Anthropologist* 96 (3): 606–33.

Ingold, T. (2007), 'Materials against materiality', *Archaeological Dialogues* 14 (1): 1–16.

James, S. (2015), '"Visual competence" in archaeology: a problem hiding in plain sight', *Antiquity* 89 (347): 1189–202.

Jeater, M. (2012), 'Smartphones and site interpretation: the Museum of London's Streetmuseum applications', in C. Bonacchi, ed., *Archaeology and Digital Communication: Towards Strategies of Public Engagement*, 66–82, London: Archetype Publications.

Mantz, J. W. (2018), 'From Digital Divides to Creative Destruction: Epistemological Encounters in the Regulation of the "Blood Mineral" Trade in the Congo', *Anthropological Quarterly* 91 (2): 525–49.

Maxwell R. and T. Milligan (2013), 'The Material Cellphone', in P. Graves-Brown, R. Harrison and A. Piccini, eds, *The Oxford Handbook of the Archaeology of the Contemporary World*, 699–712, Oxford: Oxford University Press.

Miller, D., L. A. Rabho, P. Awondo, M. de Vries, M. Duque, P. Garvey, L. Haapio-Kirk, C. Hawkins, A. Otaegui, S. Walton and X. Wang (2021), *The Global Smartphone: Beyond a Youth Technology*, London: UCL Press.

Morgan, C. (2009), '(Re)Building Çatalhöyük: Changing Virtual Reality in Archaeology', *Archaeologies* 5 (3): 468–87.

Morgan, C. (2019), 'Avatars, Monsters, and Machines: A Cyborg Archaeology', *European Journal of Archaeology* 22 (3): 324–37.

Morgan, C., H. Petrie, H. Wright and J. S. Taylor (2021), 'Drawing and Knowledge Construction in Archaeology: The Aide Mémoire Project', *Journal of Field Archaeology* 46 (8): 614–28.

Morgan, C. and H. Wright (2018), 'Pencils and Pixels: Drawing and Digital Media in Archaeological Field Recording', *Journal of Field Archaeology* 43 (2): 136–51.

Moshenska, G. (2014). 'The archaeology of (flash) memory', *Post-Medieval Archaeology* 48 (1): 255–9.

Perry, S., L. M. Dennis, H. Fredheim and T. Smith, T. (forthcoming), 'Digital field-schools as Seedbeds for Transformative Heritage Practice', in E. Watrall and L. Goldstein, eds, *Digital Heritage and Archaeology in Practice*, Gainesville: University Press of Florida.

Perry, S. and C. Morgan (2015), 'Materializing Media Archaeologies: The MAD-P Hard Drive Excavation', *Journal of Contemporary Archaeology* 2 (1): 94–104.

Powlesland, D. (1986), 'On-Site Computing: In the Field with the Silicon Chip', in J. Richards, ed., *Computer Usage in British Archaeology*, 39–43, Birmingham: Institute of Field Archaeology.

Reilly, P., S. Todd and A. Walter (2016), 'Rediscovering and modernising the digital Old Minster of Winchester', *Digital Applications in Archaeology and Cultural Heritage* 3 (2): 33–41.

Reinhard, A. (2018), 'Adapting the Harris Matrix for Software Stratigraphy', *Advances in Archaeological Practice* 6 (2): 157–72.

Robb, J. (2021), 'The mobile phone in late medieval culture', *Internet Archaeology*, https://doi.org/10.11141/ia.56.7.

Schofield, A. J., G. Beale and J. Austin (2018), 'The Archaeology of the Digital Periphery: Computer Mice and the Archaeology of the Early Digital Era', *Journal of Contemporary Archaeology* 5 (2): 154–73.

Tringham, R. (2012). 'Households through a digital lens', in B. J. Parker and C. P. Foster, eds, *New Perspectives on Household Archaeology*, 81–120, Winona Lake, IN: Eisenbrauns.

Tsing, A. (2009), 'Supply Chains and the Human Condition', *Rethinking Marxism* 21 (2): 148–76.

Van Meter, P. and C. M. Firetto (2013), 'Cognitive model of drawing construction', in G. Schraw, M. T. McCrudden and D. Robinson, eds, *Learning through Visual Displays*, 247–80, Charlotte, NC: Information Age Pub., Inc.

Wright, H. (2011), 'Seeing Triple Archaeology, Field Drawing and the Semantic Web', PhD thesis, University of York, UK.

6

Walking and Talking around the Bombsites of Bloomsbury

Gabriel Moshenska

Introduction

When I walk, keep up. When I talk, shut up.

Moshenska, apocryphal

This chapter is a critical reflection on a teaching tool that I devised more than a decade ago, and have been using and developing ever since. The walking tour 'Bombsites of Bloomsbury' is a two-hour-long guided journey around sites in the central London borough that are associated in some way with bombing, across a time span of some 120 years. The walk forms the introductory session to a graduate module on the archaeology of modern conflict, and aims to give students an overview of some of the most important concepts in this unusual interdisciplinary course.

This graduate module – 'Archaeologies of Modern Conflict' – is the first course that I designed from scratch and taught solo. My PhD research focused on the archaeology, material culture and memory of the Second World War, with a practical focus on the remains of the London Blitz. This included studies of air-crash sites, air-raid shelters, urban bombsites and the tangled post-war heritage of conflict commemoration, traced onto the memorial landscape of the city (Moshenska 2010). During my postdoctoral research fellowship I was encouraged – with a firm but friendly nudge – to develop a taught module based on my PhD research. This was an excellent opportunity for which I remain extremely grateful. I was aware from the start that the course would need a far more international perspective than my own research to that point, and while the Bombsites of Bloomsbury tour remains myopically London-centric, it introduces a module that grows more truly global, radical and wide-reaching with each iteration.

My aim in this chapter is to describe the roots and routes of this tour, to consider the pedagogical values and limits of walking, and to explore some of the relevant themes and ideas in contemporary archaeology, public archaeology and heritage that this case study feeds into. I have included quite a lot of details of the stops on the tour itself – enough for the reader to take a mini-self-guided tour if they so wish. One of the founding pillars of the walk and of my teaching philosophy as a whole is the radical people's history notion that anybody can write or rewrite history, often starting in their home, school or workplace, as a way to claim a sense of place, power and belonging. Equally, it would be wrong to ignore the fact that in the case of Bloomsbury I have been blessed with an unusually rich body of material to work with.

Beginnings in Bloomsbury

Bloomsbury is a district of north-central London defined by convention rather than firm municipal boundaries (de Freitas 2018). It is bounded to the north by Euston Road, to the east by Grays Inn Road, to the south by Theobalds Road and New Oxford Street, and to the west by Tottenham Court Road. At least, this is my definition. The area is well known for many different reasons, and these are reflected in the many walking tours already available in the area. One can tour literary and artistic Bloomsbury and learn of the 'Bloomsbury Set': Virginia Woolf, Lytton Strachey, Vanessa Bell, John Maynard Keynes and friends, who famously lived in squares, painted in circles and loved in triangles. One can walk the Bloomsbury of famous women, of political radicals, modern architecture, LGBT+ heritage and of curious urban geology (National Portrait Gallery n.d.; Siddall and Kirk 2017)

Within the bounds laid out above lie several major universities and research institutes, the British Museum, several hospitals including Great Ormond Street, Heals department store, a sadly dwindling number of occult bookshops, social housing and luxury mansion flats and the children's park at Coram's Field. From 2001 to 2009 I studied in Bloomsbury; since 2009 I have worked there. I have stayed in squatted or occupied houses around the university district, and occasionally in occupied spaces within the universities themselves. For two years, from 2007 to 2009, I lived on Gower Street in a university-owned house as a live-in warden. In these two decades of living, working and studying, I have never stopped walking around Bloomsbury and exploring the streets, squares, alleys, underground tunnels, basements, crypts, bunkers and boiler-rooms. I have wandered hungrily, lingered in bookshops, strolled alone and with others, lounged in pubs, killed time, played in the snow, and engaged in other exotic antics. All of this has built up a personal map of my own Bloomsbury, augmented by extensive reading. With my interests in the heritage of violence, I naturally began to trace the bombsites of Bloomsbury.

Sources

My research for the Bombsites of Bloomsbury walk is better described as a slow accretion of fragmented knowledge: I would not dignify it with the term 'method'. Many of the stops on my tour are things that I walked past, noticed and then Googled when I got home. Others are the result of late-night Wikipedia click-throughs, and Googling various street and place names along with the word 'bomb'. A huge amount of information, much of it questionable, is just a quick keyword search away. One of the early iterations of the walk was delivered as an activity during the 2013 Contemporary and Historical Archaeology in Theory (CHAT) conference, with lively audience participation.

The most valuable sources for the walk are the extraordinary London County Council Bomb Damage Maps, a set of high-resolution maps annotated by LCC architects throughout the Second World War to record bomb damage to buildings across London (Saunders 2005). The damage is colour-coded from mild blast damage in yellow – broken windows and doors – through to purple for destroyed beyond repair, and black for total annihilation. The resulting maps are palimpsests of several years of bombing, including the night Blitz of 1940–1 and the V1 and V2 missile attacks of 1944–5. In many places individual bombs can be traced by the bruise-like colours of black and purple at the centre, fading to washed-out red and yellow at the fringes. A few hard-hit areas are overwhelmingly coloured in the heavy, dark colours, while some entire streets among them sit eerily unscathed. I have pored over these maps for hours: first in the 2005 bound volume in the history library, then the many expensive colour photocopies I took, later still in the rather inferior but more affordable reprint volume published in 2016, and finally online where they can now be browsed freely (Ward 2016). I have discovered the surprising histories of houses where I have lived and of favourite pubs, and I have traced the bombed East End streets that both of my grandmothers' families fled. In Bloomsbury, the bomb damage maps shed light on post-war buildings inserted into gaps in terraces, on the few gaps that remained, and on entire areas such as the present-day Brunswick

Centre built on heavily-damaged blocks and streets. There is a risk of creating teleological 'just-so' stories here: many post-war buildings said to be built on Blitz rubble, including in heavily bombed cities such as Coventry and Plymouth as well as London, are in fact the work of pre- and post-war slum clearances and lucrative development projects (Tiratsoo 2000). More convenient to blame the Nazis and trust in local memory to assent.

A final word on sources: the memoirs and published diaries and letters of Bloomsbury notables such as Richard Attenborough, Graham Greene and Virginia Woolf provide remarkable insights into the experience of bombing from the ground up (Attenborough 2008; Bell 1984; Greene 2008). The shock of seeing one's urban environment transformed so suddenly and violently inspired many thoughtful responses and reactions. How else would I have learned that amongst the material casualties of the Blitz on Bloomsbury was London's premier banjo factory?

Walking and learning

What are the pedagogical values of a walking tour? Perhaps this is the wrong question, or at least starts from the wrong premise. I have worked in public archaeology and community archaeology for decades, much of it involving school and university students of different ages. This has given me a great deal of experience in developing learning programmes 'outside the classroom', and I found the 2006 *Learning Outside the Classroom Manifesto* and associated resources to be an encouraging and inspiring starting place. Similarly, in the archaeological excavations that I have run, many of them with a strong public-facing dimension, I have made explorations of the wider landscape context a central part of the work, from research design through to dissemination. This work has incorporated walks of various kinds: informal strolls to explore an area; walkover surveys to get a more detailed sense of a specific place; fieldwalking on plough-soil to collect surface artefacts; and walks to introduce new team members to the research area and its palimpsests of history, geology, archaeology, ecology and memory. These walks have sensory and embodied elements beyond the crudely intellectual or pedagogical: I want to encourage my students and team members to dwell, feel and think in spaces and moving through spaces.

Is walking a part of the much-vaunted student experience? Karein Goertz has considered the 'student as walker', from the campus orientation tour to walking for better mental health and well-being. Her survey of the intellectual history of walking-to-think ranges from Aristotle and Rousseau to Thoreau and Woolf. Goertz's own teaching includes a class that intersperses short walks with creative writing sessions, and describes a bunch of ways that walking might be integrated into a liberal arts curriculum, from podcast lectures to walking-based assessments (2018: 62).

Walking as method and pedagogy has a rich radical tradition, and I have drawn inspirations from these histories. I have experimented with Debord and the Situationists' notion of the *dérive*, drifting through urban landscapes in small groups, and drawn on Ingold's related idea of *wayfaring*, tracing lines through space (Debord 2006; Ingold 2007). I have come to view these and similarly abstract approaches to walking through the critical lens of Massey's work on place-making as relational, agential and contingent (e.g., Massey 2005). Bombsites of Bloomsbury is not an exposition of my research or a direct alternative to a lecture: it is a shared experience of space that incorporates method and learning.

Another radical foundation for walking-as-practice is the people's history movements of the 1960s and later, which aimed not only to tell the stories of ordinary people's lives but to put the means of writing history into their own hands. I have taken inspiration from writer Sven Lindqvist's 'dig where you stand' manifesto (*Gräv där du star*), which focused on researching one's own workplace using the tools and skills of your labour (Lindqvist 1979). The university sits at the heart of the Bloomsbury of my walking tours (I am aware that Lindqvist was not addressing academics!). The wider point is the idea of walking as a method that is open to all: as part of the Bombsites of Bloomsbury walk, I describe my research on Wikipedia and local community forums, oral history interviews and personal memories, the patchwork of things noticed in passing and places explored in depths. With these methods anybody can create a historical walk of their own, and claim authority and ownership in the spaces where they live and labour.

Inspirations

Two books in particular inspired my work and encouraged me to explore Bloomsbury in search of bombsites. The first is *Rebel Footprints* by the socialist historian Dave Rosenberg. Subtitled *A Guide to Uncovering London's Radical History*, this is the book form of a series of different walking tours that Rosenberg has run across London for many years (2006). With a strong focus on the East End, these tours cover centuries of political lives and movements, and even make it as far as Bloomsbury, subject of the 'No Gods, No Masters' walk. I have taken part in Rosenberg's tours of Cable Street and of Spitalfields, and I have covered some of his other walks myself with his book in hand. One of the lessons that I took from his tours is to get to know your fellow-travellers: there is a good chance that somebody on your walk has personal or familial links to the places and events that you are describing – that's probably partly why they're there – and might be able to contribute context and colour.

The second book that inspired my works and walks is another of Sven Lindqvist's works. *A History of Bombing* is a fascinating, kaleidoscopic tumble through the political, scientific, cultural and personal histories of bombing from the air, from its origins in Libya in 1911 to the nuclear terror of the Cold War (Lindqvist 2001). The book combines a fascination with the titanic impacts of aerial bombing upon geopolitics, urban architecture, technologies of death and tourism, empire and state power, and the novel notion of cities as erasable. Throughout, the book burns with a moral outrage at the impact of bombing on civilian populations and demonstrates Lindqvists's fascination with a truly global, internationalist twentieth-century history. One of the peculiarities of *A History of Bombing* is its format. The book is made up of numbered sections, most of them a few hundred words in length. One can read the book from cover to cover as a more-or-less chronological narrative history, or – more properly – one can choose a starting point and follow the guided tour, as the sections lead you from one to the next, or sometimes skipping forward dozens of pages: Lindqvist called it 'a labyrinth with 22 entrances and no exits', and exhorts the reader to 'Follow the threads, put together the horrible puzzle, and, once you have seen my century, build one of your own from other pieces' (Lindqvist 2001: v). The non-linearity of the book has provided me with inspiration to remix and remap my walks, just as the histories it contains have informed my storytelling and my understanding of bombs in all their dimensions.

Traces, tracing

The core concept of the Bombsites of Bloomsbury walk is 'trace', as both noun and verb. The nodes or waypoints of the tour, the places where I stop and talk and show and explain, are traces of bombing. The breadth of this concept of trace is key to the students' understanding of the inclusivity and interdisciplinarity of my teaching and of my conceptualization of contemporary archaeology specifically. The typology of traces (noun) includes:

- Material traces – the physical marks of bombing on surviving buildings, and the new buildings built on the ruins.
- Textual traces – the narratives told in patchy fragments on memorial plaques, monuments and other inscriptions across the urban landscape. Also the stories told in history books and historical sources.
- Mnemonic traces – my own memories of place and those that others have shared with me. An oral tradition that I am passing on through the medium of the walk.
- Absences – the gaps left by bombs, the absent buildings and the absences of the many different things planned or proposed to fill those gaps. There is a rich typology of these absences in their own right.

Trace as a verb is similarly divisible:

- Tracing or locating the marks, texts, absences and narratives that make up the waypoints on the walk.
- Tracing or the act of drawing lines on maps by moving through space, creating new iterations of the Bombsites of Bloomsbury walk through new combinations or orders of the waypoints.

What is the pedagogic value in picking 'trace' apart into these fragments? First, it illustrates the interdisciplinarity of the field of contemporary archaeology in general and contemporary conflict archaeology in particular. It highlights the integration of the material and the immaterial, texts and artefacts and memory and ruins and commemoration. The consideration of absence as a form of material and immaterial trace illuminates the destructive power of conflict, and the inclusion of memories offers a more optimistic, humanistic counterpoint. Secondly, the dual understanding of trace (verb) as method and as pedagogy demonstrates the methodological openness of contemporary archaeology, rich in precedents, and sparks a realization: I could do this myself.

Some bombsites of Bloomsbury

Where are the bombsites of Bloomsbury? What events do they mark and what traces can we trace there today? In this short chapter I cannot give a full version of the walk, or even a summary, but I can describe a few of the most significant waypoints to give a general impression of the experience.

Queen Square Gardens, 1915

Southampton Row, south of Russell Square, is a grimy, tourist-trap sort of street. On the east side a wide and rather charming alleyway, Cosmo Place, leads to the relative peace of Queen Square, overlooked by hospital buildings and close to the famous Great Ormond Street children's hospital. Queen Square Gardens, entered by one of the gates in the old-fashioned railings, is a sober sort of London park with neat flowerbeds and paths and lawns. You might not spot the bombsite unless you were looking for it: I found it by chance, but chance smiles on those who are always vaguely on the lookout for things.

To the side of one of the lawns is a circle of bricks laid into the ground, about two metres across. At their centre is a postcard-sized metal plaque. On my last walking tour we had to brush mud and leaf mould out of the inscribed text in order to read it (Figure 6.1):

> On the night of the eighth of September 1915 a Zeppelin bomb fell and exploded on this spot. Although nearly 1000 people slept in the surrounding buildings no person was injured.

Figure 6.1 Pointing out the plaque to a tour group in Queen Square, 2022. Photograph by Megan Elias.

This was London's first air raid, a mission flown by the German Navy's experienced Zeppelin commander Heinrich Mathy. Zeppelin L13 dropped several bombs across London on that night, including one close to St Bart's hospital that weighed 300kg – the heaviest ever aerial bomb at that time (Castle 2015). Casualties of the raid included twenty-two killed and more than seventy injured, alongside structural damage to a value of more than half a million pounds.

A little way to the south of Queen Square, the Red Lion pub was hit by another of Mathy's bombs that same night, killing three people. Today the rebuilt pub displays a rather battered-looking clock discovered in the wreckage, its hands stopped at 10:40, the time of the explosion.

In October of 1916, Mathy and his crew were shot down and killed over Potters Bar, north of London. Many years later I was part of a small team excavating the crash site, now a public park (Faulkner and Durrani 2008). We found nothing on that first attempt, as so often in conflict archaeology: an absence to place alongside the material trace in the Red Lion and the text of the memorial in Queens Square Gardens.

Russell Square, south-east corner, 1933

Physicist Leo Szilard liked to walk and think. On Tuesday, 12 September 1933 he was pondering the words of his fellow-physicist Ernest Rutherford, who had recently described splitting atoms as 'a very poor and inefficient way of producing energy' and that anybody promoting atom power was 'talking moonshine'. This was a blow to Szilard, and he stomped across London pondering it. At the bottom of Russell Square he waited at a traffic light to cross Southampton Row. As he began to cross, an idea occurred to him – by his own account, the moment his foot left the kerb (Jogalekar 2013; Lanchester 2005).

Szilard pictured an atom struck by a relatively low-energy neutron, and splitting into fragments – among them, two or more neutrons. These would split more atoms, the process growing exponentially. This is the nuclear chain reaction, the theoretical basis of all nuclear power, and the bridge between the equation $E=mc^2$ and the atomic bomb. Szilard calculated that the fission fragments and neutrons, together, would have a minutely smaller total mass than the original atom. This difference in mass is the 'm' in the equation; c^2 is the speed of light squared – a very big number. The tiny change in mass releases a disproportionately large amount of energy.

A year after his brainwave in Russell Square, Szilard patented a design for a basic nuclear reactor. In 1939, together with Enrico Fermi, he discovered that an

122 *Teaching and Learning the Archaeology of the Contemporary Era*

isotope of uranium was able to sustain a chain reaction, as he had theorized. The bomb born in Los Alamos was conceived in the heart of Bloomsbury.

Gower Street, 1941

Many buildings in London show the scars of bomb damage: ragged hemispherical holes in monumental stonework, pucker marks from smaller pieces of bomb casing, and the blank patchwork marks where these wounds have been repaired. The V&A has a wall famously covered in these marks, and there is a small spray across the side wall of the Tate Gallery too. St Clement Danes church on the Strand, one of many Christopher Wren churches burned in the Blitz, wears the marks of brutal bomb damage on its external walls. Brickwork is easily repaired, and rendered walls hide all sorts of architectural sins. It is on, stone buildings that these traces can most easily be seen.

The Rockefeller Building on the corner of Gower Street and University Street was not badly damaged in the Blitz. The London County Council bomb damage maps record it as suffering mild blast damage. The bomb that exploded in the middle of Gower Street in September 1940, directly in front of the door of the Rockefeller Building, sprayed hot metal into the pale grey limestone façades of the buildings on both sides of the street. Where bomb fragments hit stone walls, the craters become points of weakness and erosion. To restore the appearance of the wall, but also its strength and integrity, it was common practice to cut out the cratered section and insert a repair: either a chunk of similar stone mortared into place or a cement filling.

On the Gower Street side of the Rockefeller Building, the repairs were made with cement, mixed with ashes to match the colour of the limestone wall. The mistake the restorers made was to take the soot-stained surface of the wall as a reference for the colour: when cleaned up, the darker coloured patches stand out starkly against the pale limestone (see Figure 6.2). The effect is striking and rather attractive, but it serves to illuminate exactly where the bomb splinters hit the wall: an arc of impacts peaking in front of the doorway (Cain 2011). On the opposite side of the street the bomb damage has been repaired much more carefully and the patches are barely visible.

Tavistock Square memorial landscape

On 7 July 2005 I took a bus from my flat in south London heading north to Islington, where I was part of a team excavating a row of Victorian slum

Figure 6.2 The façade of the Rockefeller Building showing the repaired bomb damage, 2015. Photograph by author.

houses destroyed by bombs in the Second World War (Simpson 2008). On Southampton Row, just south of Russell Square, the bus was stopped, as emergency vehicles descended on Russell Square underground station and casualties of the Tube bombing began to emergence onto the street (Tulloch 2006). I left the bus and walked into Russell Square itself, where I saw a policeman on a park bench sobbing. With no public transport and rumours of bombs, I decided to head a few blocks north to UCL. Around this point, the number 30 bus on diversion through Tavistock Square exploded, killing thirteen people as well as the bomber. I walked into Tavistock Square as the police began to close it off, and saw the bus with its roof ripped off and pieces scattered in the street.

I have a memory of dark stains like blood on the walls of the British Medical Association building next to the bombed bus. Photographs of the scene do not show these – my memory is at fault here. I walked across to the university and encountered some of the walking wounded from the bus, with first aiders leading some of them around the corner to University College Hospital. I don't remember much of the rest of that morning, but early in the afternoon I started to walk home. With busses and trains cancelled, I was one of hundreds of thousands walking across London on a warm summer afternoon.

At the time of writing I am teaching the archaeology of modern conflict in a room overlooking Tavistock Square. The square itself is a commemorative landscape of a particular kind, dominated by monuments to peace and non-violence. At the centre is a statue of Gandhi, and to the north is a large stone monument dedicated to the memory of conscientious objectors to military service, or 'all those who have established and are maintaining the right to refuse to kill'. There is a tree dedicated to the memory of the dead in Hiroshima, often decorated with strings of origami cranes. Many of the trees and benches in the park bear inscriptions invoking peace and international socialism (Lal 2005).

The 7/7 bus bomb monument fits a little awkwardly into this landscape. Some years ago a plaque with the names of the victims was affixed to the railings close to where the bus exploded. A few years later it was moved down the road a little; today it is gone. Instead, there is a memorial slab in the flowerbed of the gardens, with a simple inscription:

7 JULY 2005
OPPOSITE THIS PLACE
A BUS WAS BOMBED
KILLING ...

The names of the victims are listed on the edge of the memorial.

Recently, somebody who took part in a Bombsites of Bloomsbury walk in 2013 reminded me that I had described seeing broken glass from the explosion scattered in the flowerbeds. I don't remember seeing this, nor do I remember claiming to have seen it. But I don't trust my memory of that day very much, and nor do I trust the memorials, which seem to change every time I look away.

Takeaways

The driver of the 30 bus, so I was told, began to walk west, in the aftershock of the explosion, still covered in blood. He walked for seven miles, through the hallucination of London, deaf to the sound of the city, until he found himself in Acton. Geography was confused. His bus shouldn't have been in Tavistock Square. It had been diverted. Only walking, entering the dream, could repair the hurt.

Sinclair 2005

The waypoints outlined above give a sense of the variety of narratives and of material and immaterial traces that we encounter when we walk the bombsites of

Bloomsbury. This diversity and openness to different forms is a lesson in itself, and it is why I make this walk the opening session of my course. Archaeology is a well-established part of learning outside the classroom, but contemporary archaeology in its playful approaches to method and material can present challenges. By walking the bombsites of Bloomsbury I try to take up some of those challenges: to promote embodied learning, to upend all forms of linearity, to cast aspersions at memory in all its forms, and to invite an echo of the twentieth century's whirlwind of violence into the green squares and cosy seminar rooms.

I have taught the archaeology of modern conflict, including the bombsites of Bloomsbury, for more than a decade. In that time the walking tour has evolved through numerous iterations – but so has the rest of my teaching. Over time I have reduced the length of my lectures to allow more discussion time, to the point that the module is now wholly seminar discussions of pre-assigned readings. While conflict archaeology remains dominated by academics from the Global North, with an enduring and understandable focus on the world wars, I have made a conscious effort to include more seminar readings from outside these categories, to teach a truly global conflict archaeology. My reading list is a work in progress and there is still room to improve, with more good research published each year.

Would I encourage others to teach with walking tours? Sure, but there is much more potential here than I have explored so far. A walk could serve as a platform for end-of-course evaluation, feedback and discussion. A walk (designed or delivered) could form part of a portfolio assessment. In any case, there are plenty of things to consider. Bloomsbury is flat and well equipped with dropped kerbs and raised junctions, but still the need to consider accessibility arises, for example around the audibility of talks delivered next to busy roads. Safety is also a consideration: for some, a guided walk is interpreted as a total abrogation of responsibility for one's own survival when crossing roads, for example. But the fundamental democratic pedagogical value of the walking tour lies in the fact that almost anybody can create one, almost anywhere, on a dizzying range of topics and themes. Claim your space and trace your mark on it.

References

Attenborough, R. (2008), *Entirely up to You, Darling*, London: Hutchinson.
Bell, A. O. (1984), *The Diary of Virginia Woolf, Volume 5: 1936–1941*, London: Harcourt Brace and Co.

Cain, J. (2011), *No Ordinary Space: Historical Notes on the Grant Museum of Zoology's New Home at University College London, STS Occasional Papers number 1*, London: UCL Department of Science and Technology Studies.

Castle, I. (2015), *The First Blitz: Bombing London in the First World War*, Oxford: Osprey.

Council for Learning Outside the Classroom (2006), *Learning Outside the Classroom Manifesto*, London: Department for Education and Skills.

Debord, G. (2006), 'Theory of the Dérive', in K. Knabb, ed., *Situationist International Anthology*, 62–6, Berkeley, CA: Bureau of Public Secrets.

de Freitas, R. (2018), *Three Men and a Field: Bloomsbury North of Tavistock Place*, London: Marchmont Association.

Faulkner, N. and N. Durrani (2008), *In Search of the Zeppelin War: The Archaeology of the First Blitz*, Cheltenham: History Press.

Goertz, K. K. (2018), 'Walking as Pedagogy', in C. M. Hall, Y. Ram, and N. Shoval, eds, *The Routledge International Handbook of Walking*, 55–64, Abingdon: Routledge.

Greene, R., ed. (2008), *Graham Greene: A Life in Letters*, London: W.W. Norton & Co.

Ingold, T. (2007), *Lines: A Brief History*, Abingdon: Routledge.

Jogalekar, A. (2013), 'Leo Szilárd, a Traffic Light and a Slice of Nuclear History', *Scientific American*, https://blogs.scientificamerican.com/the-curious-wavefunction/leo-szilard-a-traffic-light-and-a-slice-of-nuclear-history/.

Lal, V. (2005), 'The Tavistock Square Gandhi and the War on Terror, War on Non-Violence', *Economic and Political Weekly* 40 (30): 3242–3.

Lanchester, J. (2005), 'Story of a Street', *Guardian*, https://www.theguardian.com/uk/2005/jul/12/july7.features11.

Lindqvist, S. (1979), 'Dig Where You Stand', *Oral History* 7 (2): 24–30.

Lindqvist, S. (2001), *A History of Bombing*, London: Granta.

Massey, D. (2005), *For Space*, Thousand Oaks, CA: Sage.

Moshenska, G. (2010), 'Charred Churches or Iron Harvests? Counter-Monumentality and the Commemoration of the London Blitz', *Journal of Social Archaeology* 10 (1): 5–27.

National Portrait Gallery (n.d.), 'Bloomsbury and Fitzrovia tour', https://www.npg.org.uk/visit/walking-tour/fitzrovia-bloomsbury-tour/.

Rosenberg, D. (2006), *Rebel Footprints: A Guide to Uncovering London's Radical History*, London: Pluto Press.

Saunders, A. (2005), *The London County Council Bomb Damage Maps, 1939–1945 with an Introduction by Robin Woolven*, London: London Topographical Society and London Metropolitan Archives.

Siddall, R. and W. Kirk (2017), 'The Urban Geology of UCL and the University of London's Bloomsbury Campus', *Urban Geology in London* 1, https://www.ucl.ac.uk/~ucfbrxs/Homepage/walks/UCL&UoL.pdf.

Simpson, F. (2008), 'Community Archaeology Under Scrutiny', *Conservation and Management of Archaeological Sites* 10 (1): 3–16.

Sinclair, I. (2005), 'Theatre of the City', *Guardian*, https://www.theguardian.com/uk/2005/jul/14/july7.politicsphilosophyandsociety.

Tiratsoo, N. (2000), 'The Reconstruction of Blitzed British Cities, 1945–55: Myths and Reality', *Contemporary British History* 14 (1): 27–44.

Tulloch, J. (2006), *One Day in July: Experiencing 7/7*, London: Little, Brown.

Ward, L. (2016), *The London County Council Bomb Damage Maps, 1939–1945*, London: Thames & Hudson.

Part Three

Working with Communities

7

Over, Under and In Between: Collaborative Learning from Landscapes using Contemporary Archaeology

April M. Beisaw

Introduction

In America, the notion of progress is so strong that its people often express confusion when new construction is said to be threatening something that existed there before. As an idea, 'progress' is the assumption that humanity is moving in a desirable direction (Bury 1920). Frampton's history of twentieth-century architecture reveals how this idea helps developers ignore discrepancies in what is sold as 'harmonious and continuous' development, that is to the advantage of everyone (Frampton 2007: 9). With 'progress' as the assumed reality, all new construction is 'development' and whatever came before must not be as important as what is about to arrive. More recently, the abstract desire for sustainability has become intertwined with 'progress' in ways that justify urbanization and the mass consumption that goes with it (Li 2019). So much of what is considered 'progress' is really just change, 'modification of existing status' which is not certain to have a positive effect on humanity (Papadopoullos 1978: 144). Technological progress has brought benefits that come with under-appreciated trade-offs 'in terms of social inequalities and ecological degradation' (Hornborg 2019: 253).

This chapter uses three specific examples from New York State to show how contemporary archaeology can challenge ahistorical notions of progress. In New York's Hudson Valley, where I have lived and worked for over a decade, the widely held assumption is that new construction makes good use of previously unused or unproductive land. My research, teaching and community service regularly confronts the ignored 'underlying conflicts and discrepancies'

(Frampton 2007: 9). I believe that acknowledging that which is being destroyed in order to build a future is crucial to understanding how the present came to be and why the utopian future is always out of reach. When archaeologists, students and community members work collaboratively to explore land use histories, they are participating in critical and emancipatory pedagogy. According to Hamilakis (2004: 296), the cornerstone of such pedagogy in archaeology is the unsettling of common-sense preconceptions and the demolishing of stories that suit dominant practices and identities.

The examples presented here represent contemporary archaeology done at various geographic scales. At the state level, I explore the redevelopment of land which was once used for New York's county poorhouses. More than fifty county poorhouses were built and maintained from the mid-1800s to the mid-1900s, when some were converted into elder care facilities and others demolished. Erasing these places, and their associated graveyards, from landscapes serves 'progress' by eliminating the history of poverty. At the regional level, I explore the destruction of rural communities to create the watershed of New York City, the largest city in the state and the most populous of the United States. Using contemporary archaeology, a century of forced displacement by a city government becomes undeniably visible. The city markets its watershed as managed wilderness, replete with natural beauty, and describes those forced out as being better off. At the local level, I explore a counter-example: a recent battle over the proposed construction of a shopping mall and entertainment complex. Many locals opposed the development, which they believed would destroy a revolutionary war headquarters run by the man who became America's first president, George Washington. Traditional archaeology, subsurface testing for intact deposits, does not actually support this concern. It suggests that Washington's headquarters was demolished decades ago, when an earlier shopping centre was constructed nearby. For this case, contemporary archaeology can address the discrepancy by acknowledging that the property has become a historical site through generations of storytelling.

These case studies are examples of how contemporary archaeology can work differently to traditional archaeology in that the primary methodology deployed is community mapping. When archaeology involves someone else's heritage, 'it must be collaborative or nothing at all' (Atalay 2008: 133). Making maps for and with students and community members is an iterative process that allows all participants to engage with and revise a map in ways that tell their stories and their relationships to a place and its heritage (Howland et al. 2020). The explanatory power of a map is bolstered by its malleability. Maps can be co-created in ways that ensure the interests and concerns of multiple stakeholders are heard and represented. Maps can be shared and held onto. They can be used to generate new discussions and settle disputes when the evidence is convincing. Whereas artefacts used to be the things that archaeologists brought to the public, maps can now be our main output. This is now possible because geographic information systems (GIS) have become more public in their means of output and input.

Community mapping can take many other forms. Participatory mapping recognizes that spaces can be defined through power relations. Mapping therefore might distinguish spaces to which people are invited or spaces that people claim as their own (Chambers 2006: 2). Counter-mapping can take the form of an intervention into the "violence of mapping and its concomitant process of enclosure" (Carney, Chess and Rascon-Canales 2022: 446). Counter-mapping is less about producing spatial knowledge and more of a political project. (Re)mapping is often deployed as a form of spatial decolonization, as can occur when Native epistemologies and social relations are used to generate new possibilities (Goeman 2013). The maps produced for the archaeological projects described in this chapter are more participatory than counter-mapping and (re)mapping initiatives, but still reinforce the epistemological power of community members and students: those outside of engineering firms, government agencies and land development companies. As summarized by Parker (2006) in *The Professional Geographer*, community maps familiarize all who view them with the potential for radical social change.

Pedagogy of community heritage archaeology

According to Hamilakis (2004: 297), a 'critical archaeological pedagogy' should collapse the divide between teaching and research, which community-based archaeology does. Instead of using the 'deficit model' that archaeologists need to teach others to value the past, community archaeology uses the 'multiple perspective model' that acknowledges that non-professionals are central to our knowledge generation (Howland et al. 2020). Interactive storytelling is a powerful way to connect with audiences who can use, and contribute to, archaeological knowledge with the power to inform their lives (Kristensen et al. 2020). When using a narrative format, the overarching lesson from archaeology is usually that 'present conditions are historically contingent and explainable' and often that 'things could have been otherwise' (Hamilakis 2004: 296).

Archaeology that counters ahistorical notions of progress is inherently about how things can still be otherwise; new is not always better, and what came before can be an important part of guiding where we are going.

Community-based archaeology creates partnerships where knowledge production flows in all directions, not just from 'teacher' to 'student' or professional to non-professional. These partnerships are 'based on plurals, interconnectivity, and relationality, rather than linear, singular possessive concepts of knowledge' (Atalay 2019: 526). Surface-Evans recommends a heartfelt approach to community-based work, 'because it requires decentering of the researcher as "expert" and foregrounds community needs, interests, and voices' (Surface-Evans 2020: 72). This is also part of an anti-racist archaeology, which 'is committed to forging sustainable and nurturing connections among archaeologists of all backgrounds, as well as with communities impacted by archaeological work, community organizers and activists, and those working with smaller historical societies that are also fighting to preserve local histories' (Flewellen et al. 2021: 231). Anti-racist pedagogy acknowledges that students and community members who may lack formal credentials can be teachers, and that learning often occurs outside of the classroom (Kishimoto 2018). Community mapping, therefore, can be a tool of anti-racist archaeology.

When learning is achieved by doing and experiencing, the role of the teacher is that of a facilitator (Oland 2020: 3). By becoming a facilitator and co-collaborator, archaeologists can democratize the practice of learning, promote respectful dialogue and show that interpretations of the past are enriched by multivocal perspectives (Surface-Evans 2020: 77). Collaborative and group learning experiences that link archaeology to the present day, and to contemporary politics, have been shown to provide meaningful experiences. For example, an assessment of Brown University's Archaeology of College Hill programme included the following student comment: 'the class really developed my sense of what it means to live in a place where others have lived before' (Dufton et al. 2019: 314). Similarly, an assessment of Indian River State College's 'Field Methods in Cemetery Archaeology' course indicated that students developed 'a deeper appreciation for the history of the area' and an appreciation of opportunities 'to be actually out doing the project, serving others and still developing all of our skills ... I think we need to be doing more of this ...' (Freund, Clark and Gidusko 2019: 10). The success of community-based work should, however, be measured by more than student evaluations. It depends on whether or not the project produced knowledge useful to descendant communities, stakeholders and the archaeological community (Atalay 2008).

County poorhouses

The counties of New York State began creating poorhouses in the 1820s, in response to the passage of Poor Laws. These institutions were intended to centralize care and offer training to those who were physically able to work. In total, fifty-one New York county poorhouses were created (Higgins 2001). The buildings and campuses of poorhouses changed with philosophical and legal definitions of poverty and indolence. The 1891 State Charities Aid Report noted a capacity of 5,049 individuals in the county poorhouses. These institutions gradually and unevenly shifted towards becoming elder care homes. The Dutchess County poorhouse (Beisaw et al. 2021) added a new building in 1938 and became known as the County Home, shortly after passage of the Social Security Act. An additional wing was added for elder care in 1961, shortly before the creation of the Medicaid programme that provided health coverage for low-income Americans. These government programmes served to decentralize the care of the poor, and the county homes gradually disappeared.

While the former locations of these institutions are generally known to locals, no state-wide map exists. The 'discovery' of poorhouse ruins is a common topic among urban explorers, who trespass to explore and obtain photographs and videos of abandonment and decay (cf. Freaktography 2015). Such ruin-porn (Mullins 2012) celebrates abandoned institutions without much context beyond the assumption that they were places of horrible mistreatment. Many of New York's county poorhouses no longer linger as ruins, having been demolished to provide other county services, like fairgrounds or colleges, or repurposed as for-profit nursing homes or apartment complexes. Such developments disconnect poorhouse cemeteries from their histories, and unmarked or poorly marked grave locations are forgotten. Subsequent development disturbs the dead, when they are rediscovered and subsequently removed (cf. Rowe 2002; Liberatore 2022).

Using a contemporary archaeology approach, dozens of Vassar College students have helped me compile a database of New York's county poorhouses and what is known about those who lived and died there. We have two public interactive maps, posted on the internet (Beisaw 2021, 2022) that enable collaborative exploration of historic poorhouse locations. Recent satellite imagery can be used as the basemap, such that the former footprints of poorhouses are easily overlayed onto current landscapes. A'ishah Cerrato, a geography and anthropology major at Vassar and my paid research assistant, is currently working on integrating the map and the database so that clicking on a poorhouse will reveal basic statistics of use and abandonment. We hope that this collation of information will assist those involved in creating or critiquing new construction plans, but also allow urban explorers and their fans to see the complex histories of poorhouses and similar institutions.

To create the statewide poorhouse webmap (see Figure 7.1), students helped me georeference maps of the United States Geological Survey (USGS). Georeferencing is the process by which a paper map can be accurately displayed within GIS software to allow extraction of selected features and relatively accurate placement onto a new map. Each area of the United States has corresponding USGS maps, which were produced and updated at irregular intervals. The earliest USGS maps date to the late 1800s, at the same time that poorhouses were in operation, yet most for New York State do not identify county poorhouse locations until the late 1940s and early 1950s, when poorhouses were being repurposed, abandoned or slated for demolition. Using these circa 1950 USGS maps, and historic Sanborn Fire Insurance Maps, which mapped urban areas, it was possible to depict the last known footprint of forty-six New York county poorhouses. While I focused on compiling the historic map locations, A'ishah compiled poorhouse data shared by community members in the Facebook group 'Poorhouse and Asylum Cemeteries and Buildings of New York State' and posted elsewhere on the internet. We share our progress with that Facebook community and they have access to our webmap. Vassar students who are enrolled in archaeology courses sign up to work with A'ishah to transcribe poorhouse census records from the early 1900s, to document who lived (and often died) in these institutions.

The process of creating this map revealed one reason why New York's poorhouse cemeteries are often discovered through new construction. With only a few exceptions, these cemeteries were not documented on USGS maps, even when the poorhouse and its buildings are depicted. Figure 7.1 includes an example. This 1962 map depicts the Dutchess County Home and cemetery, but the cemetery is identified only as an unlabelled green rectangle, south of the Home buildings. Not labelling the cemetery may have been unintentional; USGS cartographers used aerial photographs to map as opposed to interacting with the landscape directly. Poorhouse cemeteries generally have small markers, large enough only to hold a number or alphanumeric code. Aerial photography cannot capture the rows of small stones scattered about a grassy landscape. Not being able to see the cemetery from above meant there was nothing to map. But such erasure can recast that green rectangle as an unused place, ripe for development, even though the last burial made at the Dutchess County Home's

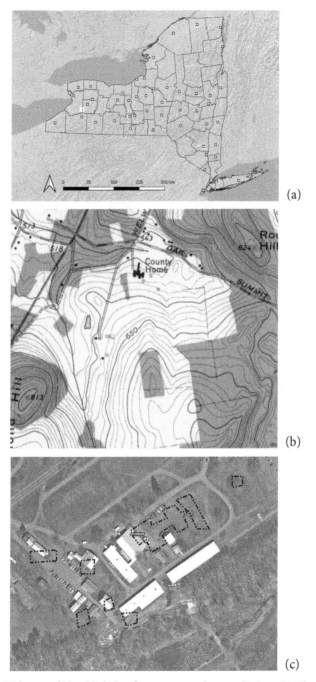

Figure 7.1 Webmap of New York State's county poorhouses (Beisaw 2022), with an example of the USGS map data used to generate it (United States Geological Survey 1962) and an example of how poorhouse building footprints (dashed line) can be projected on the current landscape. Created by April M. Beisaw, 2022.

cemetery was just a few years earlier, in 1955. In total, 800–1,000 people are buried in that cemetery.

Over an almost twenty-year time span, a team of local government officials, residents and college professors and students worked to recover the Dutchess County poorhouse cemetery from the woods and brambles that had swallowed it. Research began with archival and geophysical explorations, but the sources of data remained disparate. Then the county government cleared the overgrowth, which allowed for an archaeological pedestrian survey of the cemetery. We documented each and every marker that remained (fewer than 300) and created a traditional archaeological typology to explore patterns for the shape, size, colour and glaze observed on the markers. That allowed us to understand how the cemetery was filled and connect known burials to specific markers or general areas. The process and results of our community-mapping project was recently published (Beisaw et al. 2021). A webmap now preserves the names and locations of the individuals buried there, which may help to protect this place from new construction.

Thankfully, the Dutchess County poorhouse cemetery is not currently threatened by development, but many of the poorhouse buildings have been demolished recently. That erasure clears the landscape in such a way that makes it easier to forget what was here and consider the property available for new construction. Less than a mile (1.61 km) from the cemetery, a long-standing ruin of a college is currently being demolished for residential development (Callahan 2021). More newcomers will lead to more redevelopment of lands into grocery stores, doctors' offices and health clubs. They may not recognize those small numbered markers as a cemetery population that deserves respect. They may not see the history visible on the landscape's surface like a contemporary archaeologist.

City watershed

The New York City water system is fed by nineteen engineered reservoirs and controlled lakes, some of which are more than 100 miles (160 km) from the city's centre. Construction began in the 1830 and continued until the 1960s (Board of Water Supply, New York 1950; Burrows and Wallace 1998; Committee 1917; Galusha 1999; Koeppel 2000; Soll 2018; Stradling 2009; Tompkins 2000; White 1913). But the city continues buying properties and demolishing buildings in the name of water protection. Contemporary archaeology within watershed communities reveals the cultural costs of an urban water system (Beisaw 2022b).

Official counts of the destruction necessary to build this water system are available for just seven reservoirs (Board of Water Supply, New York 1950; Finnegan 1997). People made homeless: 4,464. People dug out of cemeteries: 8,093. My archaeological research is tabulating the destruction associated with all city reservoirs. I expect the total number of cemeteries destroyed to be in the hundreds, and buildings in the thousands. Yet the dominant narrative of the water system is that it transports natural water from the wilderness to the city (NYC Water Staff 2019). Residents of the city use an average of 118 gallons of water per day, many times the average for most cities (New York State Office of Information Technology Services 2022). Would city residents practise more responsible water consumption if they knew how much destruction their water system necessitates?

The ruins of city-water are conveniently hidden by the forest regeneration of abandonment. This has helped to naturalize the watershed through the forgetting of what came before. Because engineers took advantage of natural topography to create basins that would hold water runoff flowing through valleys, many reservoirs were built upon the fertile lands and crossroads of rural communities. Flooding that land and its adjacent foothills also necessitated the demolition of roads and railroads that connected peoples and places, supporting regional economies. Around each reservoir, contemporary archaeology can document the ripple effects of destruction, as surrounding communities struggled to survive (Beisaw 2022b).

Without archaeological documentation of the destruction that has occurred on land, attention remained focused on the desire to see ruins poking out of reservoir water during times of drought (cf. Foderaro 2002). That romantic sense of drowned sacrifice served to obscure the reality that the ruins of city-water are all around: there is nothing romantic about the almost 200-year-long programme of destruction and decay. Is that progress? Students, community members and I hike the watershed landscape and document ruins of homes, barns and businesses strewn around the New York City-owned lands that are far from the city itself. We use GIS mapping technology to overlay historic maps onto the current satellite imagery to interpret that which we find. Resulting maps are shared with community members and local historians, who provide corrections and suggestions (Beisaw 2021b). Together we have mapped the landscape of loss created when the Ashokan Reservoir (1907–15) was built upon the heart of the town of Olive. A series of maps that resulted from this contemporary archaeology now hang inside the local history museum, on the south shore of the Ashokan Reservoir.

Before these maps were complete, it was difficult to compile stories and information about the changes brought to Olive by reservoir construction. Older place names have been reapplied to new locations as communities moved upslope from the valley floor that was submerged. This complicated discussion, as few persistent landmarks remain and today's generation disagreed as to what they were told by their parents and grandparents regarding the demolished communities. The archaeological maps provided a tangibility that allowed for new questions and lesser-known stories to emerge. For example, approximately 25 per cent of the land taken by the city for construction of the Ashokan Reservoir in 1907 was woman-owned (see Figure 7.2). That statistic counters widely-held notions that female property ownership was rare in the early twentieth century. More personally, community members taught me about a man whose cabin was on our map. I was told that he left there and died a resident of the county poorhouse. I was able to offer the storyteller information about the poorhouse and its cemetery. My projects began to blend together because my archaeology is not site-specific but instead regional and therefore more nimble than traditional archaeology ever allowed me to be.

Figure 7.2 Women-owned properties in the town of Olive, taken by New York City in 1907 to construct the Ashokan Reservoir. Created by April M. Beisaw, 2022.

Suburban shopping

For the last fifty years archaeologists have been conducting cultural resource surveys for an area highly prized by developers because it sits at the intersection of two major highways, on the east bank of the Hudson River. One development in particular has been a source of controversy for over a decade, and may never be built because of community resistance to the destruction of the historic landscape. The proposed Continental Commons retail complex would include stores, restaurants and a hotel, but also a museum and visitor centre to interpret the eighteenth-century history of its location in the town of Fishkill, Dutchess County, New York (Broccoli 2022). Construction would redevelop a wooded and grassy area around a gas station, between a Mexican restaurant and busy highway interchange. Abutting the interchange is the Van Wyck Homestead historic house museum – the only visible clue that this landscape was something else before. It is also headquarters for the Fishkill Historical Society. Abutting the Mexican restaurant is a small clearing and stone marker identifying the Fishkill Supply Depot Burial Ground, which is hidden from the roadway by tall trees. Both the would-be developers and the citizen group Friends of the Fishkill Supply Depot (FOFSD) acknowledge that this area was an important place during the American Revolutionary War (1775–83). But that commonality was not enough to prevent the two sides from partaking in their own battle at this place. In December of 2020, the State Supreme Court denied FOFSD's petition that the Town Planning Board failed to 'take a hard look at the proposed development's impact on archaeological resources and historic integrity of the site' (Supreme Court and Rosa 2020: 6).

Many cultural resource surveys of the land have been commissioned because this place is a seemingly promising location for new business, such as the existing gas station (Labate, Roberts and Juergens 2017; Hunter and Lee 2016; Greenhouse Consultants Inc. 2009; Chadwick 2008; Greenhouse Consultants Inc. 2000; Crozier and Tumolo 1972). When the archaeologists did not find intact archaeological deposits from the Depot, other than a small burial ground, accusations of corruption were made. The archaeologists, some argued, were paid by the developers. That is why they found nothing. The town planning board commissioned its own archaeological review, which concluded that the Continental Commons project would not have a significant adverse impact but that construction should be monitored by a qualified archaeologist and that an unanticipated discovery plan should be in place (Labate, Roberts and Juergens 2017: 59).

142   *Teaching and Learning the Archaeology of the Contemporary Era*

A concerned resident who has worked with me on other community archaeology projects asked me to provide them with an unbiased professional opinion. I read all the reports and watched a recording of a planning board presentation. While I did find many reasons for community members to be upset, including a very arrogant stance by one cultural resource professional, what was most evident to me was the disconnect between what archaeologists had found and what that implied had already been lost. Archaeological surveys documented the small cemetery, which the Continental Commons developer was willing to preserve and incorporate into plans to make this an American Revolution-themed complex. The surveys also found evidence that the land in question was the outskirts of the outpost, where animals were kept, and not the centre or heart of the complex. The majority of the architectural remnants of the Depot were likely destroyed by the building of the multi-laned highways (Route 9 and Interstate 84) to the north and west, and by the shopping centre that sits between Route 9 and the Hudson River, a water highway during the American Revolution. History and archaeology both say that there is little left in the ground at the proposed development site, except for the small cemetery. But to many community members who cannot accept that prior development has already destroyed what they wanted to protect, history and archaeology are wrong.

In the traditional archaeology sense, the Fishkill Depot is gone. That interpretation relies on the definition of an archaeological site being one that requires subsurface excavation to find a certain number of artefacts per area excavated, a certain density of evidence. But in the sense of contemporary archaeology (cf. Hill 2013; Starzmann and Roby 2016), the outpost lives on in the small wooded and grassy lot. Whatever remains there, conveniently wrapped around a gas station, is all the community has left of lands that George Washington might have walked upon. Intact archaeological deposits, such as rusty nails or broken tobacco pipes in the ground, are not necessary for them to feel the presence of the past or experience a time-slip (Surface-Evans, Garrison and Supernant 2020).

The battle over Continental Commons continues, as the developer is filing a civil racketeering lawsuit (Broccoli 2022). Meanwhile, the larger landscape is ripe for a community-based archaeology of the shopping mall that was built atop of the Depot in the 1970s, and coincidentally includes a store called The Home Depot. American shopping malls may or may not be dying (Bhattarai 2019; Petro 2019), but they are certainly locations prime for development and redevelopment, in the name of progress. They are adjacent to major roadways and are surrounded by associated services like bus routes, gas stations and apartment complexes. An archaeological assessment of the Home Depot property might provide a useful counterpoint to whether or not the tangible heritage theme of Continental Commons is worth the intangible heritage destruction that it would bring. The notion of progress as a linear movement away from the past would be greatly challenged by such a communal project.

Lessons of contemporary landscapes

Contemporary archaeology is free from the constraints of traditional archaeology's emphasis on the slow and costly recovery of artefacts from buried contexts. The more expedient exploration of landscape surfaces provides opportunities to challenge popular notions of 'progress' through construction that is labelled as 'development'. Three examples of community-engaged research illustrated ways that archaeological maps can foster discussion with students, collaborators and stakeholders. Whether it be the assessment of local development plans, the realization of systematic erasure of populations or the appreciation of infrastructure's consequences, archaeology's lessons can be deployed at any scale, in response to current or emerging public issues. I have found that mapping sites with community members can have an immediate impact on discussions, especially those where it can be difficult to reconcile multiple sources and types of information. A map provides an anchor for memories and ideas. Layers can be added or removed, to tell multiple stories and represent many constituents.

Maps can reveal the social stratigraphy of landscapes, without actually disturbing the ground. They also allow people who may never physically visit these places to learn from their communities and ruins. The ground surface usually holds what is needed to get a sense of place. There, we can find a mixing of old and new in ways that can foster remembrances or denials. The past is rarely irretrievable. The future is always out of reach. These are important lessons for us all.

References

Atalay, S. (2008), 'Pedagogy of Decolonization: Advancing Archaeological Practice through Education', in S. W. S. Silliman, ed., *Collaborating at the Trowel's Edge: Teaching and Learning in Indigenous Archaeology*, 123–44, Tucson: University of Arizona Press.

Atalay, S. (2019), 'Can Archaeology Help Decolonize the Way Institutions Think? How Community-Based Research is Transforming the Archaeology Training Toolbox and

Helping to Transform Institutions', *Archaeologies* 15 (3): 514–35, https://doi.org/10.1007/s11759-019-09383-6.

Beisaw, A. M. (2021a), 'Brier Hill Cemetery', *ArcGIS StoryMaps*, https://storymaps.arcgis.com/stories/791a6e5778ec4d169677dc51b78e7365.

Beisaw, A. M. (2021b), 'Ashokan Reservoir', *ArcGIS StoryMaps*, https://storymaps.arcgis.com/collections/14ad17ffeab9424db0ffabc4a661082b.

Beisaw, A. M. (2022a), 'NY Poorhouses/County Homes', *ArcGIS Online*, https://arcg.is/10KKbS0.

Beisaw, A. M. (2022b), *Taking Our Water for the City: The Archaeology of New York City's Watershed Communities*, New York: Berghahn Books.

Beisaw, A. M., W. P. Tatum, V. Buechele and B. G. McAdoo (2021), 'Mapping a Poorhouse and Pauper Cemetery as Community Engaged Memory Work', *International Journal of Historical Archaeology*, https://doi.org/10.1007/s10761-021-00617-4.

Bhattarai, A. (2019), 'Malls Are Dying. The Thriving Ones Are Spending Millions to Reinvent Themselves', *Washington Post*, https://www.washingtonpost.com/business/2019/11/22/malls-are-dying-only-these-ones-have-figured-out-secrets-success-internet-age/.

Board of Water Supply, New York (NY) (1950), *The Water Supply of the City of New York: A Volume Descriptive of Its Sources, Storage Reservoirs and Transportation, with Certain Construction Features of the Catskill, Delaware and Interconnected Water Supply Systems*, New York: Reproduction Section, Board of Water Supply.

Broccoli, D. (2022), 'Colonial Themed Development', *continentalcommons*, https://www.continentalcommons.com.

Bury, J. B. (1920), *The Idea of Progress: An Inquiry into Its Origin and Growth*, London: Macmillan and Co.

Callahan, C. (2021), 'Demolition Begins on Abandoned School for Girls in Millbrook', *Times Union*, 30 September, https://www.timesunion.com/hudsonvalley/news/article/Abandoned-school-for-girls-in-Dutchess-demolished-16496904.php.

Carney, M. A., D. Chess and M. Rascon-Canales (2022), '"There Would Be More Black Spaces": Care/Giving Cartographies during COVID-19', *Medical Anthropology Quarterly* 36 (4): 442–62, https://doi.org/10.1111/maq.12732.

Chadwick, W. J. (2008), *Ground-Penetrating Radar Survey to Identify Potential Grave Shafts, Fishkill New York*, Washington, DC: John Milner Associates, Inc.

Chambers, R. (2006), 'Participatory Mapping and Geographic Information Systems: Whose Map? Who Is Empowered and Who Disempowered? Who Gains and Who Loses?' *EJISDC: The Electronic Journal of Information Systems in Developing Countries* 25 (1): 1–11, https://doi.org/10.1002/j.1681-4835.2006.tb00163.x.

Crozier, D. G. and E. A. Tumolo (1972), *Archaeological Survey Operations in a Portion of the Upper Barracks Area of the Fishkill Supply Depot*, Special Report of the Archaeological Facility, Preliminary Report, Philadelphia, PA: Laboratory of Anthropology, Temple University.

Dufton, J. A., L. R. Gosner, A. R. Knodell and C. Steidl (2019), 'Archaeology Underfoot: On-Campus Approaches to Education, Outreach, and Historical Archaeology at Brown University', *Journal of Field Archaeology* 44 (5): 304–18, https://doi.org/10.1080/00934690.2019.1605123.

Finnegan, M. C. (1997), 'New York City's Watershed Agreement: A Lesson in Sharing Responsibility', *Pace Environmental Law Review* 14 (2): 577–644.

Flewellen, A. O., J. P. Dunnavant, A. Odewale, A. Jones, T. Wolde-Michael, Z. Crossland and M. Franklin (2021), '"The Future of Archaeology is Antiracist": Archaeology in the Time of Black Lives Matter', *American Antiquity* 86 (2): 224–43, https://doi.org/10.1017/aaq.2021.18.

Foderaro, L. W. (2002), '"Watery Graves" Was No Figure of Speech: A Receding City Reservoir Reveals a Turbulent Past', *New York Times*, 14 May: B1.

Freaktography (2015), *Urban Exploration: The Abandoned County Poorhouse*, https://www.youtube.com/watch?v=plT8dfXar88.

Freund, K. P., L. K. Clark and K. Gidusko (2019), 'Service Learning in Archaeology and Its Impact on Perceptions of Cultural Heritage and Historic Preservation', *Journal of Archaeology and Education* 3 (5): 1–21.

Galusha, D. (1999), *Liquid Assets: A History of New York City's Water System*, Bovina Center, NY: Purple Mountain Press.

Goeman, M. (2013), *Mark My Words: Native Women Mapping Our Nations*, Minneapolis: University of Minnesota Press.

Greenhouse Consultants Inc. (2000), *Stage 2/3 Archaeological Survey and Excavations of the Touchdown Development, Town of Fishkill, Dutchess County, New York*, New York: Greenhouse Consultants Incorporated.

Greenhouse Consultants Inc. (2009), *Further Evaluation of Potential for Cultural Resources at the Proposed Crossroads Development, Upper Barracks and Continental Stables, Fishkill, New York*, New York: Greenhouse Consultants Incorporated.

Hamilakis, Y. (2004), 'Archaeology and the Politics of Pedagogy', *World Archaeology* 36 (2): 287–309, https://doi.org/10.1080/0043824042000261031.

Higgins, R. L. (2001), 'Poverty in the Nineteenth Century: Documentary and Cemetery Studies from New York State', *Northeast Anthropology* 61: 1–9.

Hill, L. (2013), 'Archaeologies and Geographies of the Post-Industrial Past: Landscape, Memory and the Spectral', *Cultural Geographies* 20 (3): 379–96, https://doi.org/10.1177/1474474013480121.

Hornborg, A. (2019), *Nature, Society, and Justice in the Anthropocene: Unraveling the Money–Energy–Technology Complex*, Cambridge: Cambridge University Press.

Howland, M. D., B. Liss, T. E. Levy and M. Najjar (2020), 'Integrating Digital Datasets into Public Engagement through ArcGIS StoryMaps', *Advances in Archaeological Practice* 8 (4): 351–60, https://doi.org/10.1017/aap.2020.14.

Hunter, R. W. and J. S. Lee (2016), *A Historical and Archaeological Synthesis of the Fishkill Supply Depot, Town of Fishkill, Dutchess County, New York*, Trenton, NJ: Hunter Research, Inc.

Kishimoto, K. (2018), 'Anti-Racist Pedagogy: From Faculty's Self-Reflection to Organizing within and beyond the Classroom', *Race Ethnicity and Education* 21 (4): 540–54, https://doi.org/10.1080/13613324.2016.1248824.

Koeppel, G. T. (2000), *Water for Gotham: A History*, Princeton, NJ: Princeton University Press.

Kristensen, T. J., M. Henry, K. Brownlee, A. Praetzellis and M. Sitchon (2020), 'Outreach and Narratives in Professional Practice', *Journal of Archaeology and Education* 4 (3): 1–38.

Labate, J., T. Roberts and H. Juergens (2017), *Archaeological Resource Assessment and Historic Property Treatment Plan for the Proposed Contin Ental Commons Development, Town of Fishkill, Dutchess County, New York, Final Report*, New York: PaleoWest Archaeology.

Li, M. (2019), 'Reviewing the Notion of Progress in the Quest for Sustainability: The Example of Chinese Architecture', *Journal of Architecture and Urbanism* 43 (2): 174–80, https://doi.org/10.3846/jau.2019.8820.

Liberatore, W. (2022), 'New York's Poorhouses: Disturbing Warehouses for the Destitute', *Times Union*, 21 April, https://www.timesunion.com/news/article/19th-century-care-for-poor-was-filthy-17087953.php.

Mullins, P. (2012), 'The Politics and Archaeology of "Ruin Porn"', *Archaeology and Material Culture*, https://paulmullins.wordpress.com/2012/08/19/the-politics-and-archaeology-of-ruin-porn/.

New York State Office of Information Technology Services (2022), 'Water Consumption in the City of New York', *Open NY*, https://data.ny.gov/widgets/ia2d-e54m.

NYC Water Staff (2019), 'Proud to Serve the Champagne of Drinking Water', *Medium*, https://medium.com/nycwater/proud-to-serve-the-champagne-of-drinking-water-ffa0813bad21.

Oland, M. H. (2020), 'Teaching Archaeology with Inclusive Pedagogy', *Journal of Archaeology and Education* 4 (1): 1–25.

Papadopoullos, T. (1978), 'Anthropological Criteria for a Notion of Progress', in B. Bernardi, ed., *The Concept and Dynamics of Culture*, 143–65, Berlin and Boston: De Gruyter, Inc.

Parker, B. (2006), 'Constructing Community Through Maps? Power and Praxis in Community Mapping', *Professional Geographer* 58 (4): 470–84, https://doi.org/10.1111/j.1467-9272.2006.00583.x.

Petro, G. (2019), 'Shopping Malls Aren't Dying – They're Evolving', *Forbes*, 5 May, https://www.forbes.com/sites/gregpetro/2019/04/05/shopping-malls-arent-dying-theyre-evolving/.

Rowe, C. (2002), 'Forsaken in Life, Forgotten in Death', *New York Times*, 4 February, http://www.nytimes.com/2002/02/04/nyregion/forsaken-in-life-forgotten-in-death.html.

Soll, D. (2018), *Empire of Water: An Environmental and Political History of the New York City Water Supply*, Ithaca, NY: Cornell University Press.

Starzmann, M. T. and J. R. Roby (2016), *Excavating Memory: Sites of Remembering and Forgetting*, Gainesville: University Press of Florida, https://doi.org/10.5744/florida/9780813061603.001.0001.

State Charities Aid Association (1891), *Proceedings of Public Meeting Held at Chickering Hall, May 1, 1891, to Commemorate the Completion of State Care Legislation for the Insane*, New York.

Stradling, D. (2009), *Making Mountains: New York City and the Catskills*, Seattle: University of Washington Press.

Supreme Court of the State of New York, Dutchess County and M. G. Rosa (2020), *Friends of the Fishkill Supply Depot against The Town of Fishkill Planning Board and Snook-9 Realty, Inc.*

Surface-Evans, S. L. (2020), '"I Could Feel Your Heart": The Transformative and Collaborative Power of Heartfelt Thinking in Archaeology', in K. Supernant, J. E. Baxter, N. Lyons and S. Atalay, eds, *Archaeologies of the Heart*, 69–81, New York: Springer.

Surface-Evans, S. L., A. E. Garrison and K. Supernant, eds (2020), *Blurring Timescapes, Subverting Erasure: Remembering Ghosts on the Margins of History*, New York: Berghahn.

United States Geological Survey (1962), 'Millbrook, NY', https://ngmdb.usgs.gov/maps/topoview/viewer.

8

Teaching and Learning Difficult Pasts of the Twentieth Century through Community Archaeology

Tiina Äikäs,* Oula Seitsonen, Tuuli Matila and Vesa-Pekka Herva

Introduction

Difficult and dark pasts have risen into the foreground of archaeological and heritage research in recent years (e.g., McAtackney 2013; Thomas et al. 2019), including in Northern European settings (e.g., Pétursdóttir 2013; Persson 2014; Seitsonen 2021). In Finland these have ranged from the areas impacted by the Finnish Civil War of 1918, the Second World War and the Cold War, to industrial heritage sites such as abandoned factories and mines. Heritage and community perspectives on these have been increasingly studied and their importance recognized in recent years (e.g., Jones 2017; Thomas, McDavid and Gutteridge 2014). In particular, the local significance of many nationally neglected perspectives and questions have become more widely acknowledged lately: for instance, the northern war experiences and marginal communities (e.g., Herva et al. 2016; Matila, Hyttinen and Ylimaunu 2021).

Dark heritage ties together educational dimensions, remembrance and personal emotions (Biran, Poria and Oren 2011; Cohen 2011; Dimitrovski et al. 2017: 697). As it is widely accepted that emotional experiences are important for people visiting dark heritage sites (e.g., Iles 2011; Kamber, Karafotias and Tsitoura 2016), the educational aspects can be used to help people deal with the emotions raised by these visits (Dimitrovski et al. 2017: 704). Education can offer a sort of catharsis with the aim of comprehending death (Seaton 1996: 236; Dimitrovski et al. 2017: 705). Local, place-specific educational approaches have also been suggested to facilitate pedagogy for reconciliation, for example in (post-)colonial settings (Pennanen and Guillet 2020).

150   *Teaching and Learning the Archaeology of the Contemporary Era*

Heritage can also be used to teach about power relations and social justice (Kryder-Reid 2019). Teaching the dark sides of histories can reveal the power relations and inequalities in society to students but this 'pedagogy of discomfort' has also been criticized for causing resistance and distress (Kumashiro 2002; Zembylas and McGlynn 2012). When successful, these feelings of discomfort can help students to empathize with those treated unjustly (Zembylas and McGlynn 2012). Experiences with dark history can also be used with an aim of achieving more positive feelings. Drama pedagogy can be used as a way to engage people in discussion and deal with difficult topics (Gallagher, Yaman Ntelioglou and Wessels 2013). This technique utilizes embodiment, narratives and storytelling, emphasizing the importance of positive emotions and promoting a safe and caring environment (Celume et al. 2020), thus giving people the means to come to terms with dark pasts. Various forms of engagement have also been seen as vital in teaching heritage (Bender and Messenger 2019: 4).

These pedagogical approaches can be used both with students and with wider audiences. We have used community archaeology to engage people with archaeological research in order to both learn from the past and share their experiences of the past in the present. In accordance with the definition of community archaeology, we have involved members of local communities to work on the archaeology of the area where they live, hence giving them new perspectives on their local history. The locals have also contributed to the activities and outcomes of the fieldwork. Apart from excavations, we see community archaeology as an active ingredient in people's lives even after the excavation trenches have been closed, and we recognize that the community affects the archaeologists as well (cf. Thomas, Lorenzon and Bonnie 2020). Here we take as a starting point the definition of pedagogy as 'the processes and relationships of learning and teaching' (Stierer and Antoniou: 277; see also Cobb and Croucher 2020: 2) and recognize that these processes are two-way, also affecting and shaping us as teachers.

Bringing people together

In the past ten years, we have organized several excavations and surveys at sites where the darker aspects of history are present. The purpose of this fieldwork has varied from projects where broader research questions structured the work in the field to excavations organized for school children with the focus on popularizing archaeological methodologies. People have participated as volunteers at the excavations, as informants visiting the site and discussing its history, and as active organizers of different forms of remembrance.

The youngest participants have been the pupils at local schools. Classes of eleven- to thirteen-year-old students took part in our field school days organized at two sawmill sites in the Oulu region. These sawmills were in use in the late nineteenth and early twentieth centuries and their history is tied to wartime memories of bombings and prisoner-of-war camps (Äikäs and Ikonen 2020; Äikäs et al. 2021). The fact that the pupils were excavating the recent past seemed to motivate them. They were able to recognize and make interpretations of their finds and were already familiar with some aspects of the history of the area.

Vaakunakylä is a formerly working-class neighbourhood on the outskirts of Oulu city. It was first established as a military housing site by the German armed forces (see Figure 8.1), but after the war the barracks housed local people until the late 1980s when the site was torn down in accordance with a decision by city officials. We organized three weeks of excavations at Vaakunakylä, where we taught Oulu University students and engaged with the locals who visited our site. In cooperation with the city, we also collected memories from people who had lived in the region. It seemed that our excavation also functioned as a stage or outlet for peoples' spontaneous recollections about life in Vaakunakylä. Some still express ill feelings towards the city that basically forced the residents to give up their homes in the 1970s and 1980s while cleaning up the area, which was deemed to be a slum-like and irregular community in the middle of the city.

Further north, in Sápmi, the homeland of indigenous Sámi people that covers the northernmost reaches of Finland, Sweden, Norway and Russia, we have organized community and public archaeological events as part of the 'Lapland's Dark Heritage' project in 2014–20 (e.g., Thomas and Koskinen-Koivisto 2017). These activities have included public excavations and excursions at wartime sites, the latter guided by local experts; lectures for those interested in gaining more information; the collection of local transgenerational memories, both for our research purposes and for providing the local community with the recorded interviews so that the memories would be preserved for the future generations, as they requested; and the mapping of heritage sites for various research, heritage management and local purposes, such as promoting the cultural tourism potential of the wartime localities (e.g., Banks, Koskinen-Koivisto and Seitsonen 2018; Seitsonen and Koskinen-Koivisto 2018). All public aspects of the Lapland's Dark Heritage research proved to be very popular with both locals and outsiders interested in Lapland and its war and other histories. Locals felt that it was especially important that their own heritage and landscapes were acknowledged

Figure 8.1 A German soldier standing in front of the barracks in Vaakunakylä. Photo from JOKA archive, CC-BY 4.0.

in research, as there have been enduring feelings that the authorities and historians based in the dominant southern regions of the country have neglected northern histories (Ruotsala 2002; Herva et al. 2020).

In 2014, we organized small-scale excavations in Kontinkangas, close to Oulu city centre, where a memorial iron rail marks the presumed place of the last official execution by hanging in Finland, which took place on 3 October 1916. The place of death and the original burial place of the man hanged, Taavetti Lukkarinen, soon

Figure 8.2 The hanging tree memorial with its iron rail and inscription. Antti Kaarlela is pointing to a cross engraved on the tree. Photo by Tiina Äikäs, 2014.

became a place of remembrance and resistance against the Russian threat, and in 1935 an iron memorial rail was set up around a pine tree at the site. An extract of the inscription on the memorial rail demonstrates the feelings and purposes behind the memorialization: 'May the terrifying memory of this event be passed to future generations and evoke dread towards foreign terror, and may it raise courage and strength in the nation to live and die for the independence and freedom of the fatherland' (Ikäheimo, Äikäs and Kallio-Seppä 2019; see Figure 8.2). During the excavations we offered people a place to come and share their memories of the site. Since some of the contributors were unfamiliar with the real history of the site and thought the hanging tree was an urban myth, we were also approached by the relatives of Lukkarinen as well as those of a Finnish police officer who took part in the hanging. For them, the memories related to the site were part of a painful and, in the latter case, silenced family history (Ikäheimo and Äikäs 2018).

Space for dealing with emotions

A relative of Taavetti Lukkarinen, Marianne Lukkarinen, said that she had never wanted to visit the hanging place but that our work there had encouraged her to come. She described the archaeological work as 'purifying work that eases the tragedies of generations' (Ikäheimo and Äikäs 2018: 13). As the centennial of the death of Lukkarinen was approaching, an idea came up to organize a commemorative event. Janne Ikäheimo, the leader of the excavations at the hanging tree, and Marianne Lukkarinen organized an event that started at midnight at the Oulu County prison, from where the attendees walked to the hanging site after hearing of the last moments of Lukkarinen. At the hanging tree memorial, a written account of Lukkarinen's death was read, the results of the excavations explained and lanterns were lit. Finally, the attendees walked with the lanterns in hands to the cemetery and placed the lanterns on the grave of Lukkarinen.

There were around thirty people present, including four of the five great-grandchildren of Lukkarinen (Ikäheimo and Äikäs 2018: 9). Later on, some of them attended a lecture and reminiscence event organized at a local library, where Äikäs talked about the results of the archaeological research. Furthermore, the Facebook page 'Taavetti Lukkarisen hirttopuu' (The hanging tree of Taavetti Lukkarinen), set up during the excavations, is still used for sharing information, especially by the son-in-law of Taavetti Lukkarinen's brother.

Similarly, as an unexpected public-outreach outcome of the Lapland's Dark Heritage research, a commemorative event was organized that included the raising of an Orthodox cross involving the priest of the local Skolt Sámi at Kankiniemi prisoner-of-war (PoW) camps that we excavated in Inari (Inari Sámi: Aanaar Kaŋgânjargâ; Herva and Seitsonen 2021). This event, organized deep in the secluded forest, attracted a surprising crowd of more than twenty locals, for whom it offered an appropriate venue to remember the wartime fates of the Soviet PoWs at the site (see Figure 8.3). This unanticipated output resulted from some alleged paranormal encounters that volunteers from our public excavations connected to the site. While this might sound odd, supernatural stories and experiences are in fact very common at Lapland's wartime sites (Herva 2014), especially those that are directly related to death and suffering, such as PoW camps, military hospitals and mass graves. This is most likely connected to the long silence about these difficult legacies, especially on a national level, although locally they were always acknowledged, as well as to Lapland's long cultural history as a land of natural and supernatural wonders and magical entities ever since early modern times (e.g., Seitsonen 2021; Seitsonen and Matila 2022). The rationale behind organizing this memorial event was, as explained by the Orthodox priest of the Skolt Sámi, to pacify the place and cleanse it from the evil and depressing spirit that it had been imbued with during the war. According to the priest, the cross and memorial service neutralized and tamed the place, without making it holy or special, but rather approachable, and

Figure 8.3 The memorial service organized at the PoW camp in Inari. Photo by Oula Seitsonen, 2016.

was based on what he described as 'spiritual time travel': the service consoled the prisoners who had died at the site during the war *before* their death, and thus the place did not in fact become haunted in the first place. Northern Christianity is often syncretic, as illustrated by this reasoning and the various stages of the long memorial service deep in the woods, as described by Herva and Seitsonen (2020). However, the same kinds of ideas have also been used on a theoretical level in heritage studies, examining the idea of memorials 'taming' and 'exorcising' the dark past of difficult and painful places and neutralizing them by bringing them under the umbrella of recognized heritage (e.g., Edensor 2005: 836).

Cross-generational learning

As the examples above demonstrate, archaeological fieldwork can offer a safe space for sharing and dealing with difficult memories. In Vaakunakylä, one of the elderly respondents burst into tears when discussing the maltreatment of Soviet prisoners of war in Finnish camps. Our project allowed her to share something that likely could not have been brought up in the post-war years when the focus was on reconstruction, and difficult memories of war were often silenced even within families (Kivimäki 2018). In that regard, a researcher – especially one born after the immediate post-war years – may feel like a more neutral listener. Sensitivity is also needed for listening to perhaps less-conventional narratives such as ghost stories, because they can reveal quite a bit about the local emotional climate and lingering trauma (Seitsonen and Matila 2022).

Wartime memories of bombings and PoW camps have also been part of the stories collected from the older residents of the sawmills in Varjakka and Pateniemi (Juola 2020; Äikäs et al. 2021). They were shared by the local elders in the interviews conducted as a part of Pateniemi school project, 'Pateniemen raitti', in which we also participated, and by those taking part in the excavations organized for pupils at Varjakka sawmill area. We encouraged cross-generational learning during the excavations by organizing a reminiscence event, in which two elderly local people were invited to share their stories and memories with the students. The original idea was to maximize their involvement so that they would take part in the daily activities of the youths during the field day, but due to the restrictions caused by the Covid-19 pandemic, we deemed it better to have a shorter discussion event with social distancing. One of the older participants told a story about a marine accident that had occurred in 1907 leading to the drowning of twenty women and girls. Even though this had not occurred in the lifetime of the informants, it is still recalled in memorials, art and a recent novel (see Figure 8.4; Äikäs et al. 2021).

As part of the Lapland's Dark heritage research, we organized annual public meetings and open lectures at the local meeting halls and at the Sámi Museum Siida. Of these, the public excursions to pre-war and wartime sites guided by local history enthusiasts and elders, for instance in Inari, alongside our public excavations, proved to be particularly popular. During these tours, some locals commented that they had experienced places in their own neighbourhood in a new way and from a new perspective, and encountered stories related to them that they had never even thought of. This was especially true with newcomers into these northern communities, who had no ancestral ties to the land. Thus, they also became initiated into the local place-bound and corporeal memoryscapes.

On top of these events aimed at adult audiences, we have also been giving lectures to schoolchildren at village schools in our main study areas. One of the unanticipated perspectives that we realized when involved in discussions with the children was that even the relatively small kids, from about nine-year-olds upwards, were already well acquainted with the wartime ruins in their own environments and knew various stories linked to them. These were often connected to the

Teaching and Learning Difficult Pasts of the Twentieth Century 157

Figure 8.4 (a) A memorial in Varjakka harbour and (b) a work of art in the old office building on the Varjakansaari island commemorating the women and girls who drowned in the marine accident in 1907. Photos by Tiina Äikäs, 2021.

transgenerational familial and community memories, which had been passed on by their parents and grandparents during various wilderness-based activities, such as berry picking, mushroom hunting, fishing and tending their reindeer. Most people in these small, tight-knit communities encounter their surrounding nature daily, observing, using its offerings and helping out the members who practice wilderness-based livelihoods. Thus, the areas surrounding their villages are as much part of their 'home' as the houses they live in, and they are familiar on some level with their entire landscape (see Seitsonen and Moshenska 2021).

One of the themes that typically pops up when dealing with conflict heritage with teenagers is that the boys express a disproportionate interest in explosives and the potential for finding them, which we attempt to discourage in every possible way. This parallels the typical off-hand discussions with adult males about the wartime material heritage in the north: they often share anecdotes and memories of childhood games with hand grenades and other explosives uncovered from the wartime sites. The danger presented by the unexploded ordnance (UXO) is real and such items are still found regularly and detonated in northern Finland: at the end of the war, the German troops littered their retreat routes with minefields and other explosives. UXO has also caused numerous casualties throughout the post-war decades, most recently in 2013 in the case of a metal-detecting hobbyist who had collected explosives (Seitsonen 2021).

For the younger audiences, such as preschool kids and first or second graders (six- to eight-year-olds), it has been necessary to find ways of presenting the research concentrating on dark, difficult and painful subjects in other, less depressing or graphic ways. To start with, some of them do not yet have a good comprehension of the concepts of time and the past. For the smallest children, we have typically presented our research in more generalized way, discussing what archaeologists, anthropologists, historians and ethnographers do, what for and why (see Figure 8.5). But there seems to be a genuine interest, even among the smaller children, in the darker aspects of history as demonstrated for example by the *Titanic* project that was organized in the pre-school of one of the authors' kids due to the wishes of the children.

What can we learn from dark heritage?

Heritage enables us to both see and feel, to remember and forget (Welch 2016). As archaeologists we can create different forums for dealing with a difficult past: excavations, commemorative and lecture events, even online platforms (see

Figure 8.5 Children can get acquainted with archaeology by participating in various aspects of fieldwork and research, here documenting house remains in Varjakka. Photo by Tiina Äikäs, 2019.

Peuramäki-Brown et al. 2020). An investigation of the traumatic past can serve to allay anxieties around memory and forgetting (Renshaw 2011). Archaeology can help to unearth forgotten histories and provide closure (Ikäheimo and Äikäs 2018; cf. Gonzalez-Ruibal 2007: 216). It has been suggested that archaeology can function as a therapeutic act in communities with traumatic memories and histories (Schaepe et al. 2017). Archaeological place-based activities and experiential learning can also be used for developing pedagogies for reconciliation, for example in colonial and post-colonial settings to deal with difficult memories and experiences (Pennanen and Guillet 2020). In small communities this could also help in cross-generational learning and the transmission of transgenerational memories, as community-based archaeological work could bring different generations together at key localities for their community.

While we feel uncomfortable in labelling ourselves as therapists, our excavations certainly provided a space for the former Vaakunakylä residents, as well as for the descendants of Lukkarinen and those who played as kids at Kankiniemi, allowing them to be heard and for us to recognize their difficult emotions and pasts. For the archaeology students, these have been important learning experiences that highlight how the archaeology of the twentieth century is never performed in a vacuum, disconnected from local communities – archaeology and heritage can matter in many ways that they, or for that matter we, had not anticipated.

For those learning about dark heritage, it seems to be an opportunity to ponder the nature of human existence, and our endurance amidst crisis situations like wars and depressions. In Vaakunakylä, our students regularly commented on their personal connections to some of the finds. We had given them materials to read beforehand about the history of the site, which connected them to it more deeply on an emotional level, and also heightened their awareness that these materials belonged to real people with real names. Such realizations are important when developing one's professional ethics, especially at a site that was often visited by people who have lived in the very barracks we were excavating.

The educational aspect of dark sites (Dimitrovski et al. 2017: 697) was emphasized in the case of the hanging tree, where the story of Lukkarinen was used since the construction of the memorial to remind people of the perils of foreign rule. Groups of military recruits from the nearby garrisons and schoolchildren were brought to the site to learn about its past. The recruits were taken to the hanging tree, which was used to highlight to them what would happen if the country they were soon to be trained to fight for was overcome by foreign armed forces. This tradition started in the 1960s and was discontinued only after the closure of the Oulu garrison in 1998. For schoolchildren the story was more of an example of interesting local history (Ikäheimo and Äikäs 2018).

The commemorative events organized in relation to the excavations at the hanging tree and PoW camps also served as places for dealing with emotions. It has been said that continual, sometimes almost ritualistic, remembrance at chosen places can help to recover from or heal after tragic events (Tota 2005; Seitsonen and Koskinen-Koivisto 2018). This can also be true of non-recurrent events. Commemorative events tie together national and personal dimensions of dark heritage (Dimitrovski et al. 2017: 696). By commemorating, we both move beyond grief and transmit the memories to future generations. Dimitrovski et al. (2017: 698) have stated that it can be difficult for close relatives to visit a site, but an organized commemoration can motivate them to do so. For example, Marianne Lukkarinen had not visited the hanging tree before our excavations. Similarly, in the Sámi village of Vuotso (SáN: Vuohčču), we visited in the company of locals the place where an eleven-year-old boy had died from injuries caused by UXO in 1959 and where the villagers had maintained a private memorial cross built of stones (Seitsonen and Koskinen-Koivisto 2018). Our visit and mapping of the site encouraged the boy's relatives to visit the place for the first time in their lives, nearly sixty years later, as it had been a strictly forbidden location for them after the incident (Koskinen-Koivisto and Seitsonen 2019). This illustrates again how archaeological and heritage research can have unanticipated effects in the communities connected to the work.

Discussion and conclusions

Our projects have demonstrated that archaeology can function as a suitable way to bring people together to discuss local histories and heritages. Archaeology can help people feel more connected to their community and their area, and provide deeper emotional ties to, and understanding of, the darker periods of history as well as find ways to deal with their personal memories. This emotional connection, in addition to the intellectual, is part of the premise of the 'pedagogy of discomfort' (Kryder-Reid 2019: 139.) Along with Yannis Hamilakis (2004: 288), we see archaeological pedagogy not as 'the passive transfer and delivery of produced knowledge' but as 'a socially crucial and politically contested field of cultural production', where the issues taught and learnt affect the things remembered and forgotten and the way we deal with our dark heritage. Archaeology can help people to appreciate the relevance of the past and to reconcile with dark histories (Pennanen and Guillet 2020).

Our fieldwork in various contexts has served as a reminder that history is not past or unemotional for those who have a personal connection to or experience of it. Heritage – and in our case, especially dark heritage – connects past, present and future and is tied to people's identity and daily life (Bender and Messenger 2019: 3). As archaeologists we can act as facilitators in processing these difficult memories. This is also an important lesson to remember when engaging with the public. It is important to bring emotions to the front and 'to challenge and resist this privatization and pathologizing of emotions' (Boler 1999: vi). This is perhaps one of the most important roles of community archaeology, where feelings can be discussed with attentive researchers who provide the space for remembrance through excavations and fieldwork. Cobb and Croucher (2020) have emphasized the role of material culture in archaeological pedagogy. Similarly, we see that places and materialities connected to them have been important for sharing and dealing with dark heritage. For example, the role of the hanging tree of Taavetti Lukkarinen as a testimonial of past wrongs and the visit to the death site of the young boy at Vuotso both offered a starting point for public discussions and reconciliations.

Archaeology also creates opportunities for discussing the past with different age groups. Children are interested in learning about difficult pasts, and of course we as researchers will need to bear in mind the appropriate ways to approach children of different age groups with these kinds of issues. For example, technology-enabled multiplatform learning environments can offer one way to reach out to teenagers who nowadays typically have an active online presence (Peuramäki-Brown et al. 2020). Then again, the elders can have valuable personal and transgenerational insights into the dark histories, for instance, what it was like to live in and through crisis situations. Their involvement can also facilitate cross-generational learning experiences. On a more general level, dark sites can help to process difficult feelings, and ponder questions of life and death that are inevitably part of the human condition – a basic need for humans across cultures and age groups from relatively small children to the elderly.

References

Äikäs, T. and T. Ikonen (2020), 'Public archaeology and archaeologists as a part of the heritagization of northern industrial sites', *Fennoscandia Archaeologica* 37: 197–203.

Äikäs, T., T. Kuokkanen, A. Tranberg and T. Ikonen (2021), 'Oulunsalon Varjakan sahamiljöö moninaisten toimijoiden kulttuuriperintökohteena', *Tekniikan Waiheita* 39 (3): 84–114, https://doi.org/10.33355/tw.103402.

Banks, I., E. Koskinen-Koivisto and O. Seitsonen (2018), 'Public Engagements with Lapland's Dark Heritage: Community Archaeology in Finnish Lapland', *Journal of Community Archaeology and Heritage* 5 (2): 128–37.

Bender, S. J. and P. M. Messenger (2019), 'Introduction: pedagogy and practice in heritage studies', in S. J. Bender and P. M. Messenger, eds, *Pedagogy and Practice in Heritage Studies*, 1–8, Gainesville: University Press of Florida.

Biran, A., Y. Poria and G. Oren (2011), 'Sought experiences at (dark) heritage sites', *Annals of Tourism Research* 38 (3): 820–41.

Boler, M. (1999), *Feeling Power: Emotions and Education*, New York: Routledge.

Celume, M.-P., T. Goldstein, M. Besançon and F. Zenasni (2020), 'Developing children's socio-emotional competencies through drama pedagogy training: an experimental study on theory of mind and collaborative behavior', *Europe's Journal of Psychology* 16 (4): 707–26, https://doi.org/10.5964/ejop.v16i4.2054.

Cobb, H. and K. Croucher (2020), *Assembling Archaeology: Teaching, Practice, and Research*, Oxford: Oxford University Press.

Cohen, E. H. (2011), 'Educational dark tourism at an in populo site: the Holocaust Museum in Jerusalem', *Annals of Tourism Research* 38 (1): 193–209.

Dimitrovski, D., V. Senić, D. Marićand and V. Marinković (2017), 'Commemorative events at destination memorials – a dark (heritage) tourism context', *International Journal of Heritage Studies* 23 (8): 695-708, DOI: 10.1080/13527258.2017.1317645.

Edensor, T. (2005), 'The ghosts of industrial ruins: ordering and disordering memory in excessive space', *Environment and Planning D: Society and Space* 23: 829–49.

Gallagher, K., B. Yaman Ntelioglou and A. Wessels (2013), '"Listening to the affective life of injustice": drama pedagogy, race, identity, and learning', *Youth Theatre Journal* 27 (1): 7-19, DOI: 10.1080/08929092.2013.779349.

González-Ruibal, A. (2007), 'Making things public: archaeologies of the Spanish Civil War', *Public Archaeology* 6 (4): 203–26, DOI: 10.1179/175355307X264165.

Hamilakis, Y. (2004), 'Archaeology and the politics of pedagogy', *World Archaeology* 36 (2): 287-309, DOI: 10.1080/0043824042000261031.

Herva, V.-P. (2014), 'Haunting heritage in an enchanted land: magic, materiality and Second World War German material heritage in Finnish Lapland', *Journal of Contemporary Archaeology* 1 (2): 297–321.

Herva, V.-P., E. Koskinen-Koivisto, O. Seitsonen and S. Thomas (2016), '"I have better stuff at home": treasure hunting and private collecting of World War II artefacts in Finnish Lapland', *World Archaeology* 48 (2): 267–81.

Herva, V.-P. and O. Seitsonen (2020), 'The haunting and blessing of Kankiniemi: coping with the ghosts of the Second World War in northernmost Finland', in T. Äikäs and S. Lipkin, eds, *Entangled Beliefs and Rituals: Religion in Finland and Sápmi from Stone Age to Contemporary Times*, MASF 8, 225–35, Helsinki: Suomen arkeologinen seura.

Herva, V.-P., A. Varnajot and A. Pashkevich (2020), 'Bad Santa: cultural heritage, mystification of the Arctic, and tourism as an extractive industry', *Polar Journal* 10 (2): 375–96.

Ikäheimo, J. and T. Äikäs (2018), 'Hanging tree as a place of memories: encounters at a 1916 execution site', *Journal of Community Archaeology and Heritage* 5 (3): 166–81.

Ikäheimo, J., T. Äikäs and T. Kallio-Seppä (2019), 'Memorialization and heritagization: investigating the site of the last execution by hanging in Finland', *Historical Archaeology* 53 (2): 393–411, https://doi.org/10.1007/s41636-019-00183-x.

Iles, J. (2011), 'Going on holiday to imagine war: the Western front battlefields as sites of commemoration and contestation', in J. Skinner and D. Theodossopoulos, eds, *Great Expectations: Imagination and Anticipation in Tourism*, 155–73, New York: Berghahn Books.

Jones, S. (2017), 'Wrestling with the social value of heritage: problems, dilemmas and opportunities', *Journal of Community Archaeology and Heritage* 4 (1): 21–37.

Juola, M. (2020), 'Kukkaniityltä tapulitarhaan: Muistoja merkityksellisistä paikoista Pateniemen entisen sahan alueella', MA dissertation, Archaeology, University of Oulu.

Kamber, M., T. Karafotias and T. Tsitoura (2016), 'Dark heritage tourism and the Sarajevo siege', *Journal of Tourism and Cultural Change* 14 (3): 255-69, DOI: 10.1080/14766825.2016.1169346.

Kivimäki, V. (2018), 'Sodanjälkeisiä hiljaisuuksia: Kokemusten, tunteiden ja trauman historiaa', in M. Tuominen and M. Löfgren, eds, *Lappi palaa sodasta: Mielen hiljainen jälleenrakennus*, 34–57, Tampere: Vastapaino.

Koskinen-Koivisto, E. and S. Thomas (2017), 'Lapland's Dark Heritage: Responses to the Legacy of World War II', in H. Silverman, E. Waterton and S. Watson, eds, *Heritage in Action: Making the Past in the Present*, 121–33, New York: Springer.

Koskinen-Koivisto, E. and O. Seitsonen (2019), 'Landscapes of loss and destruction: Sámi elders' childhood memories of the Second World War', *Ethnologia Europaea* 49 (1): 24–40.

Kryder-Reid, E. (2019), 'Do the homeless have heritage? Archaeology and the pedagogy of discomfort', in S. J. Bender and P. M. Messenger, eds, *Pedagogy and Practice in Heritage Studies*, 129–47, Gainesville: University Press of Florida.

Kumashiro, K. K. (2002), 'Against repetition: addressing resistance to anti-oppressive change in the practices of learning, teaching, supervising, and researching', *Harvard Educational Review* 72 (1): 67–92.

Matila, T., M. Hyttinen and T. Ylimaunu (2021), 'Privileged or dispossessed? Intersectional marginality in a forgotten working-class neighborhood in Finland', *World Archaeology* 53 (3): 502–16, DOI: 10.1080/00438243.2022.2035803.

Pennanen, K. and L.-J. Guillet (2020), 'Experiential learning and archaeology: reconciliation through excavation', *Papers on Postsecondary Learning and Teaching* 4: 58–67.

Persson, M. (2014), 'Materialising Skatås: archaeology of a Second World War refugee camp in Sweden', in B. Olsen and Þ. Pétursdóttir, eds, *Ruin Memories: Materialities, Aesthetics and the Archaeology of the Recent Past*, 435–61, New York: Routledge.

Pétursdóttir, Þ. (2013), 'Concrete matters: ruins of modernity and the things called heritage', *Journal of Social Archaeology* 13 (1): 31–53.

Peuramaki-Brown, M. M., S. G. Morton, O. Seitsonen, C. Sims and D. Blaine (2020), 'Grand Challenge No. 3: Digital Archaeology. Technology-Enabled Learning in Archaeology', *Journal of Archaeology and Education* 4 (3): Article 4.

Renshaw, L. (2011), *Exhuming Loss: Memory, Materiality and Mass Graves of the Spanish Civil War*, Walnut Creek, CA: Left Coast Press.

Ruotsala, H. (2002), *Muuttuvat palkiset: Elo, työ ja ympäristö Kittilän Kyrön paliskunnassa ja Kuolan Luujärven poronhoitokollektiiveissa vuosina 1930–1995*, Kansatieteellinen Arkisto 49, Helsinki: Suomen muinaismuistoyhdistys.

Schaepe, D. M., B. Angelbeck, D. Snook and J. R. Welch (2017), 'Archaeology as therapy: connecting belongings, knowledge, time, place, and well-being', *Current Anthropology* 58 (4): 502–33, https://doi.org/10.1086/692985.

Seaton, A. V. (1996), 'Guided by the dark: from thanatopsis to thanatourism', *International Journal of Heritage Studies* 2 (4): 234–44, DOI: 10.1080/13527259608722178.

Seitsonen, O. (2021), *Archaeologies of Hitler's Arctic War: Heritage of the Second World War German Military Presence in Finnish Lapland*, Abingdon: Routledge.

Seitsonen, O. and E. Koskinen-Koivisto (2018), '"Where the F. . . is Vuotso?": heritage of Second World War forced movement and destruction in a Sámi reindeer herding community in Finnish Lapland', *International Journal of Heritage Studies* 24 (4): 421–41.

Seitsonen, O. and T. Matila (2022), 'Natseja, kultaa ja kummituksia: Toisen maailmansodan kummitteleva perintö Pohjois-Suomessa', in *Odes to Mika: Professor Mika Lavento's Festschrift as he turns 60 years old*, MASF 10, 266-77, Helsinki: Archaeological Society of Finland, http://www.sarks.fi/masf/masf_10/MASF10_31_ Seitsonen_Matila.pdf.

Seitsonen, O. and G. Moshenska (2021), 'Who owns the "wilderness"? Indigenous Second World War landscapes in Sápmi, Finnish Lapland', in N. Saunders and P. Cornish, eds, *Conflict Landscapes: Materiality and Meaning in Contested Places*, 183-201, New York: Routledge.

Stierer, B. and M. Antoniou (2004), 'Are there distinctive methodologies for pedagogic research in higher education?', *Teaching in Higher Education* 9 (3): 275-85, DOI: 10.1080/1356251042000216606.

Thomas, S., V.-P. Herva, E. Koskinen-Koivisto and O. Seitsonen (2019), 'Dark heritage', in C. Smith, ed., *Encyclopedia of Global Archaeology*, 1-11, New York: Springer.

Thomas, S., M. Lorenzon and R. Bonnie (2020), 'Living communities and their archaeologies: Northern European cases', *Fennoscandia Archaeologica* 47: 143-6.

Thomas, S., C. McDavid and A. Gutteridge (2014), 'Editorial', *Journal of Community Archaeology and Heritage* 1 (1): 1-4.

Tota, A. L. (2005), 'Terrorism and collective memories: comparing Bologna, Naples and Madrid 11 March', *International Journal of Comparative Sociology* 46 (1–2): 55–78, DOI: 10.1177/0020715205054470.

Welch, M. (2016), 'Political imprisonment and the sanctity of death: performing heritage in "Troubled" Ireland', *International Journal of Heritage Studies* 22 (9): 664-78, DOI: 10.1080/13527258.2016.1184702.

Zembylas, M. and C. McGlynn (2012), 'Discomforting pedagogies: emotional tensions, ethical dilemmas and transformative possibilities', *British Educational Research Journal* 38 (1): 41-59.

9

Beyond Zinjanthropus: Historical Archaeology Pedagogy in Tanzania

Nancy Rushohora

Introduction

Archaeological topics are the most contested parts of Tanzanian historical pedagogy. Despite the poor public understanding of the discipline, studies of archaeological theories and practices have tended to neglect pedagogy (cf. Hamilakis 2004). The public often questions the evolution of humans, which is taught in Grade 4 in primary school history and in Form 1 in secondary schools. For the period considered historical, archaeology has been left out of teaching, and historical errors have crept into areas that would otherwise have been corrected by archaeology. The most recent example of the devaluing of archaeology in pedagogy occurred in the Tanzanian Parliament on 11 May 2022. The Member of Parliament (MP) Khamis Said Gulamali of Manonga Constituency, Igunga–Tabora region, questioned the relevance of the teaching of archaeology and specifically the evolution of humanity to students of history. While understanding very little about what the topic entails, the MP reduced the topic to a tale that's equivalent to fiction. Suggestions came from other humanities disciplines that archaeologists ought to challenge or correct this perception, but to date no response has been made.

There is an obvious and well-documented lack of work in academic discourse on the teaching of archaeology (La Salle and Hutchings 2014; Mehari 2015). The case of Tanzania is thus not particularly distinctive. A few scholars, such as Mapunda and Msemwa (2005), Kessy (2016) and Mehar (2021), are examined here to exemplify the nature of archaeology pedagogy in Tanzania. To begin, Mapunda and Msemwa's edited volume consists of chapters collected under the title *Salvaging Tanzania's Cultural Heritage* (hereafter *Salvaging*) that emerged from a workshop organized by the same scholars in 2001, nearly sixteen years after the establishment of the archaeology programme at the University of Dar es Salaam. The workshop was the first collaboration of three institutions dealing with Tanzania's archaeology and cultural heritage: the University of Dar es Salaam, the National Museum and the Antiquities Department. The core of the discussion focused on adequate preparations for archaeologists and cultural heritage professionals who are entering the field either in the private or government sector. Experiences from teaching and researching archaeology were given consideration. The opening section of *Salvaging* was dedicated to the archaeology curriculum, specifically assessing the course list, content and teaching methods, while matching it to the demand for trained staff in the field of archaeology and cultural heritage (Mapunda and Msemwa 2005). Mapunda and Msemwa (2005: xv) make it clear that the contributors to the first section of the book (experiencing archaeology: teaching and research in archaeology at the University of Dar es Salaam) were asked to address the history of the archaeology programme in Tanzania, problems in pedagogy and their solutions, curriculum development (from the then unit to the current department) and the sustainability of archaeology and heritage studies curricula in Tanzania.

Most of the problems of archaeology pedagogy were highlighted in this volume, which has remained the main resource for Tanzania's archaeology and cultural heritage. However, a transformation has taken place since the time of publication, including putting into action the recommendations from the 2001 workshop. For example, there was discussion of teaching the basics of archaeology to history student teachers at the University of Dar es Salaam. During the workshop, it was established that the archaeology content that is taught in history subjects in schools is not covered well, due in part to the inadequacy of the knowledge of archaeology amongst history teachers (Mturi 2005; Mapunda 2005; Mabulla and Magori 2005; La Violette 2002). Teaching the basics of archaeology to teachers was thus introduced into training schemes and has been sustained. Moreover, since 1985, when archaeology courses were introduced in Tanzania, there has been a growing awareness of what archaeologists do and why they do it. Although human evolution remains the best-funded area of teaching and research (Kessy 2016), Tanzanian students require greater exposure to topics such as the preservation of historic sites and artefacts, working with descendant populations, interpreting archaeological findings for public audiences, and interrogating archaeological collections in museums.

The 2016 survey was written from the perspective of a member of the first cadre of Tanzanian archaeology students of the University of Dar es Salaam, who subsequently became chair/head of the archaeology unit that was to become a department in 2013 (Kessy 2016). This study examined much of what had previously escaped notice in terms of the archaeology pedagogy. For instance, Kessy (2016: 87–8) stipulates that up until the academic year 1994–5, the University of Dar es Salaam prospectus guided archaeology students to opt for science courses such as zoology, geology and statistics (among others) on the grounds that archaeology is a multidisciplinary subject. This study also considered enrolment figures, funding for undergraduate, postgraduate and PhD research, capacity building and infrastructure development. While the study situated itself challenged colonial archaeologies and examined how early human evolution studies and anthropological research were carried out under the umbrella of racial justification (Kessy 2016: 68–9), its conclusion encouraged local efforts to match the scientific advancement in modern archaeology equipment and facilities in developed countries. Unfortunately, the study ignored the state of historical archaeology in Tanzania, despite mentioning the use of the oral tradition in archaeology as one of the key developments at the University of Dar es Salaam.

Mehari (2015) examines the development of archaeological pedagogy in Tanzania from what was merely a source of historical information into a broader, more viable field. Archaeology is taught in history for secondary school Form 1 (which is equivalent to Grade 7 in the Cambridge curriculum) as a source of historical information, and it continued as such at the university level before the establishment of the archaeology unit. Mehari conducted doctoral research into the pedagogy of archaeology in Uganda and Tanzania, which is the only study I am aware of with both depth and breadth on these topics. The previous study closest to this one would have been that of Wachawaseme (2015), which examined the practices of archaeology, particularly focusing on public understanding of what archaeologists do and why they do it, but without a focus on archaeological pedagogy.

Mehari (2015) presents archaeological pedagogy in Tanzania from seed to fruit. What could be referred to as seed is the period of colonialism that saw Tanzanians trained in archaeological excavation mainly to provide cheap labour for archaeological expeditions (Bushozi et al. 2020). The fruit is the establishment of the Archaeology Department in Tanzania (see also Kessy 2016). It is at this juncture that pedagogy as a term becomes controversial. Learning and teaching can occur in many different settings and not necessarily in the classroom alone (Giroux 1991). Although historical archaeology as a set of practices features in Tanzanian archaeology, there is a tendency to shy away from naming it, and hence there is no course on historical archaeology offered to students in Tanzania

(Mehari 2015: 226). Chami's studies, for instance, have been carried out along the coast of Tanzania and its associated hinterland. These are the areas where ancient contact and written records such as the *Periplus of the Eritrean Sea* and early Arab writings such as those of Ibn Batuta exist. Chami was able to use these written records alongside excavations of the coast of Tanzania to overturn the colonial historiography of the region (Chami 2005). This study, however, has never been termed historical archaeology. In efforts to keep up with Western archaeological methodologies, as suggested by Kessy (2016), students are instead encouraged to focus on traditional Western archaeological specialisms such as faunal, lithic, pottery and metal analysis.

The disregard for historical archaeology in Tanzania has resulted in the appropriation of the past, the silencing of subaltern voices, the politicization of archaeology, and conflicts between archaeologists and community users of cultural heritage. To elaborate on these claims, this chapter examines three sites associated with the slave trade: Mgao, which is generally dated to around the twelfth to eighteenth centuries; and the twentieth-century sites at Kilwa Kivinje and Kitanda, which are associated with the colonization of Tanzania. These sites are discussed in the context of contemporary archaeology which intersects heritage, ethnography and history in relating the archaeological past to the present (González-Ruibal 2014). Specifically, the archaeological past is related to the teaching of the subject in the Tanzanian education system. The sites in question are used to illuminate the current lack of concern for archaeology and the implications for educational curricula, archaeological institutions such as museums, and the public. A short account of how I came to study historical rather than the predominant prehistorical archaeology is also added to further illustrate the lack of formal training in contemporary archaeology in Tanzania.

Mgao

Mgao, also known as Mongalo in French documents and Mangalo in Portuguese documents, is a village formed by slave traders who decided to settle on the coast while trying to escape from the towns of Mikindani and Sudi. The name Mgao, which could be translated as 'divide', signifies a stream that seems to divide the water as it enters the ocean. It is through this feature that Mgao marks the maritime border between the Lindi and Mtwara regions of southern Tanzania. The same name Mgao has been confused with a division point of slaves who were accumulated there and divided for departure to different destinations such as Mombasa, Mauritius and Reunion. Historians such as Alpers (1967) mention Mgao as an important trading centre. Enslaved people who were sold as far as Mombasa have traced their route back to there. Mgao has largely escaped notice due to its location in between the two prominent sites of Mikindani and Sudi, which have been studied by archaeologists (e.g., Kwekason 2011; Pawlowicz 2017; Ichumbaki 2015; Pollard and Ichumbaki 2017).

The remains of an early Arab settlement are visible on the site, dated to between the twelfth and eighteenth century based on the tombs, monumental remains and Swahili pottery that dominated the excavated trenches. Local oral narratives describe Mgao as an exclusively Arab settlement. They recount that before the Arabs reached Chief Makonela, the then chief of Mgao, they surveyed the coast and identified the places suitable for settlement. The Chief granted them the land they required but decided to migrate with his people some ten kilometres away from where the Arabs established their residence.

Written records establish the French as the later occupants of the Mgao site. Sir John Gray (1956: 28) argues that the French had an interest in the Swahili coast at Kilwa, Zanzibar, Kerimba, Cape Delgado, Pemba, Mafia and even Mgao, where emissaries of the French slave trade known as '*amateurs*' – literally meaning privateers or traders trading on their own accord rather than with the support of the French government – were sent. Most of these traders originated from Mauritius, which they used as their base of operations (Gray 1956). They include Morice (also mentioned in Kilwa chronicles), who is believed to have visited Kilwa in 1774 (Gray 1956), and Nicolas Comarmond, who visited Mgao in 1784 (Teelock and Rushohora 2019). The Kilwa chronicles describe the French visits:

> After a very few days great help came to the land. A Frenchman came to trade. The Sultan and all the people made friends with him because they liked him. They did not wage war because the land was suffering from famine when this Frenchman came. They[,] together with their ruler, obtained great profits. The people fetched goods such as mats, made of palm leaves and worth ten pice, and sold them to the Frenchman for a dollar.
>
> Velten 1907

Gray (1956: 36) argues that the French were interested in other commodities such as slaves to feed the ever-expanding plantation of Mauritius. They signed treaties with the slave traders to secure a constant provision of slaves. As an *amateur*, Nicolas Comarmond chose to explore Mgao at his own expense. He hired a small expedition at Mgao to go up the rivers and did a thorough survey of the area, verifying the notes made by the Chevalier de Mondevit, who had surveyed the area some years previously. Comarmond even decided to leave a ship there as well as some crew to maintain a French presence in this area. Likewise, he saw much value in the French having a trading post in Mgao to maintain a presence where there had hitherto been none.

The stratigraphic interpretation of the site points to the Arabs' presence predating that of the French, which is also attested by monumental remains. One of the graves, for example, is found about seven kilometres away from the French warehouse bearing the inscription ' الحقعبدالقبرهذه . . . الجمعةيومتاريخ . . . تـ عالـ الـ لهرحمه ١ ٢ ٠', which Othman Bakar translated as 'This is the grave of Abdil Haqqi ... year, the day of Friday ... May God have mercy on him *1207.*' In Swahili, this translates as '*Hili ni kaburi la Abdil Haqqi ... mwaka, siku ya ijumaa ... Allah amrehemu 1207.*' No encounters between the French and Arabs at Mgao are recorded in the archive or in collective memory. The present-day community of Mgao refers to the monuments as *maghofu ya Waarabu,* meaning 'Arab Ruins'. As a memorial to the slave trade, the ruins have been left bare to fade away on their own. On the government side, Mgao does not feature on the register of historic monuments and sites of Tanzania. Elsewhere, along the Swahili coast (Mingoyo, Lindi and Kilwa Kivinje), this abandonment has been explained to be the result of colonial conservation ordinances (Bwasiri 2014) or trauma associated with sites. In Lindi, for instance, the German colonial prison has been abandoned because it is considered to be a grave for those who were incarcerated there and never returned to their homes (Rushohora 2019a).

During my fieldwork at Mgao, the community remained as bystanders, anticipating that harm would occur to the research crew clearing the site and subsequently conducting excavations. It was only at the end of the fieldwork that community outreach was conducted to establish the conservation strategy for the site that would include the community as informed partners. This initiative was taken to schools, targeting in particular history teachers and students who were aware of the monuments and their link to the Arab slave trade. We introduced them to the fact that there had been more interactions, beyond the Arabs, such as that involving the French, with their interests along the coast between the sixteenth and eighteenth centuries. In terms of students learning their history and their interaction with the Mgao ruins, this narrative needed to be a part of the pedagogy. At home, the narrative is different and probably difficult to correct. The inclusion of this form of historical archaeology, relating to sites that people encounter on a daily basis, generates more interest and it is through work like this that the service of archaeology to the people can be more effectively realized.

Kilwa Kivinje

The site of Kilwa Kivinje lies in the Kilwa district, Lindi region. The prosperity of Kilwa Kivinje came from the slave trade, particularly through the long-distance trade that involved the Kamba of Kenya, the Nyamwezi of Central Tanzania and the Yao of Southern Tanzania. In the nineteenth century the Germans established their administrative headquarters (Boma) at Kilwa Kivinje in order to control the trade and eventually to abolish it (Mapunda 2016). The abolition of the slave trade was not an untroubled undertaking. The local traders who were the beneficiaries contested it: they had amassed a lot of wealth and become big men (Becker 2004). Tippu Tip, Hassan Omar Makunganya, Abushir, Bwana Heri and Machemba are some of the figures associated with the slave trade during this period. History teaching in Tanzania mentions the end of the slave trade without discussing what happened to the slave traders themselves after abolition. A few historians such as Kimambo (1967) have suggested that the circumstances of these former traders remain unclear. The case of Hassan Omar Makunganya is exemplary here. The German governor Von Trota managed to arrest Makunganya, who was tortured and executed at Kilwa Kivinje on 15 November 1895. A memorial that was erected in the 1970s to commemorate the Majimaji War (1904–8) somehow came to include the name Makunganya, whose story in Tanzania was told up until his execution (see Figure 9.1). In the German records, however, the story is extended to include the fact that Makunganya's remains were taken to Germany for racial studies (Rushohora 2021). This is not part of the current pedagogy, and neither is the memorial on which Makunganya's name is misleadingly featured.

Makunganya's execution was carried out at Kilwa Kivinje on a mango tree famous as the execution mango tree, translated from the Kiswahili *Mwembe Kinyonga*. The tree was used for execution throughout the period of German colonialism in Tanzania, and according to the Antiquity Office in Kilwa, the tree ceased to bear fruit, dried up and eventually collapsed in 1996. The Kivinje memorial was the first state-owned Majimaji War memorial constructed in the 1970s, with the aim of including all the known victims. This memorial, which highlights the history of resistance to German colonialism, is an extremely important part of Tanzania' heritage, but issues remain about the conflict and the memorial's misrepresentation – issues which have been largely ignored. The layers of names from 1895 to 1907 might also indicate a mass grave where victims of colonialism were anonymously buried (Rushohora 2019b). This is an area where archaeologies of Tanzania might prove their relevance and provide a greater service to the community, as Tanzanian archaeologists have hoped.

Figure 9.1 Kilwa Kivinje mass grave. Photo by author.

Kitanda

Kitanda is an isolated village in Namtumbo district, surrounded by miombo woodland in all directions. The land is fertile and watered by several tributaries, some leading to the Ruvuma drainage system to the south-east, others to the Ruhuhu river basin to the south-west, while others join the Rufiji drainage system to the north. The source of one of these tributaries is a small swamp, measuring about 150 km^2 and located almost fifteen kilometres north of the village. It is from this swamp that the village has obtained its name, 'Kitanda', meaning 'a small lake' (Mapunda 2010).

Kitanda was ruled by a female *Nduna* (sub-chief) who went by the name Nkomanile of Ngoni Mchope under nkosi (chief) Chabruma during the Majimaji era. The name *Nkomanile* literally means 'the one scrambled for'. Oral sources are not certain why this female *Nduna* was given this name. However, one popular story claims that she was very beautiful and that men fought for her (Mapunda 2010). The original location of the village was close to the lake and this was where *Nduna* Nkomanile lived until the outbreak of the Majimaji War (1904–8). Archaeological surveys of Kitanda revealed mounds within a regrowth of tall grasses and established Nkomanile's residence one kilometre north of the lake. The area was, and still is, on the periphery of the Nyerere National Park, an important convergence point for game animals, especially during the dry season. The entire compound measured 4 km², with mud and wattle houses, an open space at the centre and a probable entrance in the southern side. Local pottery constituted the only material scatters on the surface.

Kitanda was on a slave trade route, and Nkomanile benefited from tributes that were paid to her during the trade. During the Majimaji War, Nkomanile is known to have confiscated some of the goods that were passing in Kitanda to increase her own wealth (Rushohora 2020). Subsequently, Kitanda became one of the most important sites in the south-western part of the war zone during the Majimaji War. It was a gateway through which 'maji' (the war medicine) from Kinjekitile Ngwale passed to the Ndendeule, Ngoni, Pangwa and Bena peoples (Rushohora 2015a). Nkomanile was the first Majimaji addressee, as she hosted the messenger Omari Kinjala from Ungindo and introduced him to chief Chabruma. Chief Chabuma established Kinjala legitimacy and had the medicine examined by ritual experts, including his own diviner. Chabruma doubted the effects of the 'maji' and had it tested on a dog and then a man convicted of adultery. On both occasions, maji proved a failure. Despite this, Chabruma accepted it and ordered his people to do the same.

Following the outbreak of the Majimaji War in Ungoni, Nkomanile, as the first recipient of '*maji*' in Ungoni, was listed among the leaders most wanted by the Germans. She was later arrested and hanged. Her name is listed on the Majimaji Mass grave together with other victims of the Majimaji War who were executed on 27 February 1906. However, it is not known when exactly Nkomanile was executed. According to her family, she was executed in Kitanda, and they point to a canyon where her remains were dumped. For this reason, her relatives do not take part in the Majimaji commemorations because they believe the remains of their heroine are not together with the others in the mass grave. Given the number of human remains that have recently been located in Germany, there is a possibility that the unique case of Nkomanile could plausibly be associated with similar looting of human remains. In 2020, Germany proposed a renaming of Wissmannstrasse in Berlin in her honour. This street name change was controversial, particularly in Berlin, because of the replacement of the name of the colonizer with the colonized. Many questions remain unanswered. Who executed Nkomanile, and where? What happened to her remains?

History teaching in Tanzania has taken up the example of Kitanda in order to emphasize the role of women in the resistance to colonialism. Although

Nkomanile's name appears in the textbook, there is no acknowledgement of the enduring controversies. None of the contemporary sources, nor the textbooks, social memory or historical treatments, fully acknowledge Nkomanile's part in the Majimaji War (Schmidt 2010). Usually her role as cultural broker between messenger and ruler is accepted almost as a given. Redmond (1972), for example, wrote that Kinjala contacted her as a mere sub-chief who brought him to see Chabruma. Mapunda and Mpangara (1968) contended that Kinjala approached Nkomanile and they entered into a temporary marriage before she introduced him to Chabruma and that Kinjala revealed Maji to Nkomanile in bed! He and Bell (1950) believe that Nkomanile, a royal woman, had already been married to Kinjala before the Majimaji conflict and that Kinjala was chosen as a messenger for Ungoni based on that. These colonial explanations ought to be questioned and challenged, including through the use of archaeology to enhance and correct the colonial history of Tanzania.

One of the ways of correcting this matter is by incorporating information from oral traditions, for example about Ngoni cultural relations. Kinjala, for instance, was from the Ngoni slave-raiding zone of Liwale. The people of Liwale are known to have been terrorized by the Ngoni incursion (Bell 1950). The Germans colonization of Liwale was a result of a Liwale chief trekking to Kilwa Kivinje to beg the Germans to establish their military base in Liwale so as to protect them against the Ngoni slave raiders (Rushohora 2015a). The Ngoni were migrants from South Africa who fled to Tanzania during the Mfecane war, arriving around 1820. To maintain their kingdom, it was taboo for the Ngoni to marry people considered *sutu* (slaves). According to the oral accounts collected by this author, since Nkomanile was a ruler, it is highly unlikely that Kinjala gained any matrimonial benefits from her. Thus, the concubine story is likely pure colonial propaganda, but unfortunately earlier historians seem to have been taken in by it. In fact, it is more likely that their shared interest in removing the colonizing force enabled Kinjala to convince Nkomanile and many others, including the chief Chabruma, that decolonization was possible through the use of *maji* and this became the immediate driver for the Ngoni to join the Majimaji War.

Ways forward

So far in this chapter I have looked at historical archaeology in Tanzania together with the development of archaeological pedagogy. That archaeology is not well taught in Africa has been reported for many decades (Lane 2011), while archaeologists have also been blamed for not popularizing their discipline more effectively (Karega-Munene 1992). This chapter argues that historical archaeology is poorly taught in Tanzania, both in its basics at introductory levels and in the inclusion of sites and materials alongside other historical sources. The fact that archaeology is largely taught in schools and elsewhere by non-archaeologists has not only proven challenging, but has also rendered archaeology an alien, uninteresting and unimportant part of history for many. Although Tanzanian archaeologists and teachers of history have deliberated on these matters, as discussed earlier, to date the changes have not been meaningful. Archaeology as a fully-fledged degree is offered only at the University of Dar es Salaam, just one of the forty-seven universities in Tanzania today. This means that 'Basics in archaeology', a course designed for teachers of history, is often taught by political scientists, sociologists or historians.

In addition, these teachers encounter seven modules of the course, which have to be taught within one fifteen-week semester, including both teaching and examination. The result is a highly theorized and somewhat daunting course that is neither learned nor taught with passion or commitment. Archaeologists in Tanzania have tried to place emphasis on how learning and teaching archaeology has the potential to disseminate the value of heritage in general and to have a powerful impact on lives and futures (Mapunda and Msemwa 2005). The current emphasis on the archaeology of human evolution that began under colonial rule and within colonial racial categories (Kessy 2016) distracts from this goal. A greater focus on historical archaeology is thus important to the archaeology of Tanzania as it not only redirects the orientation of research onto colonial contexts, but also helps to contextualize the colonial-era archaeologies that were framed within political paradigms and appropriations of the past.

Landing in historical archaeology

Writing about how I became a historical archaeologist is like writing an autobiography. Although I love reading autobiographies, I am not fond of writing them (Rushohora 2015b). I take up this role here, nonetheless, to reflect on the lack of formal training in historical archaeology in Tanzania. Born and raised in Tanzania, I became a historical archaeologist by mere accident. I learned about archaeology as a source of historical information in Form 1 and that was about it. I never visited an archaeological heritage site as part of my primary or secondary school education, and thus I did not grow up knowing what archaeology entailed. When I completed my Advanced Level Certificate (the university entrance examination), my sister recommended archaeology because it was one of the courses with fewer students. The lower number of students assured me not only a government higher education loan to finance my studies but also future employment. Most African countries consider archaeology an elitist subject, preserved for tertiary education institutions, museums and foreign research teams far removed from people's every-day lives (Segobye 2005). I spent the whole of my first year looking for an exit point. I majored in archaeology courses and associated analysis such as metal, fauna, pottery and lithic analyses, but took optional courses from development studies, philosophy, environmental studies, sociology and fine art.

What led me to historical archaeology was a field school that I attended in my second year, which was part of programme associated with the Majimaji War centenary. The field school was conducted at the ignition point of the Majimaji War – Nandete. Although I was not passionate about archaeology, I did very well in my courses and qualified to undertake an independent project. I was supervised by Professor Bertram Mapunda who had started venturing into the archaeology of the Majimaji War in Ungoni (Mapunda 2010). I came up with the project titled 'An ethnoarchaeological investigation of the Majimaji War in Umatumbi' (Rushohora 2008) and ultimately this was probably one of the archaeology courses I enjoyed the most throughout my undergraduate studies.

Surprisingly, this was not the first time that I encountered the Majimaji War. It is one of the topics taught in primary and secondary schools, and the basis of common questions in progression and national examinations. These studies, however, are superficial, with a nationalistic slant (Lawi 2009; Rushohora 2020). It was through the Majimaji project in Nandete that I came to understand the Majimaji people, landscape, memory and memorialization, which are not part of the history pedagogy. Little is taught in schools beyond the fact that the Majimaji War was 'led' by Kinjekitile Ngwale, that it included a belief in a water cult (maji) and that it was in part a reaction against the Germans' introduction of forced labour in the cotton plantation. As I developed an interest in the Majimaji War, Professor Mapunda introduced me to numerous other sites in the Matumbi hills. At that time, I still did not refer to what I was doing as historical archaeology.

After my undergraduate degree, I received the University of Dar es Salaam women's scholarship to undertake a masters in archaeology. Through the African Archaeology Network – a SIDA-funded project with its coordinator in Tanzania – I was among the beneficiaries of the international field schools organized between 2008 and 2010 in Comoros and Botswana. It was through these networks, which were often multidisciplinary, that I learned about historical archaeology as a field and interacted with scholars within the discipline who were willing to supervise and train me. It was at this point that I became motivated to specialize in this field, and revisited the Majimaji War. I have also questioned the archaeology of Tanzania which has marginalized historical archaeology (Rushohora 2015c). I should also say here that during the early stages of my research, historical archaeology lacked a base at the University of Dar es Salaam. I remember writing an article on the historical archaeology of the Majimaji War exploring in particular the wealth of the archive which has never been examined as an artefact in context (cf. Wilkie 2006), which was utterly rejected. The paper interrogated text, maps and photographs on the Majimaji War which, after analysis, revealed the great potential for conveying the details of the war that lies in sites and landscapes, people, weapons and war tactics. Some of these details were difficult to find by relying solely on archaeological excavations. Given the nature of the soil, for instance, no metal weapons were found in excavations. Using photographs that were taken during the war, weapons such as spears could easily be observed to support the oral account of the type of weapons used in the Majimaji War. Part of this paper crept into what the *Journal of African Studies* published in 2017 (Rushohora and Kurman 2017), but it has also resulted in the project called 'Imagining Futures through Un/Archived Past', which has managed to negotiate the opening of the missionary archives in Ndanda and Peramiho that had been closed to the public until the writing of this paper.

References

Alpers, E. A. (1967), *The East African Slave Trade*, Vol. 3, Nairobi: Historical Association of Tanzania.

Becker, F. (2004), 'Traders, "Big men" and Prophets: Political Continuity and Crisis in the Maji Maji Rebellion in Southeastern Tanzania', *Journal of African History* 45 (1): 1–22.

Bell, R. M. (1950), 'The Maji Maji Rebellion in Liwale District', *Tanganyika Notes and Records* 28: 38–57.

Bushozi, P. G. M., C. Saanane, W. Jilala and L. Felician (2020), *Paleoanthropological Research and Cultural Heritage Management in Lindi Region, Southern Tanzania*, unpublished project report, submitted to COSTECH, Dar es Salaam.

Bwasiri, E. J. (2011), 'The challenge of managing intangible heritage: problems in Tanzanian legislation and administration', *South African Archaeological Bulletin* 66 (194): 129–35.

Chami, F. (2005), 'Current Archaeological research in Mainland Tanzania', in B. Mapunda and P. Msemwa, eds, *Salvaging Tanzania's Cultural Heritage*, 81–9, Dar es Salaam: University of Dar es Salaam Press.

Chami, F. (2021), *Peopling of the Swahili Coast Since the Last Ice Age*, Professorial Inaugural Lecture, University of Dar es Salaam.

Giroux, H. A. (1991), 'Border pedagogy and the politics of postmodernism', *Social Text* 28: 51–67.

González-Ruibal, A. (2014), 'Contemporary Past, Archaeology of the', in Claire Smith, ed., *Encyclopedia of Global Archaeology*, 1683–94, New York: Springer.

Gray, J. (1956), 'The French at Kilwa 1776–1784', *Tanganyika Notes and Records* 44: 28–49.

Hamilakis, Y. (2004), 'Archaeology and the politics of pedagogy', *World Archaeology* 36 (2): 287–309.

Hutchings, R. and M. La Salle (2014), 'Teaching anti-colonial archaeology', *Archaeologies* 10 (1): 27–69.

Ichumbaki, I. (2015), 'Monumental ruins, baobab trees and spirituality: perception of values and uses of built heritage assets of the East African coast', PhD thesis, University of Dar es Salaam.

Illife, J. (1967), 'The organization of the Maji Maji rebellion', *Journal of African History* 8 (3): 495–512.

Kessy, E. T. (2016), 'The History of Cultural Heritage Research and Teaching in Tanzania', *Tanzania Zamani* 10 (2): 65–112.

Kimambo, I. N. (1967), 'The political history of the Pare people to 1900', PhD thesis, Northwestern University.

Kwekason, A. (2011), *Holocene Archaeology of the Southern Coast of Tanzania*, Dar es Salaam: E&D Vision Publishing.

Lane, P. (2011), 'Possibilities for a postcolonial archaeology in sub-Saharan Africa: indigenous and usable pasts', *World Archaeology* 43 (1): 7–25.

LaViolette, A. (2002), 'Encountering archaeology in Tanzania: education, development, and dialogue at the University of Dar es Salaam', *Anthropological Quarterly* 75 (2): 355–74.

Lawi, Y. (2009), 'Pros and Cons of Patriotism in the Teaching of the Maji Maji War in Tanzania Schools', *Journal of Historical Association of Tanzania* 6 (2): 66–90.

Mabulla, A. Z. P. and C. Magori (2005), 'Reflections on the Archaeology Curriculum at the University of Dar es Salaam', in B. B. Mapunda and P. Msemwa, eds, *Salvaging Tanzania's Cultural Heritage*, 25–35, Dar es Salaam: University of Dar es Salaam Press.

Mapunda, B. (2005), 'Two decades of archaeology programme at the University of Dar es Salaam: The Ups and Downs', in B. B. Mapunda and P. Msemwa, eds, *Salvaging Tanzania's Cultural Heritage*, 9–24, Dar es Salaam: University of Dar es Salaam Press.

Mapunda, B. B. (2010), 'Reexamining the Maji Maji War in Ungoni with a Blend of Archaeology and Oral History', in J. Giblin and J. Monson, eds, *Maji Maji: Lifting the Fog of War*, 221–38, Leiden: Brill.

Mapunda, B. B. (2017), 'Encounter with an "Injured Buffalo": Slavery and Colonial Emancipation in Tanzania', *Journal of African Diaspora Archaeology and Heritage* 6 (1): 1–18.

Mapunda, B. B., and P. Msemwa, eds (2005), *Salvaging Tanzania's Cultural Heritage*, Dar es Salaam: Dar es Salaam University Press.

Mapunda, O. B. and G. P. Mpangara (1969), *The Maji Maji War in Ungoni*, Dar es Salaam: East African Publishing House.

Mehari, A. (2015), 'Practicing and Teaching Archaeology in East Africa: Tanzania and Uganda', PhD thesis, University of Florida.

Mturi, A. (2005), 'State of Rescue Archaeology in Tanzania', in B. Mapunda and P. Msemwa, eds, *Salvaging Tanzania's Cultural Heritage*, 293–310, Dar es Salaam: University of Dar es Salaam Press.

Munene, K. (1992), 'Dissemination of archaeological information: the east African experience', in P. Reilly and S. Rahtz, eds, *Archaeology and the Information Age: A Global Perspective*, 41–7, London: Routledge.

Pawlowicz, M. (2017), 'Mikindani and the southern coast', in S. Wynne-Jones and A. LaViolette, eds, *The Swahili World*, 260–5, Abingdon: Routledge.

Pollard, E. and E. B. Ichumbaki (2017), 'Why Land Here? Ports and Harbors in Southeast Tanzania in the Early Second Millennium A D', *Journal of Island and Coastal Archaeology* 12 (4): 459–89.

Redmond, P. M. (1972), 'A political history of the Songea Ngoni from the mid-nineteenth century to the rise of the Tanganyika African National Union', PhD thesis, University of London, School of Oriental and African Studies.

Rushohora, N. A. (2008), 'An Ethnoarchaeological Investigation of the Majimaji War in Umatumbi', BA dissertation, University of Dar es Salaam.

Rushohora, N. A. (2015a), 'An archaeological identity of the Majimaji: toward an historical archaeology of resistance to German colonization in southern Tanzania', *Archaeologies* 11 (2): 246–71.

Rushohora, N. A. (2015b), 'History teachers and the use of history textbooks in Africa – from textbook to "desa": a personal narrative of teaching history in Tanzania', *Yesterday and Today* 14: 238–43.

Rushohora, N. A. (2015c), 'Are We Not all Archaeologists? A Plea for Archaeology Beyond Excavation in Tanzania', *Journal of Contemporary Archaeology* 2 (2): S1–S4.

Rushohora, N. A. (2019a), 'Graves, Houses of Pain and Execution: Memories of the German Prisons after the Majimaji War in Tanzania (1904–1908)', *Journal of Imperial and Commonwealth History* 47 (2): 275–99.

Rushohora, N. A. (2019b), 'Facts and fictions of the Majimaji war graves in southern Tanzania', *African Archaeological Review* 36 (1): 145–59.

Rushohora, N. A. (2020), 'The Challenges of Teaching the Majimaji War in Contemporary Tanzania', in D. Bentrovato and J. Wassermann, eds, *Teaching African History in Schools*, 107–23, Leiden: Brill.

Rushohora, N. A. (2021), 'German Colonialism and Trading in African Skull: The Case of Chief Hassan Omari Makunganya of Kilwa, Tanzania', *Jahazi* 10, *Reclaiming Our Cultural Heritage*: 27–9.

Rushohora, N. A. and E. Kurmann (2018), 'Look at Majimaji! A plea for historical photographs in Tanzania', *African Studies* 77 (1): 87–104.

Schmidt, H. (2010), 'A Deadly Silence Predominated in the District: The Maji Maji War in Ungoni', in J. Giblin and J. Monson, eds, *Maji Maji: Lifting the Fog of War*, 183–220, Leiden: Brill.

Segobye, A. K. (2005), 'The revolution *Will* be televised: African archaeology education and the challenge of public archaeology – some examples from southern Africa', *Archaeologies* 1 (2): 33–45.

Teelock, V. and N. A. Rushohora (2019), 'Ensearch for Mgao', History Week and Slavery Museums Workshop, University of Mauritius.

Velten, C. (1907), *Prosa und Poetrie der Suaheli*, Berlin: n.p.

Wachawaseme, G. F. W. (2015), 'From Professionals to the General Public: Community Archaeology and the Cultural Dialects of Cultural Heritage Resources in Mtwara Region – Tanzania', PhD thesis, University of Pretoria.

Wilkie, L. A. (2006), 'Documentary Archaeology', in D. Hicks and M. C. Beaudry, eds, *The Cambridge Companion to Historical Archaeology*, 13–33, Cambridge: Cambridge University Press.

Part Four

The Personal and the Political

10

'We Want School!' Teaching and Learning Contemporary Archaeology with Displaced People in Anarchist-Adjacent Spaces in Athens, Greece

Rachael Kiddey

Introduction

About an hour by bus from central Athens, the Pampiraiki warehouse was originally built as the 2012 Olympic basketball stadium. When I volunteered there in 2019, the warehouse was being run by activists and volunteers as the main European sorting warehouse for thousands of boxes and bags of essentials, donated by people from all over Europe, to be distributed to displaced people stranded in Greece. One of my co-workers was Atash (not his real name). He told me that he ran a project on the other side of Athens called 'Our House', which he described as a form of direct-action, short-term housing for displaced homeless women and children. I explained that I was an academic researcher studying the lived experiences of forced displacement in Europe and asked if I could visit an 'Our House' apartment as part of my fieldwork.

In this chapter, I reflect upon teaching and learning contemporary archaeology in two anarchist-adjacent spaces of contemporary 'crisis' (cf. Papadopoulos and Tsianos 2013) in Athens in 2018–19. First, I provide theoretical context for the development of my British Academy-funded research project – 'Migrant Materialities' – and describe why I was motivated to co-develop a research collective. I then discuss anarchist pedagogies and their increased application to archaeological teaching and learning, before describing two anarchist-adjacent spaces in Athens in which I conducted fieldwork and where contemporary archaeology was taught and learned. Finally, I reflect on challenges

186 *Teaching and Learning the Archaeology of the Contemporary Era*

and achievements of the Made in Migration Collective and how non-traditional educational spaces can enhance teaching and learning contemporary archaeology.

The Made in Migration Collective: doing contemporary archaeology with displaced people

Since the 1970s, archaeologists have increasingly turned their attention to the material culture of the historical and very recent past (for example, Rathje 1981; Tarlow and West 1999; Graves-Brown 2000; Buchli and Lucas 2001; Holtorf and Piccini 2009; Harrison and Schofield 2010; McAtackney and Ryzewski 2017), where the 'every day' and a willingness to examine the political climate in which archaeology (and heritage) is practised are recurring themes (Battle-Baptiste 2016/2011; Auclair 2015; Conlin Casella 2016; McAtackney 2018; Atalay 2019). Drawing on theories first developed across the social sciences and spatial humanities, archaeologists have challenged ideology, conflict, power and the epistemological roots of Western science (Bourdieu 1977; Foucault 1979; Poovey 1998; Sahlins 2008); using feminist and gender theory (Wylie 1991) and Indigenous and decolonial theory (Tapsell 2011; Tuhiwai Smith 2012) to demonstrate that 'the past' is always multiple and not always behind us (cf. Nieves Zedeño, Pickering and Lanoë 2021). Contemporary archaeologies often contend with the need to transform epistemologies of the past to recognize the entangled nature of human/non-human relationships (cf. Haraway 2015; Braidotti, 2022) and respectfully engage with Indigenous philosophies of time and tradition (Alberti 2016; Betasamosake Simpson 2017).

Using critical and decolonial theory, Uzma Rizvi asks us to flip our way of thinking from one in which the archaeologist approaches the past via archaeological material to one in which the archaeologist is speculatively approached by the 'thing' (Rizvi 2019). Such an understanding is useful because, as Rizvi states, it

> ... allows archaeology to stutter, to provide openings for possible other forms of knowing and being that can act as circuit breakers within quickly closed systems of theory building. A speculative stance understands that we have to open our foundations if we require change and a different future, not just a different theory.
>
> Rizvi 2019: 157

Common throughout contemporary archaeologies is the recognition that 'things' do not merely 'inform' lived experiences, but are *fundamentally active constituents of lived experiences* (Latour 2005; Malafouris 2019). The spectrum of possible futures (Borck 2018) depends, to some extent, upon what is 'known' about materiality – past and present – and *who* is enabled to contribute to that knowledge.

Between 2016 and 2022 the official number of displaced people across the globe rose from 65.6 million to more than 100 million (UNHCR 2022a). The real number is likely far higher as many thousands of displaced people become vulnerable to exploitation by unscrupulous corporations and unavoidably part of the murky supply-chain of 'capitalist dreams' (Tsing 2012: 41). This shocking trend comes with its own 'migrant materialities' – landscapes, structures and objects – which have received increased transdisciplinary attention (Fiddian-Qasmiyeh 2020) over the past two decades, specifically from scholars of archaeology and heritage (Byrne 2016; Colomer 2017; Hamilakis 2019; Hicks and Mallett 2019); architecture and spatial mapping (Murrani 2020; Murrani, et al. 2022); and anthropology and material culture studies (Agier 2002; Dudley 2011; Yi-Neumann et al. 2022).

Between 2018 and 2022 I held a British Academy-funded postdoctoral research fellowship at the School of Archaeology, University of Oxford. The aim of my project, 'Migrant Materialities', was to work collaboratively with displaced people to study lived experiences of forced displacement in Europe. To achieve this, I spent time volunteering in and visiting squats, day centres and refugee camps used or run by displaced people, and came to meet displaced people.

The Made in Migration Collective evolved between 2018 and 2020. It is a coalition of displaced people, creative professionals and academics, based in Greece, Sweden and the UK. Not everyone in the collective identifies as anarchist but everyone agrees to making decisions using consensus models drawn from anarchist theory (further unpacked below). I was awarded funding to do the research, but the collective made the research possible – indeed, the collective *is* the research (Graeber 2002: 70; also Betasamosake Simpson 2017: 19). Due to our dispersed geographic locations, it was not always practical for the Made in Migration Collective to work together at every fieldwork site. For example, sometimes I would undertake fieldwork alone (see 'Our House', below), but data generated were always co-interpreted during in-person and online workshops.

188 *Teaching and Learning the Archaeology of the Contemporary Era*

Anarchist pedagogies, anarchist archaeologies

Over the past half century increased attention has been paid to how anarchist pedagogies might be applied in broadly educational settings. Two books which remain influential are Paulo Freire's *Pedagogy of the Oppressed* (Freire 2017/1970), which proposes a form of 'liberated pedagogy' in which everyone is enabled to pose problems, and Ivan Illich's *Deschooling Society* (Illich 2011/1977), which argues that the ultimate aim of schools and universities is to instil subserviency to the current order. Pedagogy can be a form of empowerment (cf. Giroux 1988), 'a tool for opening . . . doors of creative empathy that might point the way toward a future of peace and justice' (Amster 2002: 434). Education can be approached as a 'funnel' or a 'web' (Illich 2011/1977: 4–5). The 'funnel' is one-way, hierarchical, and produces sausage citizens, taught to passively accept what they are told without questioning how knowledge is produced (for example, see how history lessons in some Polish schools are conflated with nationalism (Jaskulowski and Surmiak 2017). The 'web' is a more egalitarian model that inspires learners to think for themselves, within and across various bodies of knowledge (Ward 1973). The latter starts from a place of respect for the learner as an individual with their own ontological experience of the world; it requires that critical thinking skills are prioritized over prescribed content. Here, Freire's important contribution to critical hermeneutics remains vital – humans make sense of the world through constant acts of interpretation which are socially and historically contingent. Knowledge is always 'situated' (Haraway 1988). To deny people the critical free-thinking skills to make sense of the world as they experience it is, for Freire, a form of violence (Freire 2017/1970; cf. Chattopadhyay, 2019). Building on approaches by Freire and particularly Illich, Robert Haworth describes the potential for 'deschooling'

> . . . to instil a different ethics of self, identity, freedom, spontaneity, discovery, curiosity, etc., thus creating arrangements of power that are productive, not oppressive, and preserve individual freedom and autonomy. These arrangements or relationships must be considered not only on the level of individual-to-individual or individual-to-community, but also individual-to-content and individual-to-structure.
>
> Haworth 2012: 68

In the context of teaching and learning contemporary archaeology specifically, anarchist theory can be applied in practical ways (cf. Angelbeck, Borck and Sanger 2018: 3) and anarchist pedagogies remain appealing for the ways in which they enable us to transcend the means/end model because the means – how we do things – *are* the non-hierarchical results that we seek (Graeber 2002: 70).

Anarchist adjacent spaces as educational facilities: Second School squat and 'Our House', Athens, Greece

Second School squat, Athens, Greece (2017–19)

Second School squat (also known as the Jasmine), was a former school building that housed more than 350 people, mainly families, when I spent time there in 2018–19 (see Figure 10.1). The combination of the 2008 financial crash, the Greek debt-crisis and resulting widespread unemployment led to a high proportion of Greek public buildings lying empty in 2015–16, which coincided with over one million people arriving in Greece, seeking refuge in Europe (UNHCR 2022b; see also Kiddey 2019, for discussion of the Greek socioeconomic context). What had been a mainly Spanish/Syrian collective in 2017 had become a predominantly Syrian/Kurdish collective by 2018.

The building incorporated three floors of classrooms and a playground. Families slept on mats on the floors of classrooms and shared the few lavatories and basins on each floor. They pooled their little money to buy vegetables and cooked together in the playground. Volunteers from the Pampiraiki warehouse distributed dried and tinned food once a week. The school building was in poor repair, with no heating or air-conditioning, furnished with what one might expect to find in a school – desks, chairs, blackboards and so on – and items of furniture that people had found on the street.

In 2018, knowing that people needed things, I arrived at Second School with as many sanitary products, first-aid items and children's toys as I could carry. I was welcomed by a Syrian woman who spoke excellent English. Fariha (not her real name) insisted that I take coffee with her and her friends. I explained that I was a researcher looking to co-develop a research collective of displaced people (online and in-person), with the aim of co-producing public heritage exhibitions to advocate for displaced people.

I spent three weeks with Fariha and her friends. Only Fariha and one other Kurdish woman chose to join the Made in Migration Collective, recognizing that it offered the chance for ongoing friendship and a creative alternative to constantly waiting for news of their asylum-applications. The women at Second School squat and I were able to communicate because Fariha translated between

Figure 10.1 Second School squat, exterior of building, 2018. Photo by author.

English and Arabic and another woman translated between English and Kurmanji (Kurdish). I was explicitly clear that participation in the project would not change the women's citizenship status and that there was no obligation to take part. On mobile phones with cracked screens, the women showed me digital photos of the people, places and things that they had left behind in Syria and Iraq. Our meetings were sporadic and unstructured, taking place when the women were available in between washing clothes, cooking and caring for children. Our communications were a 'web'-like informal exchange.

I learned as much about established methods of contemporary archaeology as I imparted – ethnographic approaches (Castañeda and Matthews 2008; Hamilakis 2011; González-Ruibal 2014: 1–6; Mills 2022), drawing (Taussig 2011; Wickstead 2013; Hale 2020) and participant observation and collaboration (Harris and Cipolla 2017). I taught the women in Second School squat that archaeology is the study of relationships between people and place, regardless of temporality, and that, as a form of material witness, archaeology can be useful in documenting tangible differences between policy and practical reality.

'Our House': short-term privately rented apartments aimed at taking women and children off the streets

'Our House' was a direct-action housing collective comprised of Atash and four other activist volunteers – two were non-European refugees, one French and one British. Atash was shocked to see so many women and children sleeping rough in Athens (2017–19). He earned money as a photographer and used it to rent apartments in affordable neighbourhoods in Athens (see Figure 10.2). The aim was to offer displaced homeless women and children short-term accommodation

Figure 10.2 Inside an 'Our House' apartment, 2019. Photo by author.

where they could be supportive to one another, sleep, shower and cook, while trying to sort out formal accommodation.

I conducted fieldwork at 'Our House' without other members of the Made in Migration Collective, but data generated were later co-interpreted by the collective (see exhibitions, below). I shadowed Atash and one of the other activists for several weeks in June and December 2019. At that time, 'Our House' rented three private apartments. The process for offering limited space to displaced homeless women and children was simple and quite alarming. Female 'Our House' activists approached displaced homeless women in Athens' city parks, explained what 'Our House' could make available and offered to take them to the apartments. 'Our House' was not formerly incorporated but agreed that only female volunteers should approach women in the parks and that no one should be taken to an 'Our House' apartment if they had not clearly understood that accommodation was very short-term and not sanctioned by the Greek government or the UNHCR. The displaced homeless women and children in Athens at that time were native speakers of a variety of languages, with French, Arabic, Dari, Farsi and Kurmanji being the most common. 'Our House' activists spoke Farsi, Arabic, French, English and a little Greek between them and so relied heavily on a bank of volunteer interpreters who were contacted via video calls.

'Our House' activists were in touch with Greek public services and local NGOs and made efforts to work with official authorities to gain formal accommodation for the women and children. Concerned by the evident safeguarding issues, I put it to Atash that because 'Our House' was not formally constituted as a housing action group, he was taking a big personal risk in financing apartments for vulnerable women and children. He laughed:

> You Europeans! You say I am unethical because I don't collect names and numbers, because I don't make the paperwork . . . But you are unethical to prefer single women and babies live in a park, where they are more scared to be raped or be made for prostitution and other very bad stuff.

It is testament to the severity of the situation at the time that public services authorized by the Greek government (for example, charities and a women's day centre) regularly contacted 'Our House' to ask if there were spaces at the apartments available for women who came to them for assistance. Everyone could see the issues around safeguarding, but 'Our House' apartments were, as Atash said, arguably safer places for the women to sleep than the city parks.

At the 'Our House' apartment, I ran drawing workshops with the children who were staying there. I took paper and pens and planned to ask the children to draw pictures of what 'Our House' meant to them. When I first arrived at the apartment there were six children aged between six and twelve. I asked the children if they would like to draw with me, having gained permission from their mothers. I started the workshop by offering the children bottles of water, peaches and biscuits, in return for them sitting around a small table. Five children were French speakers and one was a Dari speaker. We were soon joined by five more children from a nearby squat, all of whom were Farsi speakers. With eleven children and four languages (including English), the drawing workshop was erratic to begin with but paper and pens are universally recognized and the children were keen to take it in turns to use the translation app' on my phone. Some of the older children spoke enough English that they could translate for the younger ones. The Dari-speaking child understood some Farsi. My rusty French was also useful. We all waved our arms around and used the translation app', and between us, we reached understanding. It took about an hour to settle but then the children began to draw, and as they drew, they told me what they were drawing, what things meant to them (see Figure 10.3).

Figure 10.3 'I drew *Our House* building as a pencil because it is education.'

Discussion

What happened at Second School squat and the 'Our House' apartment could not be called 'education' in any formal sense, but a joyfully liberated form of teaching and learning contemporary archaeology took place. I was not always 'the teacher'. I was often the learner, as people asked me questions about the research approach and, in some cases, told me how they would prefer to do the 'work' (cf. Cook-Sather 2016). For example, one of the older children did not want to draw what 'Our House' meant to her. She preferred to describe it to me, verbally, 'so I practise my English'. I made notes as she explained that 'Our House' meant friendship, somewhere to go during the day and somewhere to get food.

In both Second School squat and the 'Our House' apartment, the work that I undertook with displaced people was *both* collaborative fieldwork and, simultaneously, teaching and learning contemporary archaeology in anarchist-adjacent spaces. A powerful part of Friere's original pedagogy of the oppressed is what Brian McKenna calls 'critical ethnography':

> . . . a methodology oriented towards clarifying the historical location of a project, a means of identifying the felt needs of all participants, and a political intervention to privilege the interests of the most disempowered.
>
> McKenna 2010

I do not feel comfortable calling the teaching and learning that took place in these precarious, insecure spaces a 'political intervention', but a prime objective of these exchanges remained to privilege the interests, needs and capabilities of those disempowered by displacement.

After Cordova (2017), in his discussion of Punk Rock Pedagogy, Noah Romero describes 'educative healing' as a process in which:

> . . . knowledge creation allows learners to unlearn and negate oppressive discourses. Punk Rock Pedagogy then impels its practitioners to act upon this knowledge and use whatever resources may be at their disposal to contribute to the creation of non-oppressive ways of knowing, being, and relating to human and non-human others.
>
> Romero 2021: 1066

Using the resources to which we had access – my 4G connected phone, some repurposed children's chairs, my own children's pens and pencils, the backyard of a squat – we created two spaces for non-oppressive ways of knowing and relating to one another. By making space and time for the women in Second

School to talk with me about the families, jobs, homes and material trappings left behind in Syria and Northern Iraq, the women were empowered to negate the oppressive discourse which paints displaced people as scroungers or victims. For a short time, the women's identities as autonomous agents were restored – as a teacher, as mothers who could provide, as a librarian.

Similarly, one of the older the children at 'Our House' commented that she had enjoyed the drawing workshop because, 'We want school! In Iran we have school but Greece, no.' At the time, there were an estimated 37,000 refugee and migrant children in Greece of whom only a third (roughly 12,800), aged between four and seventeen, were enrolled in formal education (UNICEF 2019). For the few days I was able to spend time with the children in the 'Our House' apartment they fully engaged in learning and teaching. Through practising speaking and writing in English and teaching me to write my name in the Persian alphabet, translating and helping one another to communicate ideas, through absorbing and responding to new ideas, the 'Our House' children co-curated new knowledge and related to one another and the world in new ways. This offered the children a far too brief experience of educational empowerment and enabled them to feel their individual learning (and teaching) potential. Participating freely, the children engaged in open debates and knowledge-sharing, which gave them the sense that they were as capable of flourishing educationally as their European peers.

In discussing, documenting and drawing the built and material culture which shaped their experiences of displacement, everyone involved contributed to the wider conversation and gained some 'autonomy of migration', which Yannis Hamilakis describes as 'a social and political movement that is reshaping our world, not ... a crisis moment', a phenomenon that he argues requires political solidarity rather than a humanitarian approach (Hamilakis 2019: 1372; cf. Papadopoulos and Tsianos 2013).

Only two people from Second School were able to join the Made in Migration Collective. Their contributions to the work of the collective are valued, not least in the sense that they helped to contextualize two public heritage exhibitions (reflected upon below). None of the children with whom I worked at 'Our House' joined the collective, partly because the situation at the apartment was so transient, it was impossible to remain in contact with the children's mothers (see Kiddey 2017: 64, for more detailed discussion of the difficulties associated with maintaining and using a mobile phone in situations of displacement), and partly because it would have been inappropriate to involve vulnerable children in necessarily difficult conversations.

The Made in Migration Collective is more than a vehicle by which to undertake collaborative academic research. It is a support network which empowers displaced people through solidarity and the opportunity to connect across borders. For example, one member of the collective took up the offer of free website design training from the company that built the platform for our digital exhibition (Made in Migration Collective 2021); while three members of the collective were supported to co-host our live exhibition in person at the British Academy (London). I have been privileged to write education and employment reference letters for many collective members – three of whom are now full-time university students in Sweden, while one has started her own six-week Women's Workshop, offering support and solidarity to migrant and refugee women in Plymouth (see Figure 10.4). The collective is dynamic and the co-produced work resulting from it belongs to everyone. It cannot be ensnared or commercialized because it is 'constantly changing, co-constructed by [classroom] exchanges' (Chattopadhyay 2019: 38).

Challenges and successes of the Made in Migration Collective

At the time of writing (2023), I do not know what happened to the women and children I met at the 'Our House' apartment. The exhausted mothers at the space did not volunteer to stay in touch with me after the drawing workshops, having more pressing concerns to contend with. I am truly haunted by not knowing what happened to those women and children but knowing the socio-political and economic conditions in which I left them. I hope that they received assistance and are safe. However, the 'Our House' women and children are among the most vulnerable to economic and sexual exploitation due to the precarity of forced displacement in Europe (cf. Tsing 2012).

The Covid-19 pandemic further hampered our ability to continue working with members of the collective who were based in Athens. The planned eight-day collaborative interpretation workshop in Oxford was cancelled due to travel restrictions and lockdowns. In its place, the collective developed a series of online interpretation workshops which were held weekly on Zoom. With no regular access to the internet and often several people sharing one internet-enabled mobile phone, even the most highly engaged people in Athens struggled to attend the online workshops. I remain in touch with individual people by WhatsApp. I (and other more settled members of the collective) support our colleagues so far as is possible (for example, helping them to understand complicated government websites, to complete paperwork and to locate well-being services and support groups).

Those members of the Made in Migration Collective who were able to join the online workshops (all based in the UK and Sweden) achieved a lot. In Refugee Week 2021, we launched a virtual exhibition called *Made in Migration*, which combines interpretations of the material and visual culture collected throughout the project with maps, poetry and short films (Made in Migration Collective 2021). In June 2022, we were awarded British Academy funding to co-produce *Made in Migration, IRL* [In Real Life] (British Academy 2022), a smaller 'live' public heritage exhibition which complemented the virtual show, bringing together physical artefacts, maps, films and cartoons belonging to and made by members of the collective. We are currently crowd-funding to take the live exhibition to Krokom (Sweden), a small rural town where many members of the collective now live. This event will enable the collective to present their work to wider local communities and will be held in memorial of Mimi Finnstedt, a long-term supporter of displaced people and prominent member of the collective, who tragically died in October 2022. In these ways, the Made in Migration Collective has some long-term legacy. The funded project is finished but relationships and mutual support continue, with new projects in the early stages of design (for example, a comic book aimed at eleven- to fifteen-year-olds, with images drawn by one member of our collective who is a professional cartoonist for *The Independent* (Arabia) and text co-written by other members of the collective, drawing on my research findings.

Conclusion

The teaching and learning that took place at Second School squat and the 'Our House' apartment was erratic, unstructured and free. Everyone participated for as long or short a time as they wanted. In both cases, we sat in circles to communicate, which tangibly supported the notion that these were non-hierarchical spaces in which learner expertise and ontological experience was respected (cf. Grohmann 2020: 140). The role of teacher and learner shifted. For example, the children drew pictures to explain how 'Our House' featured in their lives and taught me to write my name in Persian, helping me as I struggled to form letters which were new to me. This created a climate of mutual learning and teaching, revealing the children to be teachers and the academic to be the learner.

As both learners and teachers, we were responsible to ourselves and each other, enabling the co-production of new knowledge through helping one another with translation, understanding and production (Amster 2002: 436). I started from the position that, as people with ontological experience of displacement, the women and children knew something more than me, something valuable. The women and children kindly respected that, as a foreign academic, I knew something different from them and we reached a consensus that we would explore the web of interconnections between our ways to know.

Education as discussed in this chapter prioritized critical thinking skills, process, relationships, attitudes, well-being and moral values over content, and the effect was that everyone was able to contribute effectively at a pace that was right for them.

References

Agier, M. (2002), 'Between war and city: towards an urban anthropology of refugee camps', *Ethnography* 3 (3): 317–41.

Alberti, B. (2016), 'Archaeologies of Ontology', *Annual Review of Anthropology* 45: 163–79.

Amster, R. (2002), 'Anarchist pedagogies for peace', *Peace Review* 14 (4): 433–9.

Angelbeck, B., L. Borck and M. Sanger (2018), 'Anarchist Theory and Archaeology', in C. Smith, ed., *Encyclopaedia of Global Archaeology*, n.p.p: n.p.

Angelbeck, B., L. Borck and M. Sanger (2018), 'Anarchist Theory and Archaeology', in C. Smith, ed., *Encyclopedia of Global Archaeology*. Cham: Springer.

Atalay, S. (2019), 'Can Archaeology Help Decolonize the Way Institutions Think? How Community-Based Research is Transforming the Archaeology Training Toolbox and Helping to Transform Institutions', *Archaeologies* 15: 514–35.

Auclair, E. (2015), 'Ordinary heritage, participation, and social cohesion: the suburbs of Paris', in E. Auclair and G. Fairclough, eds, *Theory and Practice in Heritage and Sustainability: Between Past and Future*, 25–39, London: Routledge.

Battle-Baptiste, W. (2016/2011), *Black Feminist Archaeology*, Abingdon: Routledge.

Betasamosake Simpson, L. (2017), *As We Have Always Done: Indigenous Freedom Through Radical Resistance*, Minneapolis: University of Minnesota Press.

Borck, L. (2018), 'Constructing the Future History: Prefiguration as Historical Epistemology and the Chronopolitics of Archaeology', *Journal of Contemporary Archaeology* 5 (2): 229–44.

Borck, L. and M. Sanger (2017), 'An Introduction to Anarchism in Archaeology', *SAA Archaeological Record* 17 (1): 9–16.

Bourdieu, P. (1977), *Outline of a Theory of Practice*, Cambridge: Cambridge University Press.

Braidotti, R. (2022), *Posthuman Feminism*, Cambridge: Polity.

British Academy (2022), *British Academy Summer Showcase 2022*, https://www.thebritishacademy.ac.uk/events/british-academy-summer-showcase-2022/programme-exhibits/.

Buchli, V. and G. Lucas (2001), *Archaeologies of the Contemporary Past*, London: Routledge.

Byrne, D. (2016), 'The Need for a Transnational Approach to the Material Heritage of Migration: the China–Australia Corridor', *Journal of Social Archaeology* 16 (3): 261–85.

Caraher, W. (2019), 'Slow Archaeology, Punk Archaeology, and the "Archaeology of Care"', *European Journal of Archaeology* 22 (3): 1–14.

Castañeda, Q. E. and C. N. Matthews (2008), *Ethnographic Archaeologies: Reflections on Stakeholders and Archaeological Practices*, Lanham, MD: AltaMira Press.

Chattopadhyay, S. (2019), 'Infilitrating the Academy through (Anarcha-)Ecofeminist Pedagogies', *Capitalism Nature Socialism* 30 (1): 31–49.

Chomsky, N. (2005), *On Anarchism*, Edinburgh: AK Press.

Colomer, L. (2017), 'Heritage on the move: cross-cultural heritage as a response to globalisations, mobilities, and multiple migrations', *International Journal of Heritage Studies* 23 (10): 913–27.

Conlin Casella, E. (2016), 'Horizons beyond the Perimeter Wall: Relational Materiality, Institutional Confinement, and the Archaeology of Being Global', *Historical Archaeology* 50 (3): 127–43.

Cook-Sather, A. et al. (2016), 'Introduction: Learning from the Student's Perspective: Why it's Important, What to Expect, and Important Guidelines', in A. Cook-Sather et al., eds, *Learning from the Student's Perspective: A Sourcebook for Effective Teaching*, 1–20, Abingdon, Oxon: Routledge.

Cordova, R. (2017), *DIY Punk as Education: From Mis-education to Educative Healing*, Charlotte, NC: Information Age Publishing.

Coulthard, G. (2014), *Red Skin White Masks: Rejecting the Colonial Politics of Recognition*, Oxford: Oxford University Press.

Crumley, C. L. (1995), 'Heterarchy and the analysis of complex societies', *Archaeological Papers of the American Archaeological Association* 6 (1): 1–5.

de Certeau, M. (1988), *The Practice of Everyday Life*, London: University of California Press.

Dudley, S. (2011), 'Feeling at Home: Producing and Consuming Things in Kerenni Refugee Camps on the Thai–Burma Border', *Population, Space and Place* 17: 742–55.

Durrheim, K. et al. (2018), 'How racism discourse can mobilize right-wing populism: the construction of identity and alliance in reactions to UKIP's Brexit "Breaking Point" campaign', *Journal of Community & Applied Social Pyschology* 28 (6): 385–405.

El-Enany, N. (2020), *(B)ordering Britain: Law, Race, and Empire*, Manchester: Manchester University Press.

Fiddian-Qasmiyeh, E., ed. (2020), *Refuge in a Moving World: Tracing Refugee and Migrant Journeys Across Disciplines*, London: UCL Press.

Foucault, M. (1972), *The Archaeology of Knowledge*, London: Tavistock.

Fowles, S. (2010), 'A People's History of the American Southwest', in S. Alt, ed., *Ancient Complexities: New Perspectives in Pre-Columbian North America*, 183–204, Provo: University of Utah Press.

Freire, P. (1985), *The Politics of Education: Culture, Power, and Liberation*, London: Macmillan.

Freire, P. (2017/1970), *Pedagogy of the Oppressed*, London: Penguin Books.

Giroux, H. (1988), 'Critical theory amid the politics of culture and voice: rethinking the discourse of educational research', in R. Webb and R. Sherman, eds, *Qualitative Research in Education: Focus and Methods*, 190–210, New York: Palmer.

González-Ruibal, A. (2014), *Archaeology of Resistance: Materiality and Time in an African Borderland*, Lanham, MD: Rowman & Littlefield.

González-Ruibal, A., S. Yonatan and X. A. Vila (2011), 'A Social Archaeology of Colonial War in Ethiopia', *World Archaeology* 43 (1): 40–65.

Graeber, D. (2002), 'The New Anarchists', *New Left Review* 13 (Jan./Feb.): 61–73.

Graeber, D. (2004), *Fragments of an Anarchist Anthropology*, Chicago: Prickly Paradigm Press.

Graeber, D. and D. Wengrow (2021), *The Dawn of Everything: A New History of Humanity*, London: Penguin Allen Lane.

Graves-Brown, P. (2000), *Modern Material Culture*, London: Routledge.

Grohmann, S. (2020), *The Ethics of Space: Homelessness and Squatting in Urban England*, Chicago: Hau Books.

Hale, A. (2020), 'By Drawing We Unframe Scotland's Community Heritage Conference', *Journal of Contemporary Archaeology* 7 (1): 4–22.

Hamilakis, Y. (2011), 'Archaeological Ethnography: A Multitemporal Meeting Ground for Archaeology and Anthropology', *Annual Review of Anthropology* 40: 399–414.

Hamilakis, Y. (2019), 'Planet of camps: border assemblages and their challenges', *Antiquity* 93 (371): 1371–7.

Haraway, D. (1988), 'Situated Knowledges: The Science Question in Feminism and the Privilege of Partial Perspective', *Feminist Studies* 14 (3): 575–99.

Haraway, D. (2015), 'Anthropocene, Capitalocene, Plantationocene, Chthulucene: Making Kin', *Environmental Humanities* 6: 156–65.

Harris, O. J. and C. N. Cipolla (2017), *Archaeological Theory in the New Millennium: Introducing Current Perspectives*, London: Routledge.

Harrison, R. and J. Schofield (2010), *After Modernity: Archaeological Approaches to the Contemporary Past*, Oxford: Oxford University Press.

Haworth, R. H. (2012), *Anarchist Pedagogies: Collective Actions, Theories, and Critical Reflections on Education*, Oakland, CA: PM.

Hicks, D. and S. Mallett (2019), *LANDE: The Calais 'Jungle' and Beyond*, Bristol: Bristol University Press.

Hirsch, S. J. (2020), 'Anarchists and "the Indian Problem" in Peru, 1898–1927', *Anarchist Studies* 28 (2): 54–75.

Hodder, I. (1997), *Interpreting Archaeology: Finding Meaning in the Past*, London: Routledge.

Holtorf, C. and A. Piccini (2009), *Contemporary Archaeologies: Excavating Now*, Frankfurt am Main: Peter Lang.

Illich, I. (2011/1977), *Deschooling Society*, London: Marion Boyars.

Jaskulowski, K. and A. Surmiak (2017), 'Teaching history, teaching nationalism: a qualitative study of history teachers in a Polish post-industrial town', *Critical Studies in Education* 58 (1): 36–51.

Kiddey, R. (2017), *Homeless Heritage: Collaborative Social Archaeology as Therapeutic Practice*, Oxford: Oxford University Press.

Kiddey, R. (2019), 'Reluctant Refuge: An Activist Archaeological Approach to Alternative Refugee Shelter in Athens (Greece)', *Journal of Refugee Studies* 33 (3): 599–621.

Kinna, R. (2018), 'Anarchism and Feminism', in N. Jun, ed., *Brill's Companion to Anarchism and Philosophy*, 253–84, Leiden: Brill.

Kropotkin, P. A. (2017/1902), *Mutual Aid: A Factor in Evolution*, independently published.

Latour, B. (2005), *Reassembling the Social: An Introduction to Actor-Network-Theory*, Oxford: Oxford University Press.

Leone, M. (1981), 'Archaeology's Relationship to the Present and the Past', in R. A. Gould and B. C. Schiffer, eds, *Modern Material Culture: The Archaeology of Us*, 5–14, New York: Academic Press Inc.

Lewis, A. G. (2017), 'Imagining autonomy on stolen land: settler colonialism, anarchism and the possibilities of decolonization?', *Settler Colonial Studies* 7 (4): 474–95.

Made in Migration Collective (2021), *Made in Migration*, https://rachaelkiddey.co.uk.

Mainwaring, Ć. (2019), *At Europe's Edge: Migration and Crisis in the Mediterranean*, Oxford: Oxford University Press.

Malafouris, L. (2019), 'Understanding the effects of materiality on mental health', *BJPsych Bulletin* 43 (5): 1–6.

McAtackney, L. (2018), 'Where are all the women? Public memory, gender and memorialisation in contemporary Belfast', in E. Crooke and T. McGuire, eds, *Heritage After Conflict*, 176–90, London: Routledge.

McAtackney, L. and R. H. McGuire (2020), 'Introduction: Walling In and Walling Out', in L. McAtackney and R. H. McGuire, eds, *Walling In and Walling Out: Why Are We Building New Barriers to Divide Us?*, 1–24, Sante Fe: School for Advanced Research Press.

McAtackney, L. and K. Ryzewski (2017), *Contemporary Archaeology and the City: Creativity, Ruination, and Politcal Action*, Oxford: Oxford University Press.

McKenna, B. (2010), 'Exposing Environmental Health Deception as a Government Whistleblower: Turning Critical Ethnography into Public Pedagogy', *Policy Futures in Education* 2 (1): 22–36.

Mills, N. S. (2022), 'Sharing Collections and Sharing Stories: The Importance of Archaeological Ethnography in Archaeologist–Collector Collaborations', *Advances in Archaeological Practice* 10 (1): 38–48.

Murrani, S. (2020), 'Contingency and plasticity: The dialectical re-construction of the concept of home in forced displacement', *Culture & Psychology* 26 (2): 173–86.

Murrani, S., H. Lloyd and P. Ioanna-Cristina (2022), 'Mapping home, memory and spatial recovery in forced displacement', *Social & Cultural Geography*. DOI:10.1080/14649365.2022.2055777.

Nieves Zedeño, M., E. Pickering and F. Lanoë (2021), 'Oral tradition as emplacement: ancestral Blackfoot memories of the Rocky Mountain front', *Journal of Social Archaeology* 21 (3): 306–28.

Papadopoulos, D. and V. S. Tsianos (2013), 'After citizenship: autonomy of migration, organisational ontology and mobile commons', *Citizenship Studies* 17 (2): 178–96.

Poovey, M. (1998), *A History of the Modern Fact: Problems of Knowledge in the Sciences of Wealth and Society*, Chicago: University of Chicago Press.

Rathje, W. L. (1981), 'A Manifesto for Modern Material-Culture Studies', in R. A. Gould and B. C. Schiffer, eds, *Modern Material Culture: The Archaeology of Us*, 51–6, London: Academic Press Inc.

Rizvi, U. (2019), 'Archaeological Encounters: The Role of the Speculative in Decolonial Archaeology', *Journal of Contemporary Archaeology* 6 (1): 154–67.

Romero, N. (2021), 'Punx up, bros down: defending free speech through punk rock pedagogy', *Educational Philosophy and Theory* 53 (11): 1063–73.

Sahlins, M. (2008), *The Western Illusion of Human Nature: With Reflections on the Long History of Hierarchy, Equality, and the Sublimation of Anarchy in the West and Comparative Notes on Other Conceptions of the Human Condition*, Chicago: Prickly Paradigm Press.

Scheper Hughes, N. (1995), 'The Primacy of the Ethical: Propositions for a Militant Anthropology', *Current Anthropology* 36 (3): 409–40.

Shanks, M. and C. Tilley (1987), *Social Theory and Archaeology*, Cambridge: Polity Press.

Tapsell, P. (2011), '"Aroha Mai: Whose Museum?" The Rise of Indigenous Ethics within Museum Contexts: A Maori-Tribal Perspective', in J. C. Marstine, ed., *The Routledge Companion to Museum Ethics: Redefining Ethics for the Twenty-First Century Museum*, 85–111, London: Routledge.

Tarlow, S. and S. West (1999), *The Familiar Past: Archaeologies of Later Historical Britain*, London: Routledge.

Taussig, M. (2011), *I Swear I Saw This: Drawings in Fieldwork Notebooks, Namely, My Own*, Chicago and London: University of Chicago Press.

Tsing, A. L. (2012), 'Empire's salvage heart: why diversity matters in the global political economy', *Focaal – Journal of Global and Historical Anthropology* 64: 36–50.

Tuhiwai Smith, L. (2012), *Decolonizing Methodologies: Research and Indigenous Peoples*, 2nd edn, London: Zed Books.

UN (2021), *Forced Displacement at Record Level, Despite COVID Shutdowns: UNHCR*, https://news.un.org/en/story/2021/06/1094292.

UNHCR (2022), *Global Displacement Hits Record Capping Decade Long Rising Trend*, https://www.unhcr.org/uk/news/press/2022/6/62a9d2b04/unhcr-global-displacement-hits-record-capping-decade-long-rising-trend.html.

UNHCR (2022), *Operational Data Portal: Refugee Situation, Mediterranean Greece*, https://data2.unhcr.org/en/situations/mediterranean/location/5179.

UNICEF (2019), *Refugee and Migrant Children in Greece as of 31st October 2019*, https://www.unicef.org/eca/media/9281/file.

Ward, C. (1973), *Anarchy in Action*, New York: Harper.

Wickstead, H. (2013), 'Between the Lines: Drawing Archaeology', in P. Graves-Brown, R. Harrison and A. Piccini, eds, *The Oxford Handbook of The Archaeology of The Contemporary World*, 549–64, Oxford: Oxford University Press.

Williams, D. M. (2015), 'Black Panther Radical Factionalization and the Development of Black Anarchism', *Journal of Black Studies* 46 (7): 678–703.

Wylie, A. (1991), 'Gender Theory and the Archaeological Record: Why Is There No Archaeology of Gender?', in J. Gero and M. W. Conkey, eds, *Engendering Archaeology: Women and Prehistory*, 31–56, Oxford: Blackwell.

Yi-Neumann, F., A. Lauser, A. Fuhse and P. J. Bräulein (2022), *Material Culture and (Forced) Migration: Materializing the Transient*, London: UCL Press.

11

Archaeologies of the Contemporary World – A Chancy Business?

Greg Bailey

Introduction to memory work

It was suggested that for this book I might reflect on my own learning experience with archaeologies of the contemporary world. While I will go on to recount early encounters with these burgeoning studies at – what felt to me at least – a critical turning point, these are inevitably particular and personal reactions to found things and a ubiquitous, seemingly awkward, and not infrequently transgressive archaeology. Of its nature, descriptions of contemporary archaeology remain ill-defined with different approaches that engage with a variety of theoretical positions. This archaeological branch or sub-field might adopt familiar archaeological method or entirely reject it, while time-honoured disciplinary tropes are challenged or even overturned. But if like Outsider Art – with which, to my mind, it shares something of its aesthetic and much of its energy – archaeology of the contemporary era is tricky to classify, we probably know it when we see it.

To suggest that I had discovered an appreciation of contemporary archaeology as some unique moment of dramatic revelation would not be quite right. Rather, a realization that these disturbing archaeologies-of-us were a logical and necessary outcome of the historical archaeological project as a whole dawned slowly if surely. And perhaps the fact that most discarded contemporary waste for me lacked the immediate appeal of an Iron Age midden, bone fragments from Neolithic feasting, a palaeolithic cave painting or hieroglyphic Luwian would become the salient point. I would learn to see, and wonder at, what was daily before my eyes. But if an interest in archaeologies of the contemporary world did not arrive all at once, with hindsight, this playful yet serious path propelled by chance now seems absolutely necessary and quite inevitable.

Autobiography of a chancer

After a lifetime of work in TV and film, and increasingly driven by a growing preoccupation with human evolution and early prehistory, I decided to attend evening classes at Birkbeck College, London. While I had done much preparatory reading, this had hardly prepared me for the all-encompassing scope of my chosen subject – or indeed until I turned up at UCL Institute of Archaeology, that these studies were to be undertaken entirely within the discipline, tradition and culture of archaeology.

Greatly enthused, I went on to join the University of Bristol in 2004 at what seemed to me a very particular historical moment. My feet were perhaps already set on what was to be a serendipitous path. It so happened that just the previous year Angela Piccini and Dan Hicks of the department I was about to join had founded the Contemporary and Historical Archaeology in Theory group (CHAT) that would go on to sponsor publications and host annual conferences for the following several decades.

As I remember, an initial encounter with archaeologies of the contemporary world occurred in my first seminar in Bristol's archaeology department. The group was invited to choose, then discuss, something from the so-called 'black and red books'. In *Re-Constructing Archaeology: Theory and Practice* (Shanks and Tilley 1987), a chapter discussing style as ideology dealt at some length with Swedish middle neolithic ceramics. The finely detailed description and sequencing of these prehistoric TRB pots (Shanks and Tilley 1987: 155–71) was followed in the next chapter by a yet more exhaustive (or so it seemed to me) discussion of the design and differentiation of contemporary Swedish and British beer cans (Shanks and Tilley 1987: 172–86). While somewhat overwhelmed by the erudition and descriptive power of the authors, I do recall thinking that this juxtaposition of neolithic pots and twentieth-century beer cans was as much creative provocation as scientific archaeology. I would later learn that, already by 1983, Shanks and Tilley had taken a year to undertake a comprehensive study of the design, marketing and cultures of beer consumption in northern England and Sweden – collecting cans, conducting ethnographic research, visiting breweries and interviewing designers (Shanks 2022). The two archaeologists obviously took this business very seriously.

Although Gould and Schiffer had published *Modern Material Culture: The Archaeology of Us* (1981) a decade or so earlier, I had yet to read it. So perhaps the single most influential text for me and, I think, my cohort of archaeology students at Bristol and beyond arrived with *Archaeologies of the Contemporary*

Past, a wide-ranging series of papers edited by Victor Buchli and Gavin Lucas (2001). While the book's chapters ranged widely across the world of contemporary archaeology, it was perhaps the editors' own contributions that drew most comment and, for me, affected most. While it was clear that many of these writings understood archaeology as intrinsically political and a platform from which to confront or challenge historical narratives of racism, economic oppression and slavery, several chapters also reflected the discomforting, uncanny nature of contemporary archaeology and by extension that of every other single archaeological intervention.

Buchli and Lucas' chapter, 'The archaeology of alienation: a late twentieth-century British council house' (2001: 158–68), made for uncomfortable reading. Readers could not do anything other than agree with the authors' deep concern for an untraced mother and her two young children, who, for whatever reason, seem to have hurriedly abandoned their council flat. The twenty years since this research was published hardly lessens our queasiness with forensic archaeological recording of the most personal, even intimate, material: condoms, erotic lingerie, prescription for methadone, Christmas decorations. Readers are left wondering if this small family had been under physical or other serious threat, or having absconded from their council flat if they ever managed to be suitably and safely rehoused.

If rereading the paper after so many years hardly lessens the shock, its political and archaeological argument is surely as cogent and appropriate as ever. Although I now perhaps understand the piece as much about the intrusive nature of archaeology as polemic on council rehousing, it made its mark. We might then ask if archaeology can ever be neutral and what responsibilities to their subjects, alive, dead or absent, does each and every archaeologist always bear? Or even, as Laurent Olivier suggests in his own contribution to the volume discussing the memorialization of the twentieth century's worst atrocities at Auschwitz, Oradour-sur-Glane and the mass graves in Argentina and Bosnia (2001: 173–88), if contemporary archaeology could/should become 'part of the development of new forms of citizenship'?

But it is Buchli and Lucas' own introduction to *Archaeologies of the Contemporary Past* to which I repeatedly return. I believe 'The Absent Present' (2001: 3–18) and its brief coda, 'Presencing Absence' (2001: 171–4), to be key for any researcher contemplating a dive into the choppy waters of contemporary archaeology. Indeed, recalling my own ideological development, I believe it was this single text that finally convinced me of the serious intent underlying the project of, and ambition for, archaeologies of the contemporary era: 'This operation of a familiar subject/object made unfamiliar creates profound anxieties and, as such, functions as a diagnostic tool for relevant and socially engaged cultural work' (Buchli and Lucas 2001: 10).

Making friends with The Van

A particular research trajectory toward an archaeology of the contemporary era was set for me when John Schofield, then of English Heritage, came to Bristol as a visiting lecturer. For it was John who first inspired then initiated and led what became to be known as the Van Project (Bailey et al. 2009). This was an equally celebrated and castigated though forensic dismantling or – as our small team of specialists Cassie Newland, Anna Nilsson and Steve Davies would have it – *excavation* of a Ford Transit Van. Our aim was to examine a recently decommissioned archaeology work-van from the Ironbridge Gorge Museum (see Figure 11.1). While John described the project as a response to Alan Bennett's *The Lady in the Van*, he had begun building his team (initially of Cassie

Figure 11.1 This particular Transit Van. Photo by author.

and me) as a concept before we had obtained any material – car, minibus or motorhome.

In the event, the project was offered the perfect vehicle for our research, team-building and mutual affection with J641 VUJ. Here was a very particular, recently inhabited space and workplace considered not only as landmark artefact but also aggregation and type-site of late twentieth-century archaeology. Our work would also test archaeological method and practice, provoke debate within and without a specialist field and add a particular praxis-of-unmaking to contemporary archaeology theory.

My own part in this was to locate relevant documents, create a paper archive and record oral histories of the Van as both working vehicle and as site under investigation. I was also charged with making a short twenty-minute film impression of the archaeological process, or progress, of Van *in Transit* from World Heritage Site to excavation area to breakers' yard (Bailey 2006). Though any video of our work (I imagined at the time) would have a built-in timeline, as some sort of hybrid filmmaker/archaeologist I would always consider the Van, its constituents and my own footage as found objects to be considered in their own right. The bigger question that I had to address was that of the point-of-view. Who was to be the (notional) protagonist of our film? Like many at the time I was greatly inspired, even moved to tears, by *Art and Agency*, a masterwork of the late anthropologist Alfred Gell (1998). In his final chapter, Gell develops a theory of extended mind in which under certain circumstances agency is distributed through 'art' object, decoration, token, monument or building. The book ends with a discussion of a single Māori Meeting House which he suggests is indexical of '[t]he whole gamut of *Māori* Meeting houses distributed in space and time' (Gell 1998: 254).

Thus it would be for our every-Van for all seasons. Yet more telling was how Gell also stated that for its traditional builders '[t]o enter [such] a house is to enter a mind, a sensibility' (Gell 1998: 252–3). The archaeology team certainly grew to refer to the Van – which continues to affect our lives – with unusual affection. It also became clear that J641 VUJ was to be our doomed protagonist/hero.

Another text was published just in time to inform the work. This was Matt Edgeworth's edited essays, *Ethnologies of Archaeological Practice: Cultural and Material Transformations* (2006), a work that particularly reinforced my strategy. My overtly reflexive approach both to archaeology and to video-work was greatly encouraged. While in some sense its interior was still presenced by voices of many former inhabitants, though less overtly bleak than the abandoned council house of Buchli and Lucas, the Van project was also a conscious attempt to 'apply' archaeology, as method and practice, to a familiar, recently abandoned object/site/performative space. But although our invasive and ultimately destructive application of archaeology to an often fondly remembered vehicle struck a few nerves with several archaeologists, including former occupants from Ironbridge (their voices join the film's Greek chorus), for us, our Van inspired camaraderie and much laughter along with serious work. As one used to working in small creative teams under time constraints and tasked with different jobs, such unbroken harmony seemed unusual, even noteworthy.

The lightness of mood on-site seemed infectious. Together with those who knew J641 VUJ at Ironbridge, I invited passers-by and various scholars to inspect and comment on our work as part of an oral history research. Those academics (who accepted our invitation at least) and most others, interested visitors or casual strollers, seemed not only to grasp, even enjoy, our concept and practice, but more often than not, added meaningfully to the discourse. They too joined the chorus.

On reflection and after intervening years some trope of an archaeology-of-the-imminent now seems to be more pertinent than it then did. For, rather than archaeology being triggered by tractor, trace or training, that is, one jump ahead of roadworks or tower-block demolition or as investigation of a known or suspected site-of-interest by university staff and students, the not-quite-yet Van project began not with the prospect of dirt or concrete, or even pressed steel, but as a *wholly abstract idea*. This particular archaeological materialization of the immaterial – a what-would-happen-if project – seems to be something of a marker of/for archaeologies of contemporary ubiquity. This is something I would later directly confront as part of my PhD research and something I still ponder today.

'Views and Soundings' – marking boundaries

I was indeed fortunate that Angela Piccini agreed to supervise this work. Without her unfailing encouragement and daunting erudition, I could hardly have begun. And after several serious setbacks due to serious illness and my unserious propensity to flounder, without her patient support and endless imagination I never would have finished.

As something of a progress through archaeological possibilities, my thesis, 'Views and Soundings: Marking Boundaries for Archaeological Practice'

Archaeologies of the Contemporary World – A Chancy Business? 211

(Bailey 2017), developed through and with chancy material encounters. This archaeology would not be defined by method or synecdoche, by trowel or trace or arbitrary temporal boundary or as means to catalogue material or label discrete entities as in themselves worthy of particular attention or curation. In a world of possibility, I would just have to pay due attention to what I found in front of me.

The journeyman archaeologist happens upon many remarkable things in her travels, or perhaps, 'things happen' because she attends to them.

If the Van Project had tested established method and practice against a contemporary cultural assemblage, my thesis would – through processes of attentive walking, looking, listening, recording, writing and rewriting – attempt to address both the necessity and intractability of any and all contemporary archaeology. I did not arrive at my thesis questions all at once, or, in all probability, any *answers* at all. Rather, as a mature student with no vested interest in reputation or career, I came to feel I should have, *must have*, sufficient courage to question, journey and fail. I had formulated and abandoned several project designs as implausible or unrealistic, concluding that rather than setting specific research questions my research should be to discover which ones to ask.

So, while floundering with little guiding theory and even less idea of method, I more or less clung onto an initial framework – a life-raft that would involve subjective, objective and collective textual/audio/visual/material 'points-of-view'. And perhaps a methodological logjam eventually broke while making my usual pedestrian way to our department. I encountered an unwound spool of C90 cassette tape snaking suggestively across a Bristol pavement (see Figure 11.2). After a career lifetime spent spooling through, biting short-ends for a quick change, tasting and spitting, and otherwise wrestling with miles of ferrous-oxide tape, this, apparently mischievous, unspooling of a then recently defunct, standardized mass-recording medium of the late, last millennium captured my attention. It must mean something. Or, perhaps, it was my very attention, that of a by then self-styled media-archaeologist with an early twenty-first-century phone-camera in his pocket and a thesis to think about that called an insignificant, if totemic, scrap of obsolescent, composite material into significance. In many ways my unappreciated street performance re-enacted a standard archaeological transformation.

Figure 11.2 Tape tangle on a Bristol street. Photo by author.

Archaeologists notice things

And if this transient trace of something-that-happened-in-the-world seemed some sort of a personal and professional touchstone, it was also a cultural marker of abrupt and profound socio-technological change from analogue to digital, material to virtual, from a transmittable though geographically situated, electro-chemically fixed message to random access memory (RAM) somewhere/nowhere-special in cyberspace.

And as I write this a message flashes up on my screen announcing that support for the iconic Blackberry phone is to end tomorrow.

It seems that archaeologies of the contemporary era exist only when noticed. I began to record every piece of media-related stuff I subsequently encountered during routine walks (see Figure 11.3). These were photographed with my phone exactly as found in their deposited context. I did not collect or disturb any found object, tape, CD, earphone, wiring, TV, aerial, boom-box, with just a single exception. And after deliberation I decided against using intrusive scale markers in any photograph. I identified some indeterminate artefact as distributed across Random Access Memory, landfill, memory farm, sewage system, World Wide Web, as material and virtual stuff existing simultaneously across time and space. The context might now be considered as my early Samsung digital phone or digital bytes, bites and nibbles, or not.

The exception to my self-imposed 'no touch' rule was suggested by my second only find. This was a manuscript left next to waste bins on a London estate. I had chanced upon a rejected and very recently abandoned proposal for a television script written by a well-known and (usually) highly successful writer of historical/mythological TV yarns (see Figure 11.4). This one was for a prospective TV series featuring the adventures of a very unlikely team of maritime archaeologists. Although initially unaware of any significance for my research, I did pick up this

Figure 11.3 CRT television as overnight archaeology. Photo by author.

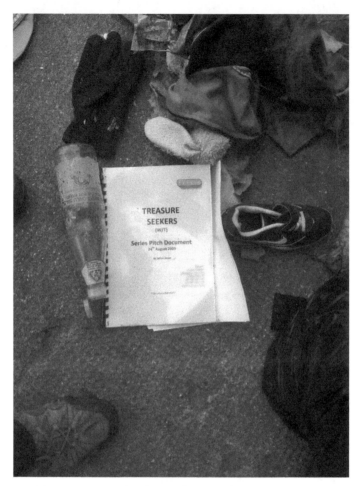

Figure 11.4 TV script proposal and part of scatter. Photo by author.

abandoned binder marked 'strictly confidential' (which remains in my possession). I photographed but then left the small surrounding scatter of material intact and untouched. On examination, this immediate context consisted of women's high-heeled court-shoes, sports or runners' shoes of approximately the same size, one Apple computer promotional or instructional booklet, a single photo (male subject tilted off-centre) of what appeared to be a 'holiday scene' of a man standing on a quay near a motorboat and water-skis, a white lace garter belt, what appears to be a small black brassiere or corset with white pearl buttons, a red-and-black fleece or sports-top garment next to a fluffy sock or slipper and a single black woollen glove. A badly deteriorated cardboard box from which the entire assemblage could have spilled lay near the middle of these items. The whole group was bisected by a long length of thin cane (which I failed to notice until writing this). An empty bottle with badly deteriorated label, later identified as 'Healthy Boy Thai Sweet Chilli Sauce 700ML', lay immediately below the TV pitch document bearing the provisional title of 'Treasure Seekers'.

Although having mentioned this find in print more than once, I have so far respected the author's injunction for privacy. This extraordinary find that a mischievous universe seemed to have put my way on that particular day seemed too much to process. While perhaps redolent of a single turbulent domestic episode, reminding me somewhat of melancholy in a hurriedly abandoned council flat, if I ever wrote further, I might (with the understanding of the script's author) look more to Kurt Vonnegut than Buchli and Lucas. Greatly encouraged, nevertheless, by a strange turn of events I continued my purposeful meander to encounter objects that stored, transmitted or received electronic messages.

Following Joanna Ulin (2009) and her pursuit of family archaeology, I went on to rummage through stuff around or near home, trusting to put together a highly personal auto-archaeological assemblage. I then called on the montage of Eisenstein (1994) and the reflexive Kino-eye of Dziga Vertov (1984) – like generations of diligent film students – to construct a subjective video account of ancestry, childhood and self. At any event, I found that while clinging to truth, and even if awkward, painful or indeed seemingly transgressive, archaeologists of the contemporary world cannot write their own person out of the collective story of us.

Lastly, I recorded ideas of heritage from communities – early morning park-drinkers, unsanctioned graffitists, outsider and pavement artists, street musicians, panhandlers and rough sleepers, food delivery cyclists, Vietnamese nail bar and Jamaican hair stylists, Gujarati grocers and Afghani 'pound-shop' proprietors, and north London's foremost and most approachable wig-makers – whose opinion from the 'cultural margins' is not generally sought or necessarily even noticed. Yet I learned the heritage that these people valued was not predominately 'museum quality' artefact or national monument (though my Afghani shopkeeper lamented the destruction of the Bamiyan Buddhas). Rather, it was a family memento, photograph, piece of hand-me-down jewellery, bicycle, pair of vintage curling tongs or street-tag of a fondly remembered artist that carried significance for these others. A distraught father sitting beneath a railway bridge had created a small shrine of photographs, letters and trinkets around his sleeping bag and a small pile of clothes. His valued heritage was declared to be a few finger rings manufactured from the ashes of his dead son. In small things – of little monetary value, no great antiquity but great personal significance – remembered. And once again I was reminded both of a professional duty of care and the particular responsibilities of any proposed archaeology of our own era.

Promising pages

An interaction with the public was subject to the necessary institutional guidelines and standard ethnographic protocol. But as with every archaeologist of the mundane, there were few, if any, rules for dealings with potentially vulnerable people, our own litter or even my own domestic detritus. Nevertheless, while I found no field manual and little other instruction in how to approach archaeology of street, shelf or self (apart from repeating an internal mantra of 'do no harm'), I did find readings that allowed me to make some sense of my wandering work. While not offering a how-to-do street manual, these at least each offered a way forward and gave permission to think and write about myself, people and things. If my wayfinding practice was initially prompted by the discarded object itself, and a method of attentive wandering was largely habitual, theory arrived piecemeal from a variety of thinkers and a variety of disciplines, and in its own time.

We might trace a theoretical spark for British contemporary archaeology to David Clarke and his impressive succession of University of Cambridge students. In his *Antiquity* paper, 'Archaeology: The Loss of Innocence' (1972), Clarke famously defined archaeology as 'what archaeologists do'. Here I have always understood this most reflective and reflexive archaeologist to be advocating a 'total archaeology' unconfined by convention, routine, apparatus or, indeed, era. I found it significant that Ian Hodder, surely Clarke's intellectual successor for archaeology and theory at Cambridge, completed the circle in providing the foreword to *Re-Constructing Archaeology*. In this, the work of his former Cambridge students Shanks and Tilley, Hodder credits David Clarke as introducing completely new paradigms along with his New Archaeology. I remember later reading Ian Hodder's 'Bow ties and pet foods' (1987), his own contribution to his book on *The Archaeology of Contextual Meanings*, published the same year as the black and red books. Hodder's writing was offered by my own MA tutor Dan Hicks as part of an informal Bristol anthropology reading group. I now consider such structured reading and discussion groups (of which I experienced far too few) as of the greatest benefit for teaching and learning.

Although I cannot now remember exactly (or at all) what I understood by it, and my notes only exist, if at all, on some forgotten memory disc, unreadable hard drive or data farm in Nevada or Mumbai, or as idealized abstractions of machine storage scattered elsewhere, I had already toyed with the idea of a 'quantum archaeology'. I was ready when Angela Piccini introduced me to Karen Barad and *Meeting the Universe Halfway: Quantum Physics and the Entanglement of Matter and Meaning* (2007). Here Barad argues convincingly for Neils Bohr's understandings of indeterminacy and the affective, co-dependent relationship of observer, experimental set-up, individual components and equipment as forming the resulting outcome. While my generation of research students were already quite familiar with the Actor Network Theory (ANT) of Bruno Latour (1993) and John Law (1994), here Barad extends intra-relational networks beyond the socio-material to some fundamental reality of nature. This is a book to read before lifting a trowel, pushing a wheelbarrow, taking a level and certainly before writing a report.

Barad would suggest that the experimenter/archaeologist is not just adjunct to or complicit in her investigation – she is herself an element in the experimental apparatus that is theory, site, context, theodolite, funding, wheelbarrow, institution, spoil-heap, use-wear of trowel, nature of breakfast, group well-being and so on, that together creates a new cut in reality (Barad 2007: 145, 174, 217).

With every justification from these and other authors, however, I was still concerned about 'finding' theory to hand when required during, or even after, the event. Fortunately, I found my decidedly odd workflow underwritten by Grounded Theory. Here was support for, or at least a recognition of, practice preceding or helping to coalesce theory. Appropriately enough my practice of attentive meander was well underway before stumbling on the works of Bryant and Charmaz (2007; and Charmaz 2010). So too with anthropologist Tim Ingold (2007) and his writings on tracks, traces and environment, whose description of wayfinding seemed to chime well with my own extemporized praxis.

I own a (for me, unusually abused) first English edition of *A Thousand Plateaus: Capitalism and Schizophrenia* (Deleuze and Guattari 2004) and had already been tunnelling through its metaphorical thickets for several years before embarking on my thesis (see Figure 11.5). The book has become a familiar text to social science and creative arts students. But in my experience many archaeologists might struggle with the book's dense and opaque language. Despite my advocacy of this book as a possible lifeline for doers and makers drowning in limitless possibility, my own archaeologist/auteur(e) postgraduate

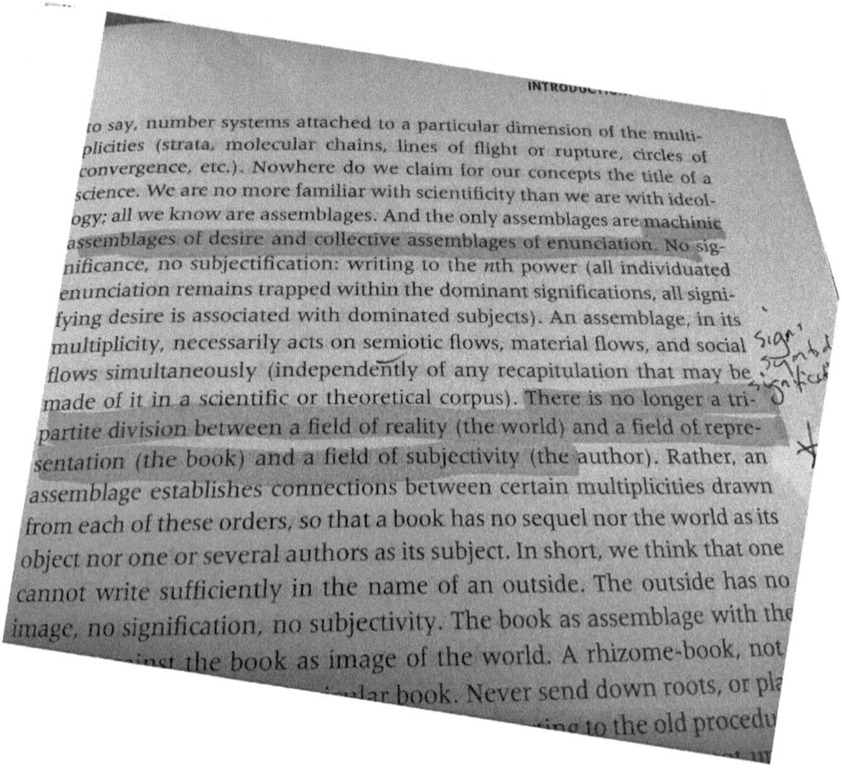
INTRODUC...

to say, number systems attached to a particular dimension of the multiplicities (strata, molecular chains, lines of flight or rupture, circles of convergence, etc.). Nowhere do we claim for our concepts the title of a science. We are no more familiar with scientificity than we are with ideology; all we know are assemblages. And the only assemblages are machinic assemblages of desire and collective assemblages of enunciation. No significance, no subjectification: writing to the *n*th power (all individuated enunciation remains trapped within the dominant significations, all signifying desire is associated with dominated subjects). An assemblage, in its multiplicity, necessarily acts on semiotic flows, material flows, and social flows simultaneously (independently of any recapitulation that may be made of it in a scientific or theoretical corpus). There is no longer a tripartite division between a field of reality (the world) and a field of representation (the book) and a field of subjectivity (the author). Rather, an assemblage establishes connections between certain multiplicities drawn from each of these orders, so that a book has no sequel nor the world as its object nor one or several authors as its subject. In short, we think that one cannot write sufficiently in the name of an outside. The outside has no image, no signification, no subjectivity. The book as assemblage with the ... the book as image of the world. A rhizome-book, not ... book. Never send down roots, or pl... to the old procedu...

Figure 11.5 Page 25, *A Thousand Plateaus* (defaced in desperation). Photo by author.

students were in open revolt against considering the poetic allusion of the book's short opening chapter as of any potential use. Their revulsion was perhaps due to some earlier admonition to always write archaeology simply and clearly. But I take comfort where I can. And for me, and recalcitrant writers/creators/explorers everywhere, this opening section, and in particular the concept of the *rhizome* and a nomadic routine of research granted permission for me to continue my wandering work.

On the surface of things

A final writing that, if not quite guided, allowed me to choose from multiple pathways was a discussion led by Rodney Harrison (2011) in the journal *Archaeological Dialogues*. 'Surface assemblages: towards archaeology in and of the present', a paper that addressed the near unanswerable, but specifically archaeological, questions surrounding the recording, reporting or otherwise noticing our encounters with our public waste in our public spaces was to the point. Harrison's central question – how to attend archaeologically to the surface scatter of our own making – and insightful though questioning replies by his respondents helped cohere my own thoughts as to the possible role of any archaeo-*flâneur*. It seemed to me that in a sea of every-thing, the problem remains firstly one of selection. The researcher could select from a well-defined, finite class of objects: pandemic-era facemasks; cigarette butts; street tags. Or she might examine, or reflect on, things tied to, or resulting from, a particular event: the closure of Woolworths or the BHS store chain; discards and perhaps lost hopes from a political campaign; remnants from some memorable sporting event (though in all these cases we note how abruptly the contemporary becomes historical). In my case, I had already chosen a theme or broadly defined category of things to care about. And by embracing, rather than despairing over, the wonderfully chancy business of archaeology, I knew not just what class of things to look for, but perhaps how to look and even how I might begin to think about them.

Choreographing chance

Cornelius Holtorf (2002) has written of the *chaîne opératoire* of a potsherd as extending beyond its manufacture, use, deposit, excavation and recording to its accession and storage in a shoebox on a museum shelf. Meanwhile media archaeologist Jussi Parrika (2015) would extend the existential 'life' of things far back into geological time. But I first took interest in the notion of agency extended between different biological entities on reading Richard Dawkins and *The Extended Phenotype* (1982). From such very different disciplines and perspectives, each of these writings suggests that organic and non-organic things continue equally to affect through time and space.

I must then return to Alfred Gell and his theory of mind extended through and between people and things, Karen Barad with Bohr's interpretation of an intra-dependent physical reality, Latour's Actor Network Theory and the *rhizome* of Deleuze and Guattari, all of which suggest that, rather than being a primary feature, boundaries are always constructed.

And if my shuffling along pavements and poking around all sorts of stuff had foregrounded this trite yet profound truth, it also seemed to me that archaeology was in the business of marking boundaries. I would then begin to think about boundary-making through and with my very own 'colossal congress of stuff and things' (Marx Brothers poster for *At the Circus* 1939).

Taking my chance

For me, writing contemporary archaeology is always first-person – I am complicit – while enacting/embodying it always leads elsewhere. If it is invariably discomforting when distance in time or exotic culture collapses and the unshielded archaeologist of nowadays is confronted with her own self, surely this now could/should become a timely validation of the discipline as a whole. It has become clear to me that we can no longer remove ourselves from all culpability in celebrating monuments to long-dead tyrants (even if bemoaning the quality of life of their subjects) while failing to properly engage with the results of past tyranny and past progress today. Their very practice implicates every archaeologist in the consequences of past and future events. However uncomfortable it might be, with archaeologies-of-now the personal is written in. I must agree with Carol Hanish that 'the personal is political'.

From Harrison (2011) I understood that to impose standard archaeological method on my street-ephemera would be a retreat into mimetic institutional security. Whereas with readings from anthropology, documentary film studies, social science and physics, I realized a possible interconnectedness in an extended agential framework of human and non-human actors. While a nomadic approach with the wayfinding of Tim Ingold and particularly the ever-continuing, chthonic *rhizome* of Deleuze and Guattari offered ways to act if not specific pathways to follow.

But without the trappings of trowel, trench and tape and the quiet comfort of an uncritical dead as central to our discipline, what remains of archaeology as commonly understood? The answer remains that archaeology supplies the material for and the platform from which we might think about and comment on the entirety of human/material/natural co-production through time (Olsen et al. 2012). To divorce material culture studies from archaeology is to lose this temporal context. Nor, I believe, should we insist on setting some arbitrary terminus for our discipline, stranded somewhere between Victorian propriety and the 'Roaring 'Twenties' or perhaps last century's two world wars? Neither a chronocentric outlook uncritically valuing the superiority of our own times nor a dehumanized past fixed as fact in 'archaeological cultures' will quite do.

What to learn?

While 'attending to things' we surely must instigate then learn from diverse, critical dialogue. This call for an inclusive, informed debate on the future of archaeologies of the present era goes largely unanswered by sceptics or those hostile to the very idea. But we surely need to have ongoing conversations with both the unconvinced and those who feel their hostility to our sub-field requires little justification. And if such a symposium were ever to be organized, I would argue that far from diminishing archaeology, such messy, partial, impertinent archaeologies-of-us might endorse and complete the whole enterprise as an integrated, serious discipline. For this research to progress we will doubtless be required to adopt or adapt our method to particular circumstances. This is perhaps the first instruction for those new to the field. And if these students might not have the literary gift of a Baudelaire or Benjamin, they no doubt carry a mobile phone with which to record notes and pictures and attend to things they encounter. I would also note that we nomadic archaeologists have access to centuries of disciplinary knowledge and millennia of the human story that gentlemen *flâneurs* could only imagine. While our colleagues studying the distant past might strive to write human lives into their narrative in studying modern material-culture, we must not write them out. As we embark on our work, we must talk to people who use, inhabit, know or neglect these things-of-ours. With contemporary archaeology, ethnographic interview might inform rather more than stratigraphic analysis.

There are few formulae to teach such wayward archaeology as I describe. But to wonder how things-happen-to-be in a particular place and in a context that the researcher herself inhabits and influences requires careful honesty and honest reflexivity. And while, on reflection, there is as much wonder in any discarded thing as there is in a rejected TV treatment, this learning is, of its nature, endless. All these things become archaeology as we archaeologists – real-life 'Treasure Seekers' – write about them. As I do and learn here. Archaeology remains what archaeologists do.

References

Bailey, G. (2006), 'In Transit' (video), *Archaeology Channel*, https://www.archaeologychannel.org/video-guide-summary/258-in-transit.

Bailey, G. (2017), 'Views and soundings: marking boundaries for archaeological practice', PhD thesis, University of Bristol.

Bailey, G., C. Newland, A. Nilsson and J. Schofield (2009), 'Transit, Transition: Excavating J641 VUJ', *Cambridge Archaeological Journal* 19 (1): 1–27.

Barad, K. (2007), *Meeting the Universe Halfway: Quantum Physics and the Entanglement of Matter and Meaning*, Durham, NC, and London: Duke University Press.

Bryant, A. and K. Charmaz, eds (2007), *The SAGE Handbook of Grounded Theory*, London: SAGE.

Buchli, V. and G. Lucas, eds (2001), *Archaeologies of the Contemporary Past*, London: Routledge.

Charmaz, K. (2010), 'Grounded Theory as Emergent Method', in S. Nagy Hesse-Biber and P. Levy, eds, *Handbook of Emergent Methods*, 155–70, New York: Guilford Press.

Clarke, D. (1972), 'Archaeology: The Loss of Innocence', *Antiquity* 47: 6–18.

Contemporary and Historical Archaeology in Theory, https://chat-arch.org/about-chat.

Dawkins, R. (1982), *The Extended Phenotype*, Oxford: Oxford University Press.

Deleuze, G. and F. Guattari (2004), *A Thousand Plateaus: Capitalism and Schizophrenia*, trans. B. Massumi, London and New York: Continuum.

Edgeworth, M., ed. (2006), *Ethnographies of Archaeological Practice: Cultural Encounters Material Transformations*, Oxford: Altamira.

Eisenstein, S. (1994), *Towards a Theory of Montage*, trans. Michael Glenny, ed. M. Glenny and R. Taylor, London: British Film Institute.

Gell, A. (1998), *Art and Agency*, Oxford: Oxford University Press.

Gould, R. and M. B. Schiffer, eds (1981), *Modern Material Culture: The Archaeology of Us*, New York: Academic Press.

Harrison, R. (2011), 'Surface assemblages: towards archaeology in and of the present', *Archaeological Dialogues* 18 (2): 141–61.

Hodder, I. (1987), 'Bow ties and pet foods: material culture and change in British Industry', in I. Hodder, ed., *The Archaeology of Contextual Meanings*, 11–19, Cambridge: Cambridge University Press.

Holtorf, C. (2002), 'Notes on the Life of a Potsherd', *Journal of Material Culture* 7: 49–71.

Ingold, T. (2007), *The Perception of the Environment: Essays in Livelihood, Dwelling and Skill*, Abingdon: Routledge.

Latour, B. (1993), *We Have Never Been Modern*, Cambridge, MA: Harvard University Press.

Law, J. (1994), *Organizing Modernity*, Oxford: Blackwell.

Olivier, L. (2001), 'The archaeology of the contemporary past', in V. Buchli and G. Lucas, eds, *Archaeologies of the Contemporary Past*, 175–88, London: Routledge.

Olsen, B., M. Shanks, T. Webmoor and C. Witmore (2012), *Archaeology: The Discipline of Things*, London: University of California Press.

Parrika, J. (2015), *A Geology of Media*, Minnesota: University of Minnesota Press.

Shanks, M. (2022), weblog 'Beer Cans', https://web.stanford.edu/~mshanks/MichaelShanks/65.html.

Shanks, M. and C. Tilley (1987), *Re-Constructing Archaeology: Theory and Practice*, Cambridge: Cambridge University Press.

Ulin, J. (2009), 'Into the Space of the Past: A Family Archaeology', in C. Holtorf and A. Piccini, eds, *Contemporary Archaeologies: Excavating Now*, 145–60, Frankfurt: Peter Lang.

Vertov, D. (1984), *Kino-Eye: The Writings of Dziga Vertov*, trans. K O'Brien, ed. A. Michelson, Berkeley and Los Angeles: University of California Press.

12

Education Is Life: Collective Experiences of Practising the Archaeology of the Contemporary Past in a Conservative Atmosphere

Maryam Dezhamkhooy and Leila Papoli-Yazdi

Introduction: a brief history of Iranian archaeology

As David Harvey states (2008: 19), 'when writing histories of institutions, one would, ideally, like to start at the beginning'. Archaeology is an imported commodity in Iran (Papoli-Yazdi and Garazhian 2012). Contracts with French archaeologists were signed by the Iranian king, Naser al-Din Shah (r. 1848–96), in the nineteenth century (Abdi 2001: 53), but later these contracts would be cancelled after the establishment of the Pahlavi dynasty in 1925 (Grigor 2018: 125). Raised between the two world wars, Reza Shah Pahlavi (r. 1925–41), the new king, commanded that the contracts with European countries be cancelled or reviewed. On 18 October 1927, just two years after the accession of Reza Shah, the French archaeological permission in Iran that had been granted forty-three years earlier was abolished (Nasiri-Moghaddam 2013: 121).

Reza Sah established a 'male nationalism; as all nationalisms are gendered' (McClintock 1993: 63); the representation of male national power played a critical role in his agenda and the development of archaeology in Iran. From the 1930s onwards, archaeologists and experts from other countries were invited to work in Iran. These included Ernst Emil Herzfeld, German by birth but a naturalized US citizen; the French architect, historian and archaeologist Andre Godard; and the American art historian and art dealer Arthur Upham Pope (Grigor 2018: 123; see Miles 1952). The French archaeologists, who were otherwise pushed to the margins, managed to take control of the National Museum of Iran, which was designed and built by Andre Godard (Gran-Aymerich and Marefat 2012).

The government and local elites established a kind of heritage modernity that was founded on ancient Iran's ruins and focused on museum archaeology (Grigor 2018: 122). Meanwhile, German and French archaeologists excavated significant landmarks such as Persepolis, Pasargadae and Chogha Zanbil between 1927 and 1979 (Mousavi 2013). Perhaps one of the most significant developments in Iranian archaeology during the reign of Reza Shah was the establishment of the Department of Archaeology at the University of Tehran (hereafter UT) in 1937 (Abdi 2001: 62), with the specific purpose of training experts to monitor the archaeological activities of foreigners (see Fallahfar 2016). A draft law of six articles was written and sent to the National Consultative Assembly to be adopted as the Antiquities Law (Ghanoun-e Atiqat), which was finally passed in 1931 (Nasiri Moghaddam 2013).

The knowledge of 'history' has a deep background in Iran. History overshadowed archaeology from the first arrival of the discipline in Iran in the late 1880s. The title of the discipline 'archaeology' was translated as the word 'bastan-shenasi', which literally means 'to understand/study ancient times' by a group of intellectuals who worked at the Academy of Persian Language and Literature, established by Reza Shah (see Bayat 1991). The very first archaeology courses were largely art-history-based and were influenced by the ideologies of the nationalist government. The early professors in the department played a crucial role in promoting nationalism in Iranian archaeology (Abdi 2001: 62).

During the 1940s and 1950s, more than half of the professors teaching in the department were from art history or history backgrounds. But in the late 1970s, the education system in Iranian archaeology was completely transformed. The syllabi were reviewed by Ezat Negahban, known as the father of modern Iranian archaeology (Negahban 2005), who was the head of the Department of Archaeology at the University of Tehran, and some other archaeologists who had studied archaeology in the US and were influenced by the New Archaeology. They revised the syllabi, added multiple courses on theoretical and methodological issues, and proposed twenty modules for field training. However, Negahban had to keep some of the art-history courses since some of the professors from the older generation had no skills to teach the modern syllabi and were opposed to such a change.

It is worth noting that Negahban intentionally endeavoured to strengthen prehistoric archaeology, as the nationalist agenda of the Pahlavi government had focused on the ancient Iranian empires. In 1971 this nationalist archaeology culminated in one of the most fantastic political uses of ancient ruins, when the last king of Iran celebrated the 2,500th anniversary of the institution of the Persian monarchy at Persepolis (Grigor 2018: 122).

After the Islamic Revolution of 1979, archaeology was attacked as royalist knowledge until a version of Shiite-nationalist archaeology emerged, supported by the government, an archaeology which ignored and still ignores pedagogic principles. In a nutshell, the art-history courses expanded while the syllabus of courses such as 'evolution' and 'theory and method in archaeology' were changed and courses such as 'the archaeology of Quran' were introduced to intensify the Islamization of humanities.

Like other fields within the humanities, archaeology was also under pressure from the Islamists in the first decade after the Revolution. The archaeology institutions were closed and sites were in danger of destruction both by fundamentalists and by the impacts of the Iran–Iraq War (see Papoli-Yazdi and Garazhian 2012). After the 2005 presidential election the discipline was again targeted by the government to produce a biased and monolithic history. The last generation of archaeologists who had developed modern archaeology in Iran was fired and, in some cases, threatened with death by the revolutionary regime (Dezhamkhooy, Papoli-Yazdi and Garazhian 2015; Van der Van 2017). The Islamists and archaeologists close to the new regime could establish their new archaeology, which was a combination of the Islamization of courses, nationalism and ethnocentrism. It is not surprising that this kind of archaeology systemically ignored minorities, women, and people of colour.

Contemporary archaeology is not archaeology!

Here, through telling our own story, we would like to open a debate on how alternative ways of teaching and pursuing education in archaeology can not only provide students and instructors with new scientific perspectives, but also help academics to introduce changes in the dominant discourse of knowledge practice and reinforce academic freedom. We started our journey on 26 December 2003, when the city of Bam was destroyed by a dramatic earthquake (Dezhamkhooy and Papoli-Yazdi 2010). On 26 December 2003 Bam was reduced to ruins by an earthquake in just twelve seconds. Approximately 40,000 people died, 30,000 were injured (Tahmasebi et al. 2005) and 100,000 were made homeless (Mann 2005: 3). At that time, we were young students of archaeology at UT who were very frustrated and dissatisfied with the nationalistic (Dezhamkhooy and Papoli-Yazdi 2018) and male-dominated archaeology. The ethnoarchaeology and contemporary archaeology projects of post-earthquake Bam (Papoli-Yazdi, Garazhian and Dezhamkhooy 2013) showed us that the possibilities existed to practice archaeology in a very different way.

Gradually we became familiar with some other students who were also dissatisfied with the syllabi and the basic foundational concepts of Iranian archaeology. From this, we built our research network and called it GAP END, including the first letters of the name of the core members (Dezhamkhooy and Papoli-Yazdi 2020). Omran Garazhian and Leila were PhD candidates by then, while the other members were either MA or undergraduate students. From the very beginning, we insisted that GAP END was a circle with a flat hierarchy for the purpose of conducting discussions in a friendly atmosphere and learning from each other. Learning theory and methodology in our circle were accompanied by some field projects which were part of Leila's PhD dissertation, 'Disaster Archaeology: Material Culture, Context and Agency in Post-earthquake Bam (South-eastern Iran)' (2008).

The Bam project was co-directed by Omran Garazhian and Leila Papoli-Yazdi and supported by the Bam Citadel Foundation. The first challenge arose when we started to think about the methodological approach to studying contemporary society. It was the beginning of a five-year journey in archaeological method and theory. In the process we held friendly discussions and meetings to revise our strategy, as self-criticism and amendments were always part of our project. Gradually we moved from ethnoarchaeology, with its theoretical and methodological challenges, to the archaeology of the contemporary past (Dezhamkhooy and Papoli-Yazdi 2020).

The methodology we were practising was neither in the syllabi we had been taught at the university nor was it recognized by the Iranian Cultural Heritage Organization, the main authority responsible for archaeological field activities in Iran. Based on the Antiquities Law, the Iranian Cultural Heritage Organization (now the Ministry of Cultural Heritage, Tourism and Handicrafts) only considers objects and monuments more than 100 years old to be archaeological. Therefore, what we were doing was simply not defined as archaeology according to the law!

Working in Bam as a contemporary site significantly changed our attitudes towards archaeology, its scope and its methods. In 2005, Omran and Leila proposed to UT to replace two very old-fashioned courses with the archaeology of the contemporary past. The proposal got a negative response. The other attempts to convince Iranian archaeological departments to consider novel approaches in theory and methodology were left in the air. Eventually, after several failed attempts, we started to teach the archaeology of the contemporary past and some other methodologies of archaeology in spaces outside of state-controlled academia; we created our own understanding of academia, independent and open to new ideas. But it should be emphasized that it is tough to establish an academic discipline in the absence of support and outside of academia.

Unfortunately, over the past decade we were not only banned from teaching the archaeology of the contemporary past in academia but received very few field-work permissions from the Iranian authorities. As a matter of fact, the authorities consider the archaeology of the contemporary past to be irrelevant and troublemaking, while its agents and practitioners are accused of being anarchists who want to foment unrest among the students (Dezhamkhooy, Papoli-Yazdi and Garazhian 2015). In spite of these difficulties, we have tried to conduct projects which challenge the fundamental issues and crises in Iran and the region, such as conflict, oppression, women's rights and environmental challenges.

Our alternative ways of teaching the archaeology of the contemporary past

As mentioned above, we had already struggled with the conservative atmosphere of Iranian archaeology. Since 2005 and after the rise of Mahmoud Ahmadinejad, the Iranian conservative politician who served as the sixth president of Iran until 2013, many intellectuals and academics confronted increasing political pressure resulting in huge waves of dismissals. In such a chaotic environment, we soon realized that we needed to establish our own independent networks to survive. We developed a set of working strategies to teach interested students and create connections with other fields in the humanities, the public and academia outside Iran.

Home conferences: self-education/self-reflection in method and theory

The nationalists who supported the Ahmadinejad government used oppression and violence against intellectuals and the minority of academics who were interested in reforms and the establishment of democratic values. Alongside this political pressure, it was the attitudes of nationalist and conservative archaeologists that forced us to rethink our relationship with Iranian archaeology. From 2009, we rarely attended the national conferences. Our last participation in Iranian archaeological events turned unpleasant: the organizers either rejected our work or when we got the opportunity to attend, we received negative and even offensive feedback. Overall, we confronted serious difficulties in sharing our studies and research.

Therefore, we organized conferences and workshops in our own homes. In late 2009, we started to hold regular home conferences. The conferences were held in Leila and Omran's house in Neyshabur city and once, in 2015, in Maryam's apartment in Tehran. From 2009 to 2012, the conferences were held once a season. Like any other conferences, the home conferences had programmes as well as abstracts and roundtables. The main participants were archaeology students, but we also invited scholars and researchers from related disciplines who were not members of GAP END at the time. The home conferences helped us create a network: a small but active community of students and researchers interested in alternative ways of thinking and observing the world.

Workshops and performances

After losing our jobs as professors, we started to look for a method that could serve to educate the public and non-archaeologists. Paulo Freire's books (1970, 1976, 1978) were translated into Persian in the 1970s and have influenced many teachers who educate the public in Iran. In one of our home conferences, it was proposed that we re-read Freire's *Pedagogy of the Oppressed* (1970).

According to Paulo Freire (1978), the purpose of education is to liberate human potential. Step by step, we adopted the framework from Freire's *Pedagogy of the Oppressed* in our work. Our experience of oppression in academia bound us together with other oppressed groups and individuals, including dismissed professors, student, and activists, helping us to strengthen our network and learn how to resist and survive.

In the second step, we familiarized ourselves with the work of Augusto Boal, an educator under the influence of Freire, and his work on the Theater of the Oppressed (TO) (2000), which is a set of dramatic techniques whose purpose is to bring to light systemic exploitation and oppression in common situations and to allow spectators to become actors. TO encourages minorities and the public to open debates on the brutal mechanisms of oppression. Remarkably, Boal's method has been developed efficiently for amateurs and can be performed by people of different body forms and ages and those with disabilities. These elements are the bedrock of the Theater of the Oppressed.

Theatre has already been used in archaeology (Pearson and Shanks 2001; Pearson and Thomas 1994) as a sophisticated means to interpret the materialistic world or to reconstruct human beings' lives from an archaeological perspective. In the absence of any other possibilities, we applied TO to the expression of oppression and our points of view about archaeology. The very first time we used Boal's method was in a theatre performance, *No one is in the garden!*, which was a free understanding of how an opposition group gathered and managed to rise and live in the Neshat Garden in the early twentieth century under Reza Shah's dictatorship (Papoli-Yazdi, Dezhamkhooy and Naeimi 2013). We staged our performance in Zahedan in 2012 at the fourth international conference of the Society of South Asia Archaeology. As expected, our novel method was not taken seriously by the archaeologists but showed us that there were alternative means of dialogue with the public.

During the following years, we applied a combination of Boal's and Freire's pedagogies. According to Paolo Vittoria (2019), Paulo Freire theorized and practised the transformation of educational relationships by overcoming the teacher–student dichotomy. From Freire's perspective, traditional content should be replaced by topics for discussion, as dialogue facilitates a critical process of social consciousness. In Boal's experimental action, spaces open up where the spectators metaphorically break the 'fourth wall' – in theatrical terms, the symbolic barrier between stage and audience – to directly participate and intervene in the action.

From the long list of Boal's techniques, we found the rainbow of desire (1994) to be one of the most useful exercises in terms of archaeological education. The rainbow of desire is a performance technique which replays situations from everyday life and reveals invisible elements of our relationships, such as mind obstacles, oppression, beliefs, desires and the relationship with the material world. We designed several exercises based on Boal's book. One activity is to ask students to take selfies in front of a monument or historical object. They can ask the other students to join them while taking selfies, smiling, laughing or doing any other 'face'. These exercises help the participants to achieve a clearer picture of their own understanding of archaeological objects and museums. Each play encourages the participants to ask more questions about their own reactions, their beliefs and the history of the mechanisms of oppression.

From 2012 to 2019, the GAP END members practised the above-mentioned pedagogy to educate different groups and age ranges, from students studying in elementary schools to middle-aged people, in multiple workshops in Bushehr (two workshops for elementary and high school students), Mashhad (three workshops for Afghan refugees, one workshop for the students of social sciences), Tehran (two workshops at UT, two workshops at the University of Culture and Science, one workshop for artists), Kerman (a workshop for the public), Sabzevar (a two-day archaeology event) and Zahedan (one workshop for teachers and one for the public) (see Figures 12.1 and 12.2). At the same time, Omran Garazhian regularly practised the Boal–Freire pedagogy in teaching his undergraduate students at the University of Neyshabour.

Making a network abroad

Gradually, we realized that working within such a conservative and oppressive atmosphere is very difficult. We needed to initiate dialogues to develop our ideas and methodologies for studying the modern world and to keep our knowledge

Figure 12.1 *No one is in the garden!*, Zahedan University, 2012. From left: Mariam Naeemi, Omran Garazhian and Arman Masoudi. Painting: Ali Roustaeeyanfard.

Education Is Life 233

Figure 12.2 *No one is in the garden!*, Zahedan University, 2012. From left: Leila Papoli-Yazdi, Maryam Dezhamkhooy and Arman Masoudi. Painting: Ali Roustaeeyanfard.

up to date. Therefore, we decided to change our strategy and make connections abroad. We mainly released our works in Persian, as we believed that we should change the conservative atmosphere, but Iranian journals did not appreciate our ideas. We changed our publication strategy and started writing more in English. It is also worth noting that we co-authored with students, especially masters and PhD candidates. We held debates before and during the writing process, which played a significant role in their learning. In addition, we corresponded with colleagues abroad who practised the sub-field and participated in international archaeological events. Though we had no opportunity to discuss our works as course materials, some articles of ours have received consideration from academia around the world (e.g., Dezhamkhooy and Papoli-Yazdi 2010, 2012; Papoli-Yazdi 2010).

Publications and events for the public

We strongly believe that archaeology should establish a dialogue with the public. We know that archaeology is produced in the present and is influenced by, and simultaneously influences, contemporary society. One result of our home conferences was a book written in Persian for the public called *Patchwork Archaeology* (Garazhian et al. 2014). The book introduces archaeological methods, theory, the history of archaeology in Iran and the branches of archaeology, and proposes how archaeology as a discipline can be involved in making the world a better place. *Patchwork Archaeology* was published online alongside the paper version, and has been downloaded over 25,000 times. After the Taliban took control of Afghanistan, we started to run online teaching to undergraduate students, and it was then we were told that *Patchwork Archaeology* had been widely read by students of archaeology in Afghanistan and was introduced by the professors to the first-semester students.

We have also held several workshops, events and lectures for the public to assess the understanding and expectations of wider society and also to receive feedback. One prominent example of this was a lecture held for Bam inhabitants after excavating ruined houses. The active participation of the local people led to provocative discussions and interesting feedback that led our team to develop a proposal for a portable museum of the Bam earthquake. However, the project was never funded after the rise of conservatives to power.

In another attempt, archaeology days were held by Omran Garazhian and his team at Tell-e Damghani in Sabzevar, north-east Iran, in 2014 and 2015, where local people were invited to visit the site and attend lectures organized by the archaeologists. In the first year, more than 4,000 people visited the site; in the second year the attendance rose to more than 6,000 people. Later, the event was prohibited due to the authorities' concerns about the size of the public gathering. In response to the variety of groups participating in our events, we incorporated different pedagogies to meet various tastes and cultures. To practice the archaeology of the contemporary past the proposed pedagogy should be flexible in order to include the public, voiceless people and those seeking their own traces in history and society.

Discussion: the archaeology of the contemporary past as resistance

The aim of this overview of our projects has been twofold: first, to demonstrate the biased nature of knowledge production in Iranian archaeology and the marginal position of the sub-field of contemporary archaeology in the broader field of archaeology in Iran; and second, to share our experiences, particularly with colleagues who experience similar situations and difficulties in other countries, and to open a debate on concrete proposals and suggestions about pedagogy in the subject.

We are indeed an oppressed group in Iranian archaeology, but structural violence has different forms. It guarantees the interests of conservative stakeholders through the marginalization of different voices. The policies of conservative governments have resulted in the massive destruction of archaeological and heritage sites, and in students becoming frustrated and usually leaving the field. Essentially, the oppression of diversity in knowledge production has resulted in the marginalization of the field. It has turned archaeology into a discipline with far less value and efficacy in society and even in legal procedures, particularly in the case of heritage and archaeological sites.

Our efforts to gain the acceptance of the Iranian archaeological establishment failed, but we found a way to start a dialogue within and beyond academia on a broader scale. The archaeology of the contemporary past provided us with a methodology to discuss the dark side of the modern world and to place the challenges and dilemmas of Iranian society in their local and global contexts. The interdisciplinary methodology and multi-source approaches of the archaeology of the contemporary past allowed us to turn criticism into transformative action.

Generally, there are two sets of reactions to the introduction of the sub-field and GAP END activities during the last decade. As we have seen, conservative archaeology considers the archaeology of the contemporary past to be a competitor. At the same time, the public, especially marginalized groups such as the working class and minorities, feel that the sub-field is able to consider their untold stories and forgotten narratives. They hope to be heard and to be seen. As a matter of fact, one reason that GAP END activities were not able to continue was due to the fact that oppressed people acknowledge the archaeology of the contemporary past. They see it as a mirror that may reflect their pains and sufferings. During our garbage project in Tehran, the impoverished people of the poor neighbourhoods appreciated our work. They simply hoped and expected that we could do something – anything – to improve their life condition.

In a nutshell, official history and archaeology has largely ignored minorities, women, children, poor and homeless people, people of colour and the disabled. They have been pushed to the margins and sometimes officially do not even exist (see Salarvand 2020; Mohajerani and Heidari 2020). To these marginalized communities the archaeology of the contemporary past plays the role of a liberator. Indeed, the sub-field could bring the subaltern into the foreground. One suggestion for the archaeologists who work amidst conflict and tyranny is to consider the archaeology of the contemporary past. It is obvious that there is no room for the sub-field in the official departments in such contexts. Still, archaeologists may use various methods of pedagogy such as performance, dialogue and consideration of the daily life of the students as well as pedagogies of the oppressed. Our experiences show that such a dialogue can exist and thrive outside official spaces.

We remain a small and marginalized group in the archaeology of Southwest Asia, but our marginalization provides a unique perspective. The feminist scholar Silvana Colella (2018: 259) considers marginality a powerful position. Marginalized people have different experiences that lead to different ways of thinking and acting. As we have shown, in many cases knowledge can be situated and produced by those in positions of relatively lesser power. However, we do not simply want to acknowledge marginality, but rather to turn marginality to active resistance, what Colella calls 'the transformative power of a critique from the edges'.

References

Abdi, K. (2001), 'Nationalism, Politics, and the Development of Archaeology in Iran', *American Journal of Archaeology* 105 (1): 51–76.

Bayat, K. (1991), 'The First Academy of Persian Language and the Difficulties in Proposing the New Persian Words', *Nashr-e Danesh* 67: 48–51 (in Persian).

Boal, A. (1994), *The Rainbow of Desire: The Boal Method of Theatre and Therapy*, New York and London: Routledge.

Boal, A. (2000), *Theater of the Oppressed*, new edn, London: Pluto Press.

Colella, S. (2018), 'Not a Mere Tangential Outbreak: Gender, Feminism, and Cultural Heritage', *Il Capitale Culturale* 18: 251–75.

Dezhamkhooy, M. and L. Papoli-Yazdi (2010), 'The archaeology of last night . . . what happened in Bam (Iran) on 25–6 December 2003', *World Archaeology* 42 (3): 341–54.

Dezhamkhooy, M. and L. Papoli-Yazdi (2012), 'Breaking the Borders/Violating the Norms: An Archaeological Survey of an Intersex in a Traditional Society, Bam (South Eastern Iran)', *Sexuality & Culture* 17: 229–43.

Dezhamkhooy, M. and L. Papoli-Yazdi (2018), *Early Persian Empires: An Archaeological Deconstruction of Power Structures in Achaemenid and Sasanid Iran*, Oxford: Archaeopress.

Dezhamkhooy, M. and L. Papoli-Yazdi (2020), 'Unfinished narratives: some remarks on the archaeology of the contemporary past in Iran', *Archaeological Dialogues* 27 (1): 95–107.

Dezhamkhooy, M., L. Papoli-Yazdi and O. Garazhian (2015), 'All our findings are under their boots: the monologue of violence in Iranian Archaeology', in A. Gonzalez-

Ruibal and G. Moshenska, eds, *Ethics and the Archaeology of Violence*, 51–70, New York: Springer.

Fallahfar, S. (2016), *The Laws to Protect Antiquities and National Monuments*, Tehran: Avineh (in Persian).

Freire, P. (1970), *Pedagogy of the Oppressed*, New York, Continuum.

Freire, P. (1976), *Education, the Practice of Freedom*, London: Writers and Readers Publishing Cooperative.

Freire, P. (1978), *Pedagogy in Process: The Letters to Guinea-Bissau*, New York: Seabury Press.

Garazhian, O., L. Papoli-Yazdi, M. Dezhamkhooy, M. Naeemi and A. Masoudi (2014), *Patchwork Archaeology*, Isfahan: Zia Publishing (in Persian).

Gran-Aymerich, È. and M. Marefat (2012), 'Godard, André', *Encyclopædia Iranica* 11 (Fasc. 1): 29–31.

Grigor, T. (2018), 'They have not changed in 2500 years: art, archaeology, and modernity in Iran', in B. Effros and G. Lai, eds, *Unmasking Ideology in Imperial and Colonial Archaeology: Vocabulary, Symbols, and Legacy*, 121–46, Los Angeles: Cotsen Institute of Archaeology Press.

Harvey, D. (2008), 'The history of heritage', in B. Graham and P. Howard, eds, *The Ashgate Research Companions to Heritage and Identity*, 28–56, Farnham: Ashgate.

McClintock, A. (1993), 'Family Feuds: Gender, nationalism and the family', *Feminist Review* 44: 61–80.

Mann, P., ed. (2005), *Active Tectonics and Seismic Hazards of Puerto Rico, the Virgin Islands, and Offshore Areas*, Washington, DC: Geological Society of America.

Miles, G. C. (1952), *Archaeologica Orientalia in Memoriam Ernst Herzfeld*, New York: Glückstadt.

Mohajerani, M. and A. Heidari (2020), *The Outside of Tehran's Inside: Kahrizak*, Tehran: Kherad-e Sorkh (in Persian).

Mousavi, A. (2013), 'The History of Archaeological Research in Iran: A Brief Survey', in D. T. Potts, ed., *The Oxford Handbook of Ancient Iran*, 1–15, Oxford: Oxford University Press.

Nasiri-Moghaddam, N. (2013), 'Archaeology, and the Iranian National Museum: Qajar and early Pahlavi cultural policies', in B. Devos and C. Werner, eds, *Culture and Cultural Politics Under Reza Shah*, 121–48, New York and London: Routledge.

Negahban, E. (2005), *A Review of 50 years of Iranian Archaeology*, Tehran: Sobhane Noor (in Persian).

Papoli-Yazdi, L. (2008), 'Disaster Archaeology: Material Culture, Context and Agency in Post-earthquake Bam (South-eastern Iran)', PhD dissertation, University of Tehran (in Persian).

Papoli-Yazdi, L. (2010), 'Public and Private Lives in Iran: An Introduction to the Archaeology of the 2003 Bam Earthquake', *Archaeologies* 6: 29–47.

Papoli-Yazdi, L. (2020), 'Shadows of Pain: Instructions for Archaeologists Living Under Dictatorship', in J. Symonds and P. Vařeka, eds, *Archaeologies of Totalitarianism,*

Authoritarianism, and Repression: Dark Modernities, 199–217, London: Palgrave MacMillan.

Papoli-Yazdi, L., M. Dezhamkhooy and M. Naeimi (2013), 'A Report on a Party and the Guests: Archaeology of a Political Opposition, Iran, Neyshabour (1920–1940)', *Archaeologies* 9: 132–61.

Papoli-Yazdi, L. and O. Garazhian (2012), 'Archaeology as an Imported Commodity: A Critical Approach to the Position of Archaeology in Iran' [Archäologie als Importware. Ein kritischer Blick auf die Stellung der Archäologie in Iran], *Forum Kritische Archäologie* 1: 24–34.

Papoli-Yazdi, L., O. Garazhian and M. Dezhamkhooy (2013), 'Bam: archaeological and social investigations after the earthquake', in S. Monton-Subias, M. Carver and G. Bysserka, eds, *Encyclopedia of Global Archaeology*, 741–4, New York: Springer.

Pearson, M. and M. Shanks (2001), *Theatre/Archaeology*, London and New York: Routledge.

Pearson, M. and J. Thomas (1994), 'Theatre/Archaeology', *Drama Review* 38 (4): 133–61.

Salarvand, S. (2020), *It Was as if I Was Dumb: An Ethnography of Afghan Garbage Collector Teenagers in Tehran*, Tehran: Kherad-e Sorkh (in Persian).

Tahmasebi, M. N., K. Kiani, S. J. Mazlouman, A. Taheri, R. S. Kamrani, B. Panjavi and B. A. Harandi (2005), 'Musculoskeletal injuries associated with earthquake: a report of injuries of Iran's December 26, 2003 Bam earthquake casualties managed in tertiary referral centers', *Injury* 36 (1): 27–32.

Van der Van, A. (2017), '(De-)revolutionising the monuments of Iran', *Historic Environment* 29 (3): 16–29.

Vittoria, P. (2019), *Paulo Freire and Augustus Boal: Revolutionary Praxis in Theatre and Education*, London: Institute for Education Policy Studies.

Index

A Thousand Plateaus: Capitalism and Schizophrenia (Deleuze and Guattari) 22, 217–18, 219, 220
academia, teaching outside 228–9
accreditation, UK course 61–2
Aide Memoire Project, the 103, 105–9
Albers, Josef 21
'*An Talla*: Giving a Voice to the Voiceless' 25–6
anarchist pedagogies 187–9 (*see also* student-led learning)
anti-racist archaeology 134
Archaeologies of the Contemporary Past (Buchli and Lucas) 6, 109, 206–8
'Archaeology from Below' (Faulkner) 11–12
archival work 48–51, 67–9, 179
Art and Agency (Gell) 209
art and archaeology 21–35
Art and Social Practice MA (MA ASP) (UHI) 31–2
artefacts, lost in developments 141–3
Ashokan Reservoir 139–40
Assembling Archaeology (Cobb and Croucher) 3, 12, 22
assessment 20, 25, 67–8, 70–2, 93–7
Atash ('Our House' apartment) 191–3
Atchley, Wyatt 48, 54
autobiography 8–10 (*see also* biographies, object)

Bailey, Doug 22
Balbirnie stone circle 87–8
Balfarg complex 85–93
Balfarg Riding School 88–9
Bam 227–9, 234
Band, Lara, 'Lines of Rupture, Lines of Flight' 32
Barad, Karen 217, 219
Barclay, Gordon 88, 89
Bauhaus School 20–1
beer consumption 206

Beuys, Joseph 21
Bevan, Ann 24
biographies, object 8–10, 85, 109
Black Mountain College (BMC) 21
Bloomsbury 114–16, 119–25
Boal, Augusto 230–2
Bombing, A History of (Lindqvist) 118
bombsites 115, 119–24 (*see also* ordnance)
Bombsites of Bloomsbury walk 113–25
Brennan, Carmel, 'Letters to the Earth: Between Despair and Hope' 32
Buchli, Victor 6, 109, 206–8
budgets, university 43–4, 53

cable ties 2
campus archaeology 11, 41–57, 66–9, 72–3
catharsis 149
cellphones 101–10
cemeteries (graves) 136–8, 139, 142, 172, 173
Cerrato, A'ishah 135–6
children
  community participation 151, 156–8, 162
  'Our House' apartment 193, 194–5
chorography 54
Clark, L. K. 134
Clarke, David 216
climate crisis 32
Cobb, Hannah 3, 12, 22
Colella, Sylvana 236
collaboration, interdisciplinary 4–6, 19–20, 21–3, 34
collaborative learning 25, 66–7, 72, 134
colonialism 169–76
Comarmond, Nicolas 171–2
commercial archaeology 62
'Communicating Archaeology' course (University of York) 104

community archaeology 62, 133–4, 150, 172
community mapping 132–3, 135–7, 139–40 (*see also* walking)
community participation 151, 156–8, 162, 234
conflict archaeology 113, 125, 235–6 (*see also* dark heritage sites)
Contemporary Art and Archaeology MA (MA CAA) (UHI) 19–20, 23–6, 29–30, 33–5
Continental Commons retail complex 141–3
council houses 207
counter-mapping 133
course structure
    Durham University 63–6, 68, 70–1
    University of Glasgow 84–5
    University of North Dakota 42–5
    University of York 104
Covid-19 pandemic 4, 69, 83, 84, 196–7
Craft of Archaeology, The (Shanks and McGuire) 11–12
creative practice 21–35
critical ethnography 194
cross-generational learning 155–8, 159, 162
Croucher, Karina 3, 12, 22
cultural resource surveys 141

dark heritage sites 149–62 (*see also* conflict archaeology; Kilwa Kivinje; Kitanda; Mgao)
Debord, G. 117
defamiliarization 6–8
Deleuze, Gilles 22, 217–18, 219, 220
Demarco, Richard 21
dérives 70, 117
Deschooling Society (Illich) 52–3, 188
desk drawer exercise 9–10
development, land 131–43 (*see also* Balfarg complex)
Dewey, John 21
diaries 116
digital delivery of learning 4, 20, 29–31, 70–2
digital materials, archaeology of 102–3
discomfort, pedagogy of 150, 161
displaced people 187–98

Dixon, James 33
Dr Space Junk vs The Universe (Gorman) 2
drama pedagogy 150
drawing
    cellphone drawing exercise 103–8
    and learning 109
    'Our House' apartment workshop 193, 194, 195
Dumbarton Rock virtual fieldtrips 30
Dunelm House project 66–8
Durham University Department of Archaeology 63, 64–6
Durham University Observatory 68–9
Dutchess County Home 135–8

Edinburgh Arts 21
educative healing 194–5
emotional experiences 149–50, 158–61
execution trees 152–4, 161, 173

Facebook groups 136, 154
Fariha (Made in Migration Collective) 189
feedback 94
fieldtrips 30, 82–98
filmmaking 32, 209–10
Finn, Christine 9, 102
Fishkill, Dutchess County 141–2
Flinders University 7–8
Frampton, K. 131
Frederick, Ursula 25
Freire, Paolo 27, 52–3, 188, 230–2
Freund, K. P. 134

GAP END 228, 231–2, 235–6
Garzhian, Omran 228, 234
Gauntlett, David 30
Gell, Alfred 209, 219
georeferencing 136
Gidusko, K. 134
Giroux, Henry 27
Glenrothes 86–90
Goertz, Karein 116–17
Gomes-Coelho, Rui 73
González-Ruibal, A. 7
Goodman, Paul 52–3
Gorman, Alice 2, 7–8
Gould, R. A. 10
Gower Street 122
grading and ungrading 53

graves (cemeteries) 136–8, 139, 142, 172, 173
Graves-Brown, P. 6–7
Gray, Sir John 171
Guattari, Felix 22, 217–18, 219, 220

Hale, Alex 30
Hamilakis, Yannis 11, 195
hanging tree, Kontinkangas 152–4, 161
Harrison, Rodney 7, 8, 218–19
Haworth, Robert 188
Hicks, Dan 206, 216
Hill, Lisa 5–6
History of Bombing, A (Lindqvist) 118
history teaching 168
Hodder, Ian 216
Holtorf, C. 83–4, 85, 219
home conferences 230, 233–4

Illich, Ivan 52–3, 188
intended learning outcomes (ILOs) 94, 96
interdisciplinary collaboration 4–6, 19–20, 21–3, 34
Iran 225–36
Ireland, Tracy 25
Islamists 226–7

Jones, J. C. 83

Kessy, E. T. 168–9
Kiddey, Rachael 33
Kilwa Kivinje 173
Kitanda 174–6

Lambert, Rebecca 30
Lapland's Dark Heritage project 151–5
lectures, public 156, 234
Lee, Daniel 23, 24
Lindqvist, Sven 117, 118
'Loveable' assignment 8
Loveless, Natalie 29
Lucas, Gavin 6, 109, 206–8
Lukkarinen, Taavetti 152–4, 159, 160, 161

MacColl, Eòghann 28
Made in Migration Collective 187, 189–91, 195–7
Majimaji War 173–6, 178–9
Makunganya, Hassan Omar 173

mapping 132–3, 135–7, 139–40
Mapunda, Bertram 167–8, 178
marginalized groups 235–6
Mathy, Heinrich 121
McKenna, Brian 194
media-related artefacts 211–16
Mehari, A. 169
Mehler, N. 14
memorials 50, 124, 152–3, 155, 173, 175
Mercer, Roger 86
Mgao 170–2
'Migrant Materialities' project 187
Miller, D, et al. 103, 109–10
Modern Material Culture: The Archaeology of Us (Gould and Schiffer) 10–11
Msemwa, P. 167–8
music 25–6

NASA satellite tracking station (Orroral Valley) 2
Negahban, Ezat 226
Nelson, R. 26–7
New York State poorhouses 135–8
New York watershed 132, 138–40
Ngoni people 176
Nilsson Stutz, Liv 34
Nkomanile 174–6

Ogilvie, Aileen 25–6
Olive (New York State) 139–40
Olivier, Laurent 207
online learning 4, 20, 29–31, 70–2
oppression 229–32, 235
ordnance 158, 160–1 (*see also* bombsites)
Orkney College 23–30
Oulu 150–4, 160
'Our House' apartment 191–5, 196
outcomes, pedagogical 52–4, 94, 96

Patchwork Archaeology (Garazhian et al) 233–4
Penrose, Sefryn 104
Permar, Roxane 31
Perry, Sara 102, 104
Piccini, Angela 27, 206, 210
poorhouses 132, 135–8
practice-as-research 26–9
prisoner-of-war (PoW) camps 151, 154–5, 156

'progress' and building developments 131–2, 143
prompt cards 91–3
Punk Rock Pedagogy 194

QAA Benchmark Statements 61, 82–3, 84
'quantum' archaeology 217
Queen Square Gardens 120–1

rainbow of desire 231
Rathje, W. 10, 41
Re-Constructing Archaeology: Theory and Practice (Shanks and Tilley) 206
(re)mapping 133
remembrance 51–2, 149, 153–5, 158–9, 161–2
replicas at Balfarg 85–93
reservoirs 138–40
Ritchie, Graham 87–8
Rizvi, Uzma 186
Romero, Noah 194
Rosenberg, Dave 117–18
Russell Square 121–2, 124
Russell-White, Chris 88

safeguarding 192
Salvaging Tanzania's Cultural Heritage (Mapunda and Msemwa) 167–8
Sápmi 151
sawmill sites 151, 156
Sayre Hall, Wesley College 42–3, 48–51
Schiffer, M. B. 3, 10–11, 41
Schofield, John 7, 8, 9, 102, 208
scrapbooks 93–7
Second School squat 189–91, 194–5
Shah, Reza 225–6
Shanks, M. 206
shopping malls 141–3
skills gap 14
Skolt Sámi priests 154–5
slave trade 170–6
slow archaeology 53–4
Speirs, Douglas 91
storytelling 133, 156
street ephemera 211–21
student-led learning 45–57
supernatural stories 154, 156

Surface-Evans, S. L. 134
Szilard, Leo 121–2

Tanzania, archaeological pedagogy in 167–70, 176–9
tape, cassette 211
Tavistock Square 122–4
Theater of the Oppressed (TO) 230–2
therapy, archaeology as 149–50, 158–61, 194–5
Tilley, C. 91, 206
traces (noun and verb) 118–19
training in archaeological methods 13–14, 41–2, 61–2
transgenerational learning 155–8, 159, 162
trees, execution 152–4, 161, 173
Twitter conferences 71–2

'Underpasses are Liminal Places' project 30
University College London 104
University of Arizona 41
University of Bristol 206
University of Dar es Salaam 169, 178–9
University of Glasgow 81, 84–5
University of North Dakota (UND) 42–4
University of Tehran (UT) 226, 228
University of the Highlands and Islands (UHI) 19–20, 23–6, 28–35
University of York 104

Vaakunakylä 151, 155–6, 161
Van Project, the 208–10
Varjakka 151, 156
Vassar College 135, 136
Velten, C. 171
'Views and Soundings: Marking Boundaries for Archaeological Practice' (Bailey) 210–12
virtual fieldtrips 30
visuality in archaeology 27
Vuotso 160–1

walking
    Balfarg 89–93
    Bloomsbury 116–17, 118–19, 124–5
    and recording 211–16

Index

Wall, Gina 30
Wallis, L. 7
Washington, George (headquarters) 132
Washko, S. 83
wastebasket exercise 9–10
Wesley College Campus 42–52
Wickstead, Helen 27

Wilk, R. 3, 10–11, 41
Wilkie, Laurie 41
Wittgraf, Michael 54
women and colonialism 175–6

Yeoman, Peter 89

Zimmerman, Larry 9–10